Charles Paul MacKie

With the Admiral of the Ocean Sea

A narrative of the first voyage to the western world, drawn mainly from the diary of

Christopher Columbus

Charles Paul MacKie

With the Admiral of the Ocean Sea

A narrative of the first voyage to the western world, drawn mainly from the diary of Christopher Columbus

ISBN/EAN: 9783337197230

Printed in Europe, USA, Canada, Australia, Japan

Cover: Foto ©ninafisch / pixelio.de

More available books at **www.hansebooks.com**

Charles Paul MacKie

With the Admiral of the Ocean Sea
A narrative of the first voyage to the western world, drawn mainly from the diary of Christopher Columbus

ISBN/EAN: 9783337197230

Printed in Europe, USA, Canada, Australia, Japan

Cover: Foto ©ninafisch / pixelio.de

More available books at **www.hansebooks.com**

WITH THE ADMIRAL OF THE OCEAN SEA

A Narrative of the First Voyage to the Western World

DRAWN MAINLY FROM THE DIARY OF
CHRISTOPHER COLUMBUS

BY

CHARLES PAUL MAC KIE

> When newes were brought that Don Christopher Colonus, the Genoese, had discovered the coasts of India, whereof was great talke in all the Court of King Henry the 7, who then raigned, . . . all men with great admiration affirmed it to be a thing more divine than humane, to saile by the West into the Easte, where the spices growe, by a chart that was never before knowen. — SEBASTIAN CABOT

CHICAGO
A. C. McCLURG AND COMPANY
1891

TO

My Friends in the United States Navy,

*IN RECOGNITION OF MANY KINDNESSES RECEIVED
IN SOUTHERN SEAS.*

PREFACE.

IN preparing this narrative we have preferred to deal only with the accounts left by Columbus himself and those directly associated with him in the enterprise which placed him among the true Immortals. Our effort has been, by following as closely as might be the language of the actual participants, to present a living picture of the events connected with that stupendous achievement. If in so doing we have lost somewhat of the dignity of graver methods, and departed in sundry particulars from those presentations of the great exploit which are deservedly familiar, our apology is that we have adopted the errors of the actors themselves. It has seemed well to the critical spirit of our day to question the accuracy of Columbus in more than one respect; but that he and those who were his fellow-workers by land and sea did not faithfully relate what passed in connection with the discovery of the Indies, we have not the temerity to assume. Their written reports and the testimony given by many of them under oath lie before us as we write, and we have found no cause to doubt the exactness of their contents. That these reports are seldom artistic, often confused, and not infrequently prolix in what now appear to be trivial matters, may be with propriety alleged; but our object would not be attained were we to trim the language of the Admiral and his companions to suit our ideas of proportion. They planned the voyage and made it, and we are content to follow their account of what befell.

The diary, letters, and other remaining writings of Columbus picture for us with rare fidelity the man himself. As we turn over their leaves and read his words, — penned in a Latin, Spanish, or Italian whose very want of polish is its most palpable charm, — their author ceases to be a character in history about the disposition of whose bones fierce controversies have raged, and becomes once more the earnest student, skilful mariner, and fearless explorer whose acts have freed his memory from limitations of time and place. We feel, as we follow his artless periods, that we are looking past the pen into the heart of the man, and recall with a new appreciation that he was the contemporary of the Great Captain and of Bayard the Matchless, in the days when great deeds were simply done and yet more simply told by their doers. Concerning himself, as freely as concerning others, he relates both good and bad alike; his times of weakness as well as of strength, his failures as well as his success. When we remember that nearly all of his existing writings were addressed to his royal patrons of Castile, we may admire the naked frankness with which he speaks, while we must regret the simplicity which trusted blindly to those who would so naturally regard their own interest rather than their servant's.

Some of the incidents incorporated in our narrative have been found in the official documents bearing upon the Discovery; others are drawn from the testimony in the lawsuit brought against the Spanish Crown after the death of Columbus, by his son Diego, for the full recognition in the latter's person of all the dignities and emoluments originally conferred upon his father but in later years so greatly abridged by King Ferdinand. Whatever the source, we have confined ourselves to the evidence of eyewitnesses, and have desired to be exact rather than elaborate. The conversations attributed to the Admiral are such as are reported, by himself or his companions, to have taken place. In his diary he usually entered them with sufficient fulness to permit their reconstruction; but in those given in the prefatory chapters, which are merely recorded by the physician Garcia Fernandez and others as having occurred, without details being given, we have put into dialogue form such extracts from Columbus's letters as illustrate his attitude toward the subjects discussed. The words placed in his mouth are, in this case, substantially those which his hand transcribed.

No large portion of the reading public has either the time or the inclination to delve into the many tomes which, chiefly by the liberality of the Spanish Government and the devoted labors of Muñoz, Navarrete, and their successors, have been made available for the students of Columbus's life and works; and yet, if we are not wholly in error, it is only from these original sources that any lifelike conception of the great discoverer's character can be formed. It is to this larger world of readers, who would gladly read the story of the renowned event of 1492 in the words of the chief actors, that our narrative is addressed.

The Appendix contains a few notes upon the main points in dispute concerning Columbus and his career. Without wishing to enter into matters of controversy, it has seemed best to offer this small contribution toward the solution of the questions at issue.

We have preferred to retain the Spanish form of the Admiral's name, Cristóval Colon, as being more in keeping with the spirit of our narrative than the anglicized Christopher Columbus.

CONTENTS.

CHAPTER		PAGE
I.	THE FATHER SUPERIOR'S SAILOR GUEST	11
II.	THE SHREWD IDEA OF THE YOUNG PHYSICIAN	20
III.	NOTABLE MISSION OF THE EX-PRIVATEERSMAN	32
IV.	THE FAMOUS MULE OF JUAN THE HARD-HEADED	42
V.	BARGAINING FOR A WORLD	53
VI.	"I, THE KING!" AND "I, THE QUEEN!"	67
VII.	THE HEAVY HAND OF JUAN DE PEÑALOSA	76
VIII.	THE SEA-BREEZE OUTSIDE THE BAR	89
IX.	IN THE PATH OF THE SUN	100
X.	WHAT THE MOON DISCLOSED	113
XI.	UNDER THE BANNER OF THE GREEN CROSS	128
XII.	AMONG THE ISLES OF IND	140
XIII.	IN SEARCH OF FAR CATHAY	153
XIV.	THE EMBASSY TO WHOM IT MIGHT CONCERN	166
XV.	THE EVIL DEED OF MARTIN ALONZO	180
XVI.	ALPHA AND OMEGA	193

CONTENTS.

CHAPTER		PAGE
XVII.	HIS UNCLAD MAJESTY	207
XVIII.	A GLOOMY CHRISTMAS	219
XIX.	THE FIRST FRONTIERSMEN	233
XX.	THE RETURN OF THE "PINTA"	247
XXI.	NORTHEAST BY EAST, FOR SPAIN AND IMMORTALITY	264
XXII.	"THERE WERE NO TEMPESTS IN THE INDIES"	279
XXIII.	THE GRACES OF CIVILIZATION	290
XXIV.	KING AND COMMONS	302
XXV.	HIGH NOON AND THE TIDE AT FLOOD	317
XXVI.	AFTERWARD	329

APPENDIX 343

WITH THE ADMIRAL OF THE OCEAN SEA.

I.

THE FATHER SUPERIOR'S SAILOR GUEST.

IN the little refectory of a tiny Franciscan convent, dedicated to Our Lady of the Madness, which still stands in the remote corner of Southern Spain where our narrative begins, two men sat conversing earnestly together on a certain sunny afternoon many a long year gone by. The one, a monk wearing the coarse gown and cowl of the Order of Saint Francis, was rather over forty years of age; the other, a layman clad in the ordinary dress of the period, — somewhat the worse for wear and travel, — seemed to be ten years older. Against the tall back of the chair occupied by the older man, and listening respectfully to all that was said, leaned a lad of thirteen or fourteen years, whose features plainly proved him to be his son. A flagon of the common red wine of the country stood on the table before them, with the remains of a loaf of bread, a piece of cheese, and a broiled fish, — evidence that some one had been eating, although it was long past the hour for the simple midday meal of the worthy friars.

The room was barren of all ornament. Its only furniture consisted of a dozen or more ponderous chairs and stools, all more or less carved and covered with embossed leather, which stood against the whitewashed walls, and a heavy table of some hard polished wood which occupied the centre of the smooth stone floor. Bare though it was, the exquisite cleanliness of everything around gave to the room an attractiveness of its own, which was heightened by the contrast between the fresh coolness of its shaded atmosphere and the quivering heat of the glaring Andalusian sun outside. From where the boy was standing he could look through the open doorway into the little courtyard of the convent, where the fig-trees and pomegranates stood motionless in the hot sunshine; or, by turning his head, could see through the grated windows of the refectory the great waves of the mighty western sea lazily rolling landward, waiting to be whipped into dancing whitecaps later on by the brisk breezes of the afternoon. But as he listened to the older men before him, his eyes sought oftenest the plain of heaving waters; for their talk was wholly of that vast world of unknown ocean which stretched far out of sight toward the setting sun, and of what might lie beyond the level mocking line which lay between sea and sky, and ever receded, as now and then some daring sailor sought to reach its limits and learn what was there concealed.

"Your Worship is not of Spain, I take it, Señor," the monk had said, when father and son had finished their light meal; "if I do not offend in asking the question?"

"No, Father," the layman answered, "I am from Genoa; a true son of Saint George, — may he ever defend me!" he added, crossing himself devoutly.[1] "I was born Christoforo Colombo, though here in Spain men call me Cristoval Colon; an unworthy servant, ever at your orders, reverend sir."

"I hold myself happy in knowing your Worship, Señor Cristoval," the monk replied. "The sailors of our coast here often speak of your famous voyages to distant seas, and I have heard your name as well in the gossip from the Court."

[1] For Columbus's statements concerning his birthplace, see Note A in the Appendix.

"Your own kindness exaggerates my deserts, good father," said Colon. "Some of the hardy seamen from the southern ports have sailed with me on voyages of some length, 't is true; and it is but natural that they should bear in mind the hard knocks and scanty fare they found while on their travels."

"Your present journey is not a long one, Señor Cristoval, if I may judge by your boy accompanying you?" the monk again queried, with a kindly glance at the young lad standing against his father's chair.

"We come now but from Seville," the latter responded; "and 't is no great distance, — the more as we have walked at ease, good father. Please God, our journey ends at Huelva, your neighboring town. But as we broke our fast betimes this morning, and have still some hours of road before us, we have trespassed thus upon your hospitality which has been so bountiful."

"You must stay now under our poor roof, Señor, at least until your boy has had some rest. It will be no easy thing to reach Huelva this evening; and in the morning we can get a boatman to put your Worship across the bay, if you needs must leave us. Whatever Juan Perez, the humble superior of this little cloister, can do for your comfort, worthy sir, you may count upon as already done."

"I thank your Reverence warmly," Colon replied; "and we will tax your kindness still further, since you are so good. But Diego here is no court-bred youngster who cannot travel on his own legs. Which were the harder life in these days of war on sea and land, the life of the camps or that on shipboard, it were not easy to say; but I have led both since he was born, so the colt has learned to go with the sire. Moreover, his lady-mother — may God give her rest! — came of the stoutest-hearted stock in Portugal, and the lad should be no weakling. Mayhap you know one Pedro de Muliar, a townsman of Huelva, reverend father? He married a sister of my dead wife, — may God rest her soul! — and 't is he I seek on this present journey."

"Seek you him, Señor? Then I greatly fear your labor will be fruitless; for only lately I heard it said he was going on a cruise to the Levant, with a brave company of seamen from our neighboring ports along shore,—Palos and Lepe and Huelva and Ayamonte. Still, he may not yet have sailed."

A shade of annoyance crossed the frank brow of Colon at this news.

"So much the worse for me, Father," he said. "I counted much on seeing him; and God only can tell when he will be back now, or whether at all. Who sails the Mediterranean in these troublous times, be he Christian or Moor, should leave his testament ready made behind him. Yet will Pedro go in good company, for stouter men never handled rope than those from these shores."

He sat some moments in silence, looking intently at the table. Then, turning his head upward toward his son, he said,—

"Well, Diego, my son, and what shall I do with thee, now that thine uncle is gone? It were too long a journey to take thee with me to France."

"Yet would I gladly go, Señor, if you will but take me," the boy replied eagerly. "Surely I could serve you well as page, and help you often in your journey."

Colon nodded, seeming pleased with the lad's spirit. Then putting his hand on the leathern wallet which hung at his belt, and giving it a shake, he said with a touch of bitterness,—

"'T is scanty fare therein for one, my son, and I should ne'er see his Majesty of France were two to travel on it. The lad too is touched with the madness of the sea," he added, half sadly, as he turned again to the friar.

"I grieve to hear you speak of leaving Spain, Señor Cristoval," the latter answered. "Surely their Highnesses our gracious sovereigns can ill spare such men as your Worship in these times of strife and trouble."

Colon raised himself erect in his chair, and grasped its carven arms nervously with his hands, as he looked straight at the monk out of his clear blue eyes.

"Their Highnesses of Spain have no more faithful or devoted servant in their kingdoms than I, good father," he said with emphasis, "stranger though I be. To the noble Queen Isabella I am beholden for great favors, and a kindly sympathy more valued still. May the holy saints ever have her Majesty in their safe keeping!" and again he crossed himself. "But for six long years have I been suitor at their court, asking of them no grace save to take at my hands all the wealth of Asia, and to bring under their dominion and that of the holy Christian faith the lands of the heathen which now languish in hateful idolatry. Is not that a task fit for the kings of Castile and of Aragon, the conquerors of the Moors, think you, good father? Nor was my only hope with them; for I myself placed in the queen's hands the letters of three other princes, bidding me to their courts and proffering me the aid I sought. Yet their Highnesses of Spain will none of it! The cares of the war in Granada; the intrigues of the emissaries of Portugal, who seek to retain a monopoly of sailing distant seas and searching for new lands; the ignorance and apathy and timidity of those who advise their Highnesses, — all these and a thousand more pitiful reasons have resulted in my suit being rejected, or, what is harder still to bear, being postponed and deferred from month to month and year to year until I have grown weary and hopeless. Now that their Majesties have pitched their camp before Granada, there is neither time nor disposition to hear of aught save war, and I go to the Court of France, whose king has said he would give me the ships and men I need to find the world which lies beyond yon western horizon."

He gazed toward the ocean, which heaved and sank beneath the afternoon sun, with a look in his eyes as though he clearly saw some distant headland lying low in the hazy west.

"Something of this have I heard, Señor Cristoval," said the friar, with an air of sympathy, "but had thought ere this your suit had prospered. Your Worship may not know that our good queen honored me for several years as her Highness's confessor. At the Court they called me the Fray Antonio of Marchena."

"Say you so, Father?" Colon replied with interest; "then I hold myself doubly fortunate in meeting your Reverence. Often has that most excellent lady her Grace of Maya spoken of you, and wished you at Court to further my petition. Yet had I good friends and powerful among their Highness's counsellors, and their number increased each year, as my proposals became more and more understood. But, Father," and he leaned toward the monk almost with an air of supplication, "the years are passing, and I grow old. It is God's will that I should make this voyage to the west, to find the great continent of Asia and bring its people to a knowledge of the true faith. If I wait on and on, it may be too late, and I shall go to my grave with my task undone."

The monk looked at his guest with a frank admiration. The stranger's eye was kindling as if from the inspiration of some noble thought, and the whole expression of his face was that of a lofty determination to dare all in doing the duty he felt to be plain before him. Such a light had the good friar often seen, when he followed the camp of Isabella, in the faces of the knights of Santiago as they set spurs into their chargers and dashed, lance in rest, against the Moorish horsemen, with a great shout of "Saint James for the Holy Cross and Spain!"

His heart was stirred now at the sight of his guest's enthusiasm; but he spoke quietly enough as he answered Colon, —

"There is wisdom in the words of the son of David, that much waiting weareth the soul, good sir; yet doubt I not it would sorely grieve our gracious sovereigns were this quest to be made under any banner save that of the Lions of Castile. I am but a layman in the arts wherein you are master, Señor Cristoval; still, I have given much thought and study to the writings of the ancients who held that there is a lost continent far out in yonder Atlantic, and our sailors at times have told me strange tales of distant lands they have spied from the shores of the Canaries and Azores. To me, who know so little, it seems likely enough;

for I remember that the Canaries themselves were only found in our fathers' times, though the ancients knew them well and called them the Fortunate Isles. Therefore glad would my heart be, Señor, if my poor services could avail you anything. If it please your Worship, I would crave your warrant to bring to you my learned friend the physician Garcia Fernandez of Palos, hard by, who, albeit young, has studied deeply the science of the earth and the heavens, and conferred much with the sea-faring men who frequent our ports. His judgment and counsel are weighty beyond his years, Señor, or I should not give your Worship the labor of meeting him; and we should hold it a high privilege to know more of your project."

"It is no trial for me to meet those who use the minds that God has given them in trying to learn more of His works than what lies under their noses," Colon answered with vigor. "'Tis those who do not think, not those who differ from me, who have made my labors of none effect till now. Fourteen years did I pass at the Court of Portugal, ever pressing my plan save when I was on voyages. They took my charts and writings from me, saying they would ponder them; but secretly they sent out the ships they had denied me. God drove them back on their own coasts, and punished their treachery; but I could no longer trust them. Two years I spent with that noble man the Duke of Medina Celi, and he would have gladly given me the ships I asked, but feared to affront the Crown by seeming bolder than his sovereigns. Six years have I spent at the Court of Castile, as I said but now, and all without result. In twenty years, Father, I have met scarcely more men than could be numbered twice on my fingers who have believed in that western land as I believe in it. You shall judge, therefore, whether I count it a toil to converse with those who seek to share my faith."

The monk rose as he said, "I will myself go to the village for my friend, Señor. Will your Worship go with me? It is but a short half-league, and the brothers will see that the lad gets the rest he seems to need;" and he nodded smilingly toward Diego, who had seated himself on the arm of his father's chair and fallen fast asleep.

"Willingly," Colon replied, "for I would gladly learn what I may about some of the men from this coast who sailed with me years and years ago."

As they crossed the courtyard and passed through the portal of the convent into the space outside, they met the strong, steady press of the sea-breeze which had sprung up as the sun declined on its last quarter. The sharp swish of a few glittering palm-tops tossing overhead, sounded above the softer murmur of the light gale blowing through the pine-trees farther off. Away over the sea the white crests were riding landward, with here and there a glance of blinding sunbeams as some smoother wave cast back the nearly level rays. The sky was everywhere without a cloud, save that some few soft masses of rounded vapor hung on the sea-line directly in the path of the sun. A lovelier day never drew to its close even in favored Andalusia.

As his practised eyes half closed to veil the brilliant light reflected from sea and sky, Colon drew his tall figure up to its full height, and laying one hand on the friar's arm, stretched out the other toward the dim outlines of the cloud-piles lying along the western horizon.

"Saw you ever fairer scene than yonder ocean, Fray Antonio? Yet shall you find nineteen men in every score, be they seamen or men learned in the arts, who will maintain that that fair ocean is filled with all the horrible monsters of hell; and that he who sails more than a few hundred leagues from this same coast on which we stand, even if he escape them, shall fall into Chaos, or be burned up by the sun's heat, or wander forever like another accursed Jew, over a trackless waste of waters."

The monk smiled kindly at his companion's enthusiasm, as he replied, —

"But who better than yourself, Señor Cristoval, knows the fickleness of this now so comely sea? 'T is not on days like this that our mariners dread its terrors, or our scholars weave their legends; but when the skies close down in leaden gloom, and the sea is naught but yawning gulfs of blackest pitch. Then the stoutest heart may well fear what lies ahead of the narrow distance the eye can pierce."

"True, Father," said Colon, thoughtfully; "yet who trusts in God and weathers the storm, shall find ever the sun shining on smooth seas beyond."

And in friendly chat the two men passed down the winding path which led through the pines to the little village of Palos below.[1]

[1] For the historical basis of this and the following chapter, see the Appendix, Notes C and D.

II.

THE SHREWD IDEA OF THE YOUNG PHYSICIAN.

THAT evening, shortly after vespers, the lamp which flickered on the table in Fray Antonio's room lighted up a group of men whose combined worldly possessions probably did not amount to one hundred of the dollars of our day; and yet they were planning, in all simplicity, to accomplish the greatest work for their fellow-men the world has seen since the fishermen of Galilee laid down their nets and followed Him they called the Nazarene. Though the good father was superior of the convent, and therefore chief among the brethren, the bareness of his room showed that his vows of poverty and abstemiousness were no mere words. A low pallet-bed, with a crucifix on the whitewashed wall above it, a few straight-backed armchairs like those in the refectory below, a water-jar and basin of coarse earthenware, and a massive table completed the furniture of the apartment. At one end of the table sat Colon, with a parchment map of no great size spread under his hands; and on either side of him, following closely all he said and bending down to distinguish the crabbed letters in the uncertain light, were Fray Antonio and his friend the physician of Palos, Garcia Fernandez. The latter was much younger than either of his companions, being scarcely more than thirty years old; and with the graceful courtesy of Spanish breeding, he showed a marked deference in manner and speech toward his seniors. But when he did speak it was with a clearness and conviction which showed that he had reflected much on the subject in hand, and had sought to increase his knowledge from every source open to him.

"This chart I had from my very learned friend and master in the geographical art, the Doctor Paolo Toscanelli of Florence, who sent it to me some fifteen years ago when I was seeking at the Court of Portugal the means with which to discover the lands which lie in the western ocean."

As Colon said this, the young physician remarked that he spoke of the existence of those unknown lands as a certainty, not as being merely probable or possible.

"In drawing it, that wise and ingenious man has brought together all that the ancients knew of the world we live in, and has added to it what has been discovered in our own times of the coast of Guinea, and the islands which are found on the course thither. I myself have made some few additions to it, and in particular have laid down the great island of Cipango and the mainland of Cathay somewhat nearer to the shores of Europe than my learned master had done. You will, I fear, consider it but presumption on my part, good sirs, to amend the work of so great a scholar; but all the computations I have made, and all the knowledge I have been able to gather, strengthen my belief that the confines of Asia which stretch farthest to the east are nearer to our European shores than any of our maps now show."

Colon laid his finger on the chart at a spot distant by the scale some three thousand miles west of the coast of Portugal, where a large island was roughly drawn and marked "Cipango." About half-way to it, in the middle of what we now call the Atlantic Ocean, lay another uncertain outline lettered "Island of the Seven Cities;" while far to the south, near the equator, was a third, charted as "St. Borondon's Isle." The space we now know to be covered by North America was filled with a multitude of other islands; Java and the Celebes were placed nearly on the site of South America; and the continent of Asia reached clear across the wide space where rolls the vast Pacific. There was no Africa south of Sierra Leone, nearly the whole of the map being marked as "unknown seas;" while in the remote North, where hardy modern voyagers have sought the Pole, lay the island of Thule, the Iceland of now-a-days.

The monk and the physician studied intently that portion of the chart to which Colon had pointed.

"If this distance be in any measure exact, Señor Cristoval, naught can be plainer than that the shortest track to the Golden Indies lies in sailing west," said Fray Antonio. "But, with your Worship's permission, it seems to me that the chief danger is in your finding no land after sailing a thousand leagues to the west, and being unable to return to these shores. I have heard men who were no idle chatterers, but men of thought and sense, say that beyond the limits of the known sea the ocean slopes so toward the west that no ship can hope to return eastward once it has passed the farthest line."

"I treat lightly the opinion of no man who has thought much or seen much, good father," replied Colon. "Should that slope of which men speak lie really there, I could but sail on and on until we reached our bourn."

"Then you hold of no weight the tale some mariners tell of a great zone of dead calms lying in the west, where ships may lie as if at anchor from century to century?" the physician asked. "That seems to me a grievous peril, Señor, though I frankly grant there may be land somewhere to the west of us."

Colon settled himself back in his chair before answering. When he spoke it was in the tone of one who weighs carefully his words in the hope of carrying conviction, —

"Señor Doctor, once you are satisfied the land is there, all else seems little. There is no navigating without its share of peril, and he who would make sure of dying in bed must not go to sea. That there is no zone of calm I do not affirm, since he is but foolish who denies all he has not seen. Rather, it seems to me that such a zone must lie far to the south, where the heat is greatest; for when I sailed to the Guinea coast with the Portuguese, we found the airs grow lighter as we journeyed toward the Southern

Pole. And unless I err in every thought, and my life has been spent thus far in vain, the land I seek is to be found by sailing ever west on the line of these our shores, or, at the most, that of the Canary Islands."

The young physician spoke eagerly as Colon finished, — "Your own voyaging hitherto has then confirmed your faith, Señor? You have encountered naught to cause you to doubt?"

"Thirty years as boy and man have I followed the sea, worthy sir," Colon replied; "and wherever keel has ploughed in the known world of waters, there have I sailed. I say it not boastingly; but, as you know, much travelling on the ocean inclines a thoughtful man to ponder over its many and profound secrets. From the Pillars of Hercules to the farthest isles of Greece I have crossed and recrossed the Mediterranean Sea times without number, and visited all its coasts, whether of Africa, Europe, or Asia. To the English islands I have sailed more than once, and years ago I went to the utmost verge of the western sea which the ancients called Ultima Thule, but the people who dwell there call the Land of Ice. As far as men have sailed along the western coast of Africa I have also been on divers voyages, and passed much time in the islands the Portuguese name Azores, and in the Spanish archipelago of the Canaries. Wherever I have been I have sought to learn both from sailors and from learned scholars; priests and laymen, Latins and Greeks, Jews and Moors, — all these and many of other sects have I known and had conversation with. And to this day, good sirs, I have met none who could show one good cause why, by keeping a straight course to the setting sun, I should not reach the boundaries of Asia and the empire of the Great Khan. Much to the contrary, month by month and year by year my belief has been strengthened and increased, until now I know I but follow the way the finger of God marks out for me to go."

"There is, indeed, a mariner of our village, Señor Cristoval," said the physician, with some diffidence, "one Pedro Velasco, who has followed the sea for many years, and declares that starting from the Azores some years ago he and his companions sailed due west for several days, and found the ocean ever the same in all its aspects as those it bears nearer home."

"You must do me the service of procuring me speech with your neighbor, Señor Garcia," said Colon, with interest, "for from such men I have learned much. When I was before on this coast, under the protection of my noble patron, his Grace of Medina Celi, in his port of Santa Maria, a one-eyed sailor, who from his appearance must have had a stormy life, told me that on a certain voyage when he was bound for Ireland, which is one of the English isles, his ship was blown far off its course by constant easterly gales, until they came in sight of a western land they supposed to be the shores of Tartary. Being afraid to land, and the winds having changed, they made their way back again across the wide sea to these shores. Whether in fact they reached so far as Asia, or only lost their reckoning and sighted some nearer land, I cannot determine. But afterward I met in Murcia a Portuguese sailor who had been on this same voyage, and he confirmed all the other had told me. I see nothing extravagant in their tale; but they could find no other to believe them."

"Others of our seafaring men have told me that returning from Guinea they have seen the dim outlines of some unknown land lying far in the western sky. Saw you anything of this, Señor Cristoval?" asked the younger man. "I trespass, perhaps, too far on your Worship's kindness in repeating such idle mariners' tales," he added, as if in apology.

"'Tis a kindness done, not one you ask, young sir," Colon responded with heartiness. "These reports have I heard both in the Azores and in the Canary Islands, as this afternoon I was saying to his Reverence here; but I never saw with my own eyes aught that looked like land. Some filmy shadows there sometimes were, to say truth; but they seemed to my sight to be but distant clouds or some trick played by the sea-haze upon us. Clearer tokens that something lay beyond our vision in that direction were to me the strange trees and plants which from time to time the sea has cast on the shores of those islands. The father of my dead wife — may God have her in his glory! — was governor for the Crown of Portugal of the island of Porto Santo for many years; and when I was there his son showed me some canes or reeds of the thickness of a man's thigh, which had come ashore in a gale, and avowed to me that he himself had talked with those who had found the bodies of two men cast up by the ocean on the isle of Flores, who had yellow faces and straight black hair, such as we know the people of Asia to have. These evidences, and others which have been given up by the waves, weigh more with me, Señor, than the doubtful tales of lands which have been seen so near and never found."

Fray Antonio had listened with close attention to all that passed between his friend Garcia Fernandez and the stranger, nodding his head now and then as if to show that he agreed with some remark of one or the other. Now he turned to Colon and said, —

"Then you see no cause to doubt that men may have already crossed this western sea, Señor Cristoval, albeit no record remains of their voyages?"

"It were much to say, reverend father, that since God made the world or since men have sailed the sea no gale has driven their ships westward to shores we know not of," Colon answered with an air of modesty; "yet of this we know naught for certain; nor have we any sign of men coming eastward over those western waters, save those two dead bodies on the beach at Flores Island.[1] You both have read the ancients, worthy sirs, and will doubtless remember that in their writings is frequent mention of a western continent, which they called Atlantis, but which cannot be else

---

[1] That Columbus was aware of the vague tales concerning involuntary voyages across the Atlantic appears from various references in his writings. His position in regard thereto, and his possible debt to the Norsemen, or to later voyages in the Sea of Darkness, are alluded to in Note E of the Appendix.

than that side of Asia which lies nearest to us on that course."

The father superior answered, with a glance of sly amusement at the physician, —

"This young student by your side, Señor Cristoval, has given me many a sleepless night with his disputations over that very point, and his attempts to establish the geography of Pliny and Strabo and Herodotus by the tales of our sailors here, or of some wandering merchant who has come from the far Orient."

"Nay, Father; you are malicious," the younger man answered, laughing as he spoke. "You too were startled by the prophecy in the book my kinsman Martin Alonzo brought from Rome."

"'T is true, my friend," said the friar, soberly; "I had forgotten that. Know you of such a book, Señor?" he asked, turning to Colon. "Martin Alonzo Pinzon, our neighbor of Palos, who owns both lands and ships, and has been much at sea, returned not long since from a voyage to Rome, and brought a book which he says he had from a gentleman of his Holiness's own household, and which is of the time of King Solomon. In that book it is written: 'Whoever shall sail by the Mediterranean Sea to the end of Spain, and from there toward the setting of the sun for fourteen hundred leagues, keeping always along a middle course between the north and the south, shall come to the land of *Campanso*, which is very fertile, and abounding in all good things; and with it he shall conquer all Africa and Europe.' I may err in the words, but the sense is as I say."

Colon leaned forward eagerly, as the monk repeated the paragraph.

"I know not that book, good father, and shall be much your debtor if you will bring me to converse with this Señor Martin Alonzo," he replied. "Howbeit the distance named is twice too great; for all my computations place the island of Cipango at only seven hundred, or at the most eight hundred, leagues from the Spanish coast; and I doubt not the land called *Campanso* shall be the port of Quimsay in Cathay, which our later travellers to India — Marco Polo the Venetian and the monks who went before him to the remote East — have placed not far beyond Cipango, as you may see by this chart."

He laid his finger on the spot as he spoke, and sat musing for a few moments.

"Nevertheless," he continued with emphasis, "that prophecy is not more notable, Señores, than the one of Seneca, who wrote in the times of Nero, — ' In the later years of the world shall come the days when ocean shall loosen the bonds of the unknown, and a great country shall be opened up. Another mariner like him who guided Jason shall discover a new world, and then shall Thule cease to be the limits of the earth.' "

As he recited the sonorous lines of the Latin poet, Colon's face lighted up again with a look of lofty purpose, which seemed to his companions akin to the fire of inspiration. Lowering his voice slightly, he continued, —

"Almost in our own times, worthy sirs, we have this assurance repeated by the English knight Sir Mandeville, who, following the footsteps of Maestro Marco, penetrated through the Holy Land and India to the farthest bounds of Asia and the remotest islands of the eastern seas ; for after he had gone from his own land of England through all of Europe and Asia until, according to his count, he had covered by land more than three fourths of all the distance around the globe of the earth, he returned after thirty years by a like weary journey to his home. And of this long pilgrimage he has said : ' I tell you for a surety that if you but have good ships and men and prudent guidance, you may sail around all the world of this earth, as well on the side we inhabit as on the other, and return safe and sound to your own country ; and everywhere you shall find men and countries and islands there as well as in our own part of the world.' Much more besides this does this wise and sagacious man say from the abundance of his knowledge to prove that the earth is round, and that he who will sail across the western ocean will find the distant lands he himself saw or heard of, and that by a voyage but one third as long as the mighty travel he made. This same belief is also held by my learned master Paolo Toscanelli, Señores," continued Colon; " for in sending me this present chart, he wrote to me, saying: ' Nor should men wonder that I call the Occident the region where the spices grow, which commonly is named the Orient; for whoever shall sail by the ocean to the west shall find those same countries, and those who journey by land to the east shall come to them likewise, for they are but one and the same.' "

"Wherefore, good sirs," added Colon, after a moment's pause, " for all these reasons, and for an infinite many more taken from the writings of the ancients, both sacred and profane, and from the voyages of travellers by land and sea in these later days, and from the knowledge God has given me, the humblest of His servants, have I maintained for all these years, and ever must maintain, that he who will but venture to the west shall have the lands of the heathen for his possession; for He has called me to this work, in giving me from my earliest days a love for the knowledge of strange lands, and in making me learned in the secrets of the sea and of the stars, and in vouchsafing to me wisdom in geometry and arithmetic, and skill in the making of charts and globes, and in leading me to study the writings of the wise men of old in their chronicles and histories and philosophies, and all else that was needful for this labor; and to this knowledge and experience has He added His calling and commandment that I should undertake this enterprise, and given me the strength and heart to accomplish it with His aid. To Him be the glory to the latest of the ages. Amen."

As Colon concluded, he made the sign of the cross, and remained gazing beyond the narrow circle of light into the gloom of the room beyond, as if he saw there the land he spoke of.

Fray Antonio had sat during the greater part of his guest's remarks with his face half covered by his hand, leaning his elbow on the arm of his chair. He now looked up and said, with some emotion in his voice, —

"And all this you have laid before our gracious sovereigns, Señor Cristoval?"

"All this and more, reverend father, — both to their Highnesses in person and before the council they summoned to hear my cause at Salamanca. But it was the same there as it had been in other years with the council called by the Portuguese king, — some few believed, many remained in doubt; but most laughed at me as a visionary, and ridiculed my proposals as the dream of a madman. Yet feel I still the fire from God burning in my heart, and until I cease to breathe must I follow His bidding."

"May it not be, worshipful sir," inquired the physician, with much respect, "that their Highnesses cannot now sustain the costs of so great an undertaking, seeing that their realms are exhausted by the wars against the Moors?"

"That did I weigh most heedfully, Señor," replied Colon, with emphasis. "I asked them for but two or three small ships, — such as sail along our coasts; for these I deem the best for a voyage of discovery. His Grace of Medina Celi had such a fleet, which he gladly would have given me were it not for the reasons I already named."

"Two or three small ships," repeated the younger man, musingly; "that were a small venture for such a vast return."

"You say right, Señor Garcia," said Colon, sitting upright, with his former look of exaltation kindling in his eyes; "you say right. While the fleets of the King of Portugal are slowly creeping from headland to headland along the coasts of Guinea, getting here a little gold dust and there a few negro slaves, their Majesties of Spain would secure the direct road across the western ocean to the incalculable wealth of Asia. How long would it take, think you, for the gold and pearls, the gems and spices and silks of the golden Indies to repair all the costs of the Moorish wars, and make their Highnesses the chiefest powers of Christendom? Yet is this the least part of the glory which awaits them; for while the ministers of the true faith taught the way of life to the countless hordes of Asia, their Highnesses, with the vast treasure which would pour into their ports with every returning ship, would have the means to crown their pious work of driving the infidel Moors from Spain with the infinitely more blessed one of freeing the Holy Sepulchre from the foul grasp of the vile dogs of Mahomet. This," continued Colon, his rising voice echoing through the bare room, — " this is the grandest task ever given to Christian kings to accomplish; and by doing this our noble king and queen would secure the high approval of Almighty God and the gratitude of endless generations. As for me," he added in a lower tone, " I have vowed to the Holy Trinity that in so far as lies in my power all the benefits from my discovery shall be dedicated to the rescue of Jerusalem from the Paynim."

No one spoke for several minutes. The lamp on the table was sputtering fitfully as the wick drank up the last drops of oil, and monstrous shadows of the three men wavered along the walls and on the ceiling of the fast darkening apartment.

The monk had followed every word spoken by Colon as though he listened to a prophet. He was the first to break the silence.

" Señor Cristoval, it grows late, and we have taxed your kindness unduly, I greatly fear. With your permission we will talk more of this to-morrow. It is barely possible that in your holy work even so humble an instrument as myself may be of some slight help. Let me show you to your chamber. 'T is no disloyalty, I am assured, to say that the poor convent of La Rabida is this night honored as though their Majesties themselves were sharing its lowly shelter."

After conducting Colon to the room where his boy was sleeping, Fray Antonio walked to the convent wicket with the young physician. As they stood there alone in the quiet starlight, his friend said to him in a low tone, full of hidden meaning, —

" Did you mark the Señor Colon said he wanted but two

or three small ships, good father? Bear you in mind, as you ponder his words, that our port of Palos is under sentence of their Majesties' Council to furnish two ships and their crews for any service their Majesties may appoint. The cost of a third might not deter them, were two already provided."

"You speak shrewdly, Garcia," the monk said, clearly much impressed; "mayhap the hand of God is in that thought. Let us keep our own counsel for the night, and on the morrow I will come and confer further with you. Sleep you well, good friend!"

He remained a moment, watching the young physician recede into the darkness; then, stepping within the wicket, walked thoughtfully to his chamber.[1]

[1] Note H, in the Appendix: "The Three Ships of Palos."

III.

THE NOTABLE MISSION OF THE EX-PRIVATEERSMAN.

NO sooner were the services over in the little chapel of the convent on the following morning, and his simple meal despatched, than the father superior excused himself from Colon, and leaving him in charge of the other brethren, betook himself to the house of his friend in the village of Palos. Early though the hour was, the hot sun of an almost tropical summer's day beat fiercely on the path he had to traverse, and rose in trembling air-waves from the low banks of the river and the red-tile roofs of the little town.

The young physician was evidently awaiting the friar's visit with impatience; for the latter had barely given him good-day and thrown himself into a chair with a sense of enjoyment at the freshness of the room, when the doctor exclaimed, —

"Tell me, good father, what think you of our friend yonder, the Señor Colon?"

"I hope that we may help him, Friend Garcia, if so it please God. Her Highness our Most Catholic Queen has ever deigned to give much heed to such causes as I have felt justified in laying before her, and this benignant condescension I have endeavored never to abuse. Now, it seems to me, were a worthy occasion for approaching her Majesty, and asking her renewed attention to the proposals of the Señor Colon, which, if they are but laid before her as a holy enterprise for the propagation of our true religion which shall greatly redound to the glory of God and the credit of Castile, I am assured will receive a new consideration. Moreover, my friend, your thought of the past night may well be used as an argument that the costs of the undertaking need prove no obstacle; that is, provided always you mistake not in your belief about the two ships."

The physician hastened to convince his friend that as to these there could be no doubt. The villagers of Palos, nearly all of whom were seamen, had more than once got themselves into trouble with the courts of the kingdom by deeds of piracy and contraband. Only lately, despite frequent warnings, they had infringed the rigid navigation laws which strictly established for the sailors and shipmasters of Spain the ports which they could visit, the goods they might carry, and prescribed every circumstance of the voyages they were permitted to make. This defiant "re-incidence" of their former offences against the Crown, as the Spanish laws called it, had exhausted the patience of the Royal Council, before which the case had come; and they had, justly or unjustly, condemned the parish of Palos to furnish and equip two ships at the cost of its inhabitants, and hold them at the pleasure of the Crown, to be sent, with the crews required, on whatever service might be ordered within the term of one year. This sentence had caused no little grumbling in Palos and its neighborhood, for no one could foretell whose ships might be selected, or on what cruise they might be sent; although the worst that could happen, so far as the knowledge of the mariners went, was that they should be sent on a voyage to the Canary Islands and back. As time passed, however, and no further commands came about the vessels, the community settled down into the belief that it was nothing more than a threat used by the Council to frighten them into better behavior. Little did the villagers imagine, as they passed the young doctor's house on that hot morning, going down to their boats alongshore or up into the vineyards on the hills above the town, or only lounging lazily toward the village wine-shop for a friendly gossip, what a plot was hatching against their wonted peace of mind!

The friar listened attentively as the physician explained just how the matter of the ships stood. Then he answered, with a smile at the thought of the clamor that would be raised, —

"I knew not all the circumstances of the affair, Garcia, and your exposition makes it clear that the ships are in truth available for the voyage the Señor Colon proposes. But our neighbors here of Palos will surely make resistance if they be consulted beforehand, and it will be best to secure a particular order from their Highnesses, if we can but obtain it. Oftentimes has my worthy brother, Fray Martin Sanchez, the curate of your parish, told me of the stubbornness of his flock. You may yourself remember, since it is not many years ago, how they rebelled against the king's command to restore the vessel they had stolen from their neighbors of the port of Santa Maria? 'T was a clear case of piracy, since our sailors seized both ship and crew while peacefully engaged, as was their right, in fishing along the coast; yet our people resisted the order of the Council, and all but revolted before they would give up the ship."

"They are loath to part with what they once hold, Father," replied the doctor, anxious to speak a word for his turbulent townsmen, "be it had by fair means or foul. But a direct mandate from our sovereigns to perform a bounden duty cannot be avoided, and they must yield in the end. Think you such an order can be had?"

"We can but try, my son; but on this matter we must hear the Señor Colon. Will you go with me to the convent?"

As soon as the force of the midday heat was past, the two friends made their way back to the cloister on the hill. They found Colon seated in the library, poring diligently over a heavy tome of one of the early fathers of the Church, apparently deeply absorbed in its contents.

In a few words the superior explained to him the suggestion made by the physician on the previous night, and the result of their conversation in the village that morning.

"Will the ships serve your purpose, worthy sir?" inquired the friar. "If they will but answer, with your consent I will gladly lay the matter privately before her Majesty the Queen, in the hope that such feeble incitement as I may use may determine her Majesty not to permit so godly a work to pass into other hands."

"The vessels in use along these coasts are such as best suit my needs, reverend father," Colon responded; "since those of greater size and deeper draught cannot approach near to shallow shores or enter the mouths of many rivers. This much have I learned in voyaging to Africa. Moreover, I look not for stormy seas or great gales, since I should maintain always the latitude of the Canary Islands, where soft breezes and moderate weather prevail. But two ships, I fear, are scanty provision with which to make such a voyage, since, should disaster overtake one, the other must return at once. Nevertheless," he added in a tone of decision, "if we can but obtain two, I shall make the voyage, putting my trust in the Holy Trinity, who have never yet forsaken me, Their servant."

"It were long to put all this our cause on paper," said the friar. "If it please you, Señor Colon, I will rather but open the matter in a letter to her Highness the Queen, and crave her gracious permission to expound the subject at greater length to her in person."

"I doubt not you do well, Father," Colon answered, "since written words, however true they be, must fall but coldly on her Majesty's sight in the press of anxieties forced upon her mind by the siege of Granada."

"Señor Garcia," the superior said, turning to his friend, "we shall need as bearer of this letter a man who is both stout of heart and discreet of mind. The road from here to the royal camp is none too safe in these days of turmoil, and it behooves us as well that our petition should reach her Majesty's hand without the knowledge of any of the Court. Know you a man whom we can trust?"

The physician reflected a few minutes, and then named two or three men of Palos and the neighboring town of

Moguer; but some objection was made to them all. Finally he said, —

"There is Sebastian Rodriguez, good father, — the pilot from Lepe. He is just now in our village, and I know him for a brave man and a prudent."

"Is not he the brawler who seized a vessel and all its contents from one of our men of Palos, within sight of the port, not many years ago, my friend?" asked the priest.

"The same, Father; but he claims that Nieto, who owned the other boat and was privateering against the Moors, had done him a grievous wrong, and that he took his vessel away in a fair trial of strength. When the Council sentenced him to restitution, he gave up his spoils without resistance. I deem him to be an honest man and faithful."

"If he took but what he believed to be his own, good father," interposed Colon, "in a fair and open contest, it should not be counted against him, think you? Such boldness is often a sign of a frank and open disposition among the men of the sea."

"Nay, my friends," replied the friar, "I know nothing to his discredit; and of a verity the ways of the sea are not as the ways of the cloister. If Garcia will bring the man to converse with us, he may prove to be the very one we need."

The superior then explained in detail his plan, and asked Colon's sanction to make the attempt. He would write a letter to the Queen Isabella, relying on his former close relations with her Majesty as her confessor, and would ask a private audience to lay before her his reasons for urging her to consider favorably and give prompt despatch to the proposals of Colon. Knowing well the enthusiastic piety of the queen, he would dwell chiefly on the vast service to be rendered to the Christian religion by opening a direct road for its spread to the immense hordes of heathen Asia, and crowning her grand work of driving the Mohammedan Moors from Spain with the evangelization of all that enormous eastern continent. The pious monk also counted, in a more worldly manner, on removing the chief obstacle that had before been urged by the queen's advisers against the project of Colon, — that is, its cost, — by showing that two vessels already lay at the orders of the Crown, and it would be an easy measure to put them at Colon's disposal for his undertaking. This he felt would have especial weight with King Ferdinand, who was disposed to be less open to the influences of sentiment than the queen. The same prudent and eminently practical monarch, the friar imagined, would realize that even as a speculation it would be worth while staking the small sum now demanded, in the hope of securing for the Spanish treasury the fabulous wealth of the Indies, which from time immemorial had come overland through the eastern ports of the Mediterranean, and enriched the sovereigns who controlled these, from Solomon of old to the merchant princes of Venice in the days of which we write. But as the good father was familiar with the manifold intrigues and jealousies of the Court, and shrewdly suspected that much of the opposition encountered by Colon had come from the latter's direct and straightforward methods and impatience of fawning and hypocrisy, he determined to deal himself with the queen alone, giving to the bearer of his letter a note to her Majesty's present confessor, the Bishop Fernando de Talavera, merely requesting the latter to see that Fray Antonio's letter should reach the queen's hands promptly, as it related to important interests of the Crown.

"In the mean time, honored sir," concluded the worthy superior, "our poor retreat of La Rabida will consider itself indeed fortunate if you will use its roof for your shelter until we hear the pleasure of our Lady Queen."

"That will I, and gladly, Father," Colon replied with heartiness. "Were it not that I feel this call so strong upon me, I would myself long before this have worn the habit of Saint Francis."[1]

"We can all serve God in our own fashion, good sir," answered the monk, with kindness. "So that we keep our hearts steadfast and our hands clean, and do the duty that

[1] In his latter years Columbus wore the habit of a lay brother of this Order.

lies before us, it matters little whether we wear gown or doublet. For my part, I should rather be the meanest of your sailors on this voyage you wish to make, than be the Superior of La Rabida. But each must do the work that is nearest his hand."

When the little conclave separated in the evening, it was settled that the physician should seek out Sebastian Rodriguez and bring him up to the convent, without telling him of the particular service wanted. Meanwhile the superior was to prepare his letters to the queen and her confessor.

The next day the doctor appeared with the pilot of Lepe. As the latter came before Colon and Fray Antonio in the latter's room, he showed a strong, well-knit frame of the middle height, a face and neck burned to a deep reddish-brown by years of scorching sun, and a frank but determined cast of features. Holding his woollen sailor's cap in his gnarled hands, he made a clumsy bow, and said, without any sign of embarrassment, —

"A poor servant of your Worships, Señores, at your orders."

"Sebastian, my son," said the superior, adopting the priestly mode of address, "I want some one to do a piece of work for me which is not easy, and must be done by one who is both deaf and dumb. Wilt thou do it for me?"

"Why not, your Reverence," answered the sailor, "if it pass not my powers?"

"'T is on land, not on the sea, Son Sebastian," continued the friar; "and it may take thee many a league from home."

"So much the worse for me, then, reverend father," the sailor replied; "for I am but half a man on dry land. Still, I will not go back on my given word."

"Look you, Sebastian!" the monk said, taking up a small packet from the table; "here is a letter for his Grace the Bishop of Avila, which thou art to give into his own hands. He is now at the camp of their Highnesses, before the city of Granada. Thou wilt have no trouble in finding his Grace, for thou hast but to go toward the royal pavilions on reaching camp, and any one will tell thee where to find him. I have marked the packet 'On their Majesties' Service;' and if any hinder thee on thy way, thou hast but to show it and say thou bearest a message to Court, to gain free passage. Make thy journey as quickly as may be, and hasten back with the reply that shall be given thee. Thou shalt have both thanks and reward. But above all, let not the parcel leave thy hands except for those of his Grace the Bishop. Here is money for thy needs." And the superior handed him some silver coins.

"Have no fear, your Reverence," the pilot said cheerfully; "the writing shall reach its haven if my legs but hold out. I ask your blessing, holy father." He bent his head as the superior bestowed it upon him, and then departed with a hearty farewell to all present.

The little group remaining thought it would take three weeks for him to go to Granada and return with a reply, allowing him a week each way and a week for detention at Court. The way was not so very long, but led over the mountains, and was rugged throughout; besides, it lay mostly through the territory from which the Moors had been expelled only the previous year; and in the confusion and disorder of military occupation it might well be that a single messenger should meet with delay.

During the days of waiting which followed, Colon was the least impatient of all the trio. He spent most of his time in the library of the convent and in conversing with the superior, though now and again he would join his son Diego in the garden, where the latter took great delight in working with the younger monks. The superior himself made no secret of the anxiety with which he attended the queen's reply; while the young physician was backward and forward between the convent and the village two or three times each day. They all agreed that it was best for Colon not to go much to the village at present, lest some suspicion of his real purpose should be aroused; for although in so small a place the presence at the convent of a stranger of his distinguished bearing could not fail to excite some remark, it was no uncommon thing in those days for men of active life to seek for a period of rest in some religious house, and so no especial meaning need attach to Colon's sojourn with the superior. He also deferred for the present his desire to meet Martin Alonzo Pinzon and converse with him about his voyages, and also his search for the old companions of his own earlier cruises. Three or four sailors from the surrounding district did, indeed, climb the convent hill to seek him out, either because they had sailed with him in bygone years, or had heard of him as a famous captain when on their own voyages; but to all such, beyond a warm welcome and an assurance of his gratitude for their offers of service, Colon only said that at present he was " in port for repairs," and could not yet say when he would command a ship again. It was no new thing for him to have to wait; and he had in every fibre of his strong heart the deep-laid conviction that all would be well "in God's own time," as he was accustomed to say.

Only two weeks had passed of the time allowed Sebastian Rodriguez to make his journey, when one morning that doughty mariner presented himself at the convent gate, accompanied by the faithful Garcia Fernandez. On hearing of their presence the superior hastened to meet them, with a great fear in his heart lest some disaster had overtaken his messenger and prevented his reaching Granada. One look at the joyful face of the physician, however, was enough to dispel all doubts. The pilot had made the journey, and returned with the queen's reply.

Sending them both to his room, the friar hastened to summon Colon before hearing Sebastian's report. When they were all together, the worthy mariner carefully drew a packet from the inner depths of his jerkin and handed it to the superior. The latter hurriedly broke its seals and ran his eye over it; then giving it to Colon, exclaimed, —

"Now, glory be to God, Señor Cristoval! Our gracious queen has ever the same noble heart."

Checking his enthusiasm at the sight of the pilot standing motionless before them, he added, —

"My son, thou must have refreshment. If thou wilt go to the refectory, the brothers will gladly serve thee, and in a little while we will hear the account of thy travels. Such reward as it is in our power to give thou shalt surely have."

"Whenever your Reverence pleases," Sebastian replied. "'T was not so hard to do as I thought." And with a look of satisfaction he turned to leave the room.

"Thou hast sailed a straighter course than thou knewest, comrade, good pilot though thou art," said Colon to him, heartily; "and I for one owe thee many thanks."

"Nay, your Worship," said the sailor, evidently flattered; "'t was but a ship-boy's cruise, — a fair wind and a smooth sea."

"Yon goes a man after my own heart," said Colon, as the pilot stepped into the courtyard.

Then spreading the queen's letter before him, he studied it intently.

IV.

THE FAMOUS MULE OF JUAN THE HARD-HEADED.

THE letter of Queen Isabella thanked the father superior cordially for the loyal and pious motives which had led him to address her, and directed him as soon as he received her Majesty's present reply to come to the royal camp before Granada and present himself before her. He was likewise commissioned to say to Colon, on the queen's behalf, that he should now be of good heart, and look forward with confidence to the speedy realization of all his hopes.

"Her Highness is indeed gracious," said Colon, as he returned the letter to the friar; "but I will recompense to the Crown a thousand fold whatever they advance for my voyage."

At the first renewed sign of promise all the bitterness and disappointment of those long twenty years of waiting had vanished. To the ardent imagination of Colon all difficulties had been overcome, the voyage successfully accomplished, and the treasures of the Indies were flowing into the coffers of the Spanish monarchs. Sanguineness is usually counted as a fault; but had this man been less sanguine he would never have done the work he did.

"Her Majesty's commands admit of no delay, my friends," the superior said, the monkish spirit of prompt obedience asserting itself. "I must start at once for the

Court, unless, indeed, the Señor Colon should have a reason why I should wait upon him?"

"Far be it from me to hold you for a single hour, Father," returned Colon, hastily. "If you will but continue the kindness to which I am already so much beholden, I will await your return, or such message as you shall send me, here among the godly brethren of La Rabida."

"The advantage will be ours, Señor," replied the friar. "But, Gossip Garcia, between us we must find some beast to carry me on the way; for it will be neither prudent nor becoming for me to make the journey to her Majesty on foot. And our little monastery is not yet so rich that it can maintain a stable," he added, with a comical look of despair.

"By no means, Father," the physician answered; "the journey must be made with all possible haste. Though," and he looked puzzled in turn, "it is not easy to find among our neighbors here a beast fit for travelling, — unless, in truth, we ask the Pinzons, and for many reasons I would not do that could we avoid it."

"You are very right, Garcia," said the superior; "until we know the wishes of her Majesty the Queen we must avoid anything which might allow a knowledge of this project to get abroad."

"It may be that herein lies a way out of the dilemma, Father," suggested Colon. "Among the old sailors who have sought me out since I have been housed under your kind roof was one Juan Rodriguez Cabezudo, who many years ago made several voyages with me. Hard-headed is Juan Rodriguez in name, and hard-headed is he by nature; but his heart is sound to the inmost core. In his offers of service, he particularly told me he had an excellent mule, which he much lauded as a good traveller. I bear it well in mind," and Colon laughed, "because it seemed to me that the old sea-wolf was anxious I should know that now he was a man of estate; and I duly wished him well of his good fortune. I doubt not the worthy man will spare the mule if he knows it is a service done to me."

"I know the good man well, Señor Cristoval," the physician said. "He has a little vineyard between Palos and Moguer, and lives now quietly at his ease; though men do say his life in other times was stormy enough."

"With his past life we have naught to do, Friend Garcia," objected the friar, impatiently, "so he but have a good travelling beast and let us have its use. Think you we can compass this, Señor Cristoval?"

Here the young physician interposed, and said that if Colon would go with him to his own house in Palos, he would send for Juan Rodriguez, and they could converse there without risk of exciting attention, and without giving Colon the needless fatigue of the long walk to Moguer and back. To this Colon assented willingly, and a messenger was sent to the old sailor to go to the physician's house as soon as he could. Then the trio sought out Sebastian the pilot, and heard his report of the adventures which had befallen him on his journey to Granada, and of the wonderful sights he had seen in the royal camp; where, according to his belief, the vast hosts of the Spanish sovereigns were going to sweep the Moors clean out of Granada and drown them all — king, knights, and rabble; men, women, and children — in the deepest waters of the blue Mediterranean. Having dismissed the honest mariner with many hearty thanks and the promised reward, the three associates discussed in detail the representations to be made by Fray Antonio to the queen. Colon gave him the fullest liberty to speak for himself before her Majesty.

"Such arguments as are familiar to my mind I have already worn threadbare before their Highnesses and their counsellors, reverend father," he said with sadness. "My main hope now is that her Majesty will hearken to your pious exhortations as to the duty of their Catholic Highnesses, as the especial champions of the Church against all infidels and heathen, to exert themselves to carry the truths of our blessed religion into those distant lands which I believe shall be found beyond the sea. Should you wish to consult with me, or should her Majesty desire my presence, I will hasten to the Court without the loss of a single moment."

The superior informed himself minutely of how this and that dignitary of the Court had stood with reference to Colon and his project. The latter stated clearly and concisely the position of the chief personages about the sovereigns regarding himself, and, in especial, impressed upon the superior that Alonzo de Quintanilla and Luis de Santangel, financial officers of the crown, and Fray Diego de Deza, tutor to the young Prince Juan, had shown themselves repeatedly to be his sincere friends and supporters; but that he had never felt that the Bishop Talavera, a prelate whom the worthy superior held in the highest esteem, was friendly to him or his cause.

"Nay, then, Señor Cristoval," the friar urged, "have no fear on that score. I shall talk with no one, be he your friend or not, about this matter, save with the Queen Isabella alone. I did but wish to be advised, so that were her Majesty to show any new scruple about the enterprise, I might discover whence it took its source and overthrow it. The Holy Book commends to us the wisdom of the serpent as well as the gentleness of the dove, my son. But under her Majesty's express injunction that you should hold high your hope, Señor, I have but little fear of a new repulse."

When the noontide heat was past, Colon and the physician walked down to the latter's house in the village to await the reply of Juan Rodriguez. They had not been long seated, when that worthy himself appeared, clattering into the little courtyard of the modest house upon the very animal they were in quest of. Dismounting with the air of a man who had been accustomed to ride all his life, he entered the open door of the room where the others were sitting, and saluted them with profound gravity.

Short of stature and dumpy of build, his weather-beaten and wrinkled face might have passed as that of a hard-working farmer, had not a certain habit of spreading his stumpy legs and a most preposterously loud voice stamped Juan as a man who knew more of ropes than of grape-vines. A head as round as any orange was set close on his shoulders by a thick and muscular neck, and covered with closely curling locks of wiry hair, which with the short, stubby beard surrounding his face, was liberally sprinkled with gray. It was not necessary for the good man to open his mouth for one to know why he was surnamed Cabezudo, or hard-headed. His whole appearance justified the title.

"Your servant, Master Cristoval, and yours, Señor Doctor," he rumbled out. "They told me your Worships wanted to see me, and here I am at your orders. Is it a cruise, Master?" he asked, turning toward Colon.

"Not so, Juan Rodriguez," the latter answered; "but I want thee to make me thy debtor by lending me thy mule for a little, since thou wert so good as to make the offer to me."

"'There is no better mule between here and Seville than mine, Master," the other replied, with a glance of pride out into the courtyard. "She has a trot as easy as a cradle."

"Then thou wilt lend me thy beast, Friend Juan?" Colon asked.

"Master, the beast is a good beast, and I would not have harm come to her."

"I will be thy warranty, Juan, against any harm befalling thy mule."

"Your Worship is somewhat over-tall for the little brute, — to make so bold, Master Cristoval," Juan said in a doubtful tone.

"'T is not I who will ride the mule, thou old fault-finder!" Colon said with a laugh. "'T is my honored friend the pious guardian of the convent up yonder, and his Reverence is less my size than thine. But I have his journey greatly at heart, Juan, for much will it advantage me; and I offered to find him a beast to ride, counting upon thy goodness. 'T is no great distance he travels, and the mule shall be cared for as though she were my own."

"They say at sea, Master, that 't is better to carry the crucifix aboard ship and leave the *padre* on shore," the old fellow said doubtfully. "I know not whether it be the same with the lading of a mule or not."

"Now leave thy profane railings for the tavern, Juan

Rodriguez," Colon answered sharply. "Thou shouldst remember I like not to hear Holy Church reviled. If thou wilt not let me have the mule, say so straightly, like the plain sailor thou art, — or used to be; but if thou wilt, be not so tedious about doing thy kindness, for it but lessens the thanks I shall have to give."

"Your Worship knows that I honor the Church, and am a humble votary of Our Lady of Montserrate," Juan said, with an attempt at looking pious; "but it is no sin to know a good beast when you see it, and care for it as it deserves, Master."

"Thou hast been so much with thy mule, Juan," Colon answered in despair, "that thou art growing like her. Wilt thou let me have thy beast or not?"

"Surely, Master Cristoval, all I have is at your Worship's service, and proud will I be to wait upon you in anything you may wish. Yet that little mule is like a child to me; were aught to befall it, I would not know where to get another."

"Then thou canst not lend me the mule, colleague?" Colon said.

"Nay, Master, I said not so."

"Then thou wilt lend her to me, Friend Juan?"

"Why, and it please you, Master, 't was what I plainly meant to say, only I have not the trick of easy speech. It would ill become me to refuse your Worship any service I can do."

"There spoke the man I used to know," Colon replied heartily. "I told his Reverence thou wouldst serve us in this, and that thy head was harder than thy heart. Thou hast my thanks, Juan Rodriguez, and I will answer that the little beast is treated as thou wouldst have her."

Having given, with many protestations of respect and excuses for his boldness, a great variety of cautions and suggestions as to the care and management of his precious mule, the old sailor trudged away. He was well satisfied with having served "the Commander;" but now and again a twinge of regret shot through his mind as he thought that for some time he must forego the proud pleasure of riding through the neighborhood "like a somebody," as he said to himself in the Spanish phrase.

Colon and Garcia Fernandez returned to the convent, whither the mule was shortly afterward brought by a neighbor of the physician. In order to avoid observation, the superior had determined to make his start after nightfall; this plan having the additional advantage of enabling him to escape the burning heat of the summer sun in crossing the plains which lie between Palos and the mountains. All was soon ready for his departure. The affairs of the convent, in his absence, had been intrusted to the brother next in rank, and Colon and his son were commended to the hospitable care of the little community. At the evening service in the chapel the superior himself had officiated, his two friends devoutly taking part in the exercises, and Colon in particular committing this enterprise of the friar's, which was of so great moment to himself, to that Divine Providence whose aid he continued to invoke until the last moment of his life. Then, the evening being well advanced, with many hearty farewells and prayers for his success, the father superior mounted the mule of Juan Rodriguez, and started on his journey in the bright starlight of the southern night.

We may be sure that he made his way as rapidly as was practicable over the broad plains and rugged mountains which lay between him and the last stronghold of the Moors in Spain; though of the incidents of his journey we have no record. Arriving at the royal headquarters, which were then established at that town of Santa Fé which the sovereigns had built close to the walls of Granada as a token that they meant not to turn their backs on the city until the Cross had supplanted the Crescent, Fray Antonio caused his arrival to be announced to the queen without loss of time.

He was soon summoned to her Majesty's presence, and greeted as a trusted friend and faithful counsellor. In as few words as possible he described the reason of his personal appeal to the queen in behalf of Colon; the deep impression made upon him by the latter; the vast field for the spread of the Catholic religion which would be opened up were the kingdoms of Asia in reality to be reached by a short cut across the western ocean; and, finally, the insignificance of the cost and preparations involved if the two vessels available at Palos were pressed into this service. For the present he purposely refrained from dwelling on the more material side of the project. He had gained an intimate knowledge of the characters both of the king and queen, when the latter's confessor, and knew that while Isabella was most easily to be persuaded to any undertaking by considerations of religion, her royal husband had ever an eye to the main chance, and would be more likely to give his approval to the once rejected proposal by the inducement of cargoes of gold and silks and spices and new dominions, which would raise Spain to a higher rank among the powers of Europe. As he had intimated to Colon, the prudent monk accordingly reserved these arguments to meet the objections he was sure would be made by King Ferdinand to any revival of Colon's scheme at that time.

The queen herself listened with evident interest to all Fray Antonio said. She did not attempt to disguise her sympathy for Colon and his aims, or her belief in their practicability. But she showed the monk, in a few frank sentences, how almost impossible it had been for her to undertake an enterprise of the magnitude of that which Colon proposed, at a time when her own realm was engaged in a life-and-death struggle with the Moorish kings, when her treasures were exhausted, and when, with few exceptions, all her most trusted advisers, including King Ferdinand himself, had opposed the project as doubtful both of execution and advantage.

"You should remember, reverend sir," the queen had said, "that for fifty years our neighbors of Portugal have been making voyages of discovery along the African coast in search of a path to Asia, and therein have spent a vast treasure and lost great numbers of their stoutest seamen, with no return in any wise proportioned to these sacrifices.

With such an experience so near our borders, it is not cause for wonderment that our Council should shrink from embarking in so perilous a venture at a season when every man and every maravedi are so sorely needed here at home."

Now, however, the queen continued, since Providence had so blessed the Spanish arms that the war was almost ended, and it was only a question of time when Granada, the last refuge of the Saracens, must yield, the queen was anxious to advance the plans of Colon, if it should be in any way feasible; and most particularly did she wish to dissuade him from making any application to the other sovereigns of Europe. All this Fray Antonio was to communicate to Colon, and to add a renewed message of hope, and the queen's pledge that as soon as the affairs of the siege permitted, his proposals should have immediate attention. Meantime the superior himself was to remain at the Court, where he could be consulted by their Majesties as they might find leisure to treat of the affair.

The good father took the first opportunity to inform Colon by letter of the friendly disposition shown by her Majesty, and the encouragement she held out to him of a speedy solution of his anxieties. The receipt of this news filled Colon with a quiet confidence and assurance of success to which his mind had long been a stranger; while the more excitable physician could hardly contain his impatience from day to day, so eager was he for further word from Fray Antonio. It came, not long afterward, in a letter to Garcia Fernandez himself, saying that the queen had sent a summons to Diego Prieto, the *alcalde mayor*, or chief officer, of the village of Palos, ordering him to appear without delay at the Court, on the service of the Crown. The superior explained to Garcia Fernandez in his letter that the object of this summons was to inquire into the convenience of fitting out an expedition for Colon from that port; but that no hint had been, or would be given as yet of its destination, it being spoken of only as "a voyage to be made in their Majesties' interests."

This piece of news proved too much even for Colon's

disciplined self-control. The convent library lost its restful charms, and he found himself wondering why he had not been sent for by the queen, and picturing the intrigues and obstacles which would be invented by the opponents of his scheme to hinder its realization as soon as they should know that it had been revived and received with favor by Queen Isabella. Fortunately this anxiety was not to be of long duration; for within a fortnight Diego Prieto, the alcalde, himself returned from Granada, bringing with him another letter from Fray Antonio to his friend the physician, and, what interested the little community a great deal more, word that their Majesties had raked up that old sentence of the Council, and were likely at any day to demand the two ships and their crews, and send them off on a voyage somewhere.

But to all the clamorous inquiries of his fellow-townsmen as to the destination of the cruise, and the details about it, the worthy magistrate would only answer, with a plentiful show of temper, —

"Now ask that of Our Lady in your prayers, good people, for I know not. Since when did our gracious sovereigns whisper to me the secrets of the kingdom? For all I know, ye idiots, the ships are to seek the Isles of the Blessed that our sailors tell their idle tales about."

Within the harmless-looking packet which Fray Antonio had asked the alcalde to take with him "by very special favor" to his good friend the physician Garcia, was contained the explanation of the whole matter. Therein lay a letter to Colon, calling him, on the queen's invitation, to the Court without delay, and enclosing no less a sum than twenty thousand maravedies in golden florins of Aragon, to provide for the purchase of a mule for his journey and a wardrobe suitable for his appearance at Court. All this was sent under cover to the young physician, so that the recent inquiries about the ships should not be coupled with Colon's name in advance of the completion of the queen's intentions.

Where Colon found this second mule our documents do

not show;[1] but with a heavy purse and a light heart we may rest assured he did not waste as many words over it as over the first one. That his preparations were soon made we do know, and also that, leaving the lad Diego in the kind keeping of the brothers of La Rabida, and asking the young physician to see to the boy's welfare also, he bade farewell to son and friend, and set out for the Court of their Most Catholic Majesties, Ferdinand of Aragon and Isabella of Castile.

[1] Some of the more critical historians of late have derided the testimony of Juan Rodriguez Cabezudo, which was given twenty years after the incident here recorded, on the ground that it was absurd to suppose that he would remember the loan of his mule after so great a lapse of time. They overlook the fact that a good mule was worth from eight thousand to ten thousand maravedies in those days, and the owner of one was a marked man in a rural community. The evidence concerning the visit of Colon to La Rabida is directly as we have related it, notwithstanding the version given by Prescott and Irving in their brilliant volumes. Those who care to judge for themselves may find the details of the testimony in the Appendix.

V.

BARGAINING FOR A WORLD.

IN the vivid pages of Prescott and Irving and Lockhart we have a series of pictures, as clear as those of the camera, of that camp before the Moorish capital where Colon now arrived. Eighty thousand mail-clad Christian soldiers surrounded, as by a girth of iron, the "infidel" defenders, who, do what they might, could neither break the blockade and escape from their city, nor open it long enough to receive the help they so much needed from without. In those days of helmet and breastplate, of cross-bow and lance, when nearly all the fighting was still hand to hand, and the bonds of discipline were so much looser than now, an army like that of the Spanish monarchs would make a greater impression on the beholder than one of half a million men to-day. Add to this the vast array of camp-followers, servants and hangers-on which the military methods of the age allowed, and the large civil and ecclesiastical element present in attendance on the royal Court, and we can well believe that the plain of Granada bore a stirring appearance as Colon entered it on that autumn day, four hundred years ago.

Since their city of Santa Fé had progressed far enough to afford them shelter, their Majesties had abandoned the more exposed life of the camp pavilions for the greater security of walls of stone and roofs of tile ; and over their new palace now floated the standards of Aragon and Castile. To the king and queen this siege meant all the word implied.

It was indeed a "sitting down" before the Moorish walls; and there they plainly intended to remain until the pressure of famine or a realizing sense of the uselessness of further resistance should induce their stubborn adversary, Boabdil the Unlucky, to open his gates, own himself beaten, and give up Granada, and with it the dominion of his race in Spain.

Colon sought out the lodgings of his friend the superior, and was soon in possession of all that had passed between that good ally and the queen. Fray Antonio also related to him all that he had been able to gather as to the disposition of her Majesty's advisers toward the project, and told Colon with emphasis that he need have no fear that any opposition would now divert the queen from her determination to grant him the means he required. But, knowing the impetuous nature of the man he addressed, the friar warned Colon that he should bear in mind the excessive demands now made upon their Majesties' attention, and not yield to a feeling of impatience if delays were still encountered. Those who were in a position to be best informed were of the opinion that the war was nearing its close; that it was only a matter of a few weeks when the city must surrender, and the Moors be banished once and forever from the kingdom. This done, the queen would be free to carry into execution the proposal of Colon, and, the friar asserted, would assuredly do so. Meantime her prompt and generous response to the representations made by Fray Antonio and her summons of Colon to the Court were sufficient evidence of the sincerity of her purpose toward him.

To all of these suggestions Colon yielded a ready acquiescence. Now that he had positive assurances of her Majesty's intention to forward his undertaking, it was far more easy to wait than it had been in former years, when he was in doubt as to whether she would, after all his patience, give him the aid he solicited, or dismiss his whole scheme as impracticable. With a heart made lighter and his resolution still further confirmed by the encouraging words of his friend, Colon caused his arrival to be announced to the queen, and awaited in some impatience her Majesty's orders.

These were not long delayed. Queen Isabella commanded that he should be ushered at once into her presence. So kindly and courteous was the reception given him, that Colon never to his dying day recalled it without a declaration of his gratitude. Frankly and earnestly her Majesty set before him, as she had already done with Fray Antonio, the difficulties and embarrassments which at the moment surrounded her. Let these once but lessen somewhat, the queen said, and her attention should be devoted to the project which Colon had so much at heart. Meanwhile it was her desire that he remain attached to the Court, and as opportunity could be found she and the king would discuss with Colon the details of his enterprise. With these and many assurances of her confidence and sympathy, her Majesty dismissed him for the time being, commending him to her officers as one entitled to particular consideration and regard.

In the weeks which followed Colon for the first time fully felt the grateful sensation which was supposed in olden times to attend those fortunate beings who enjoyed their sovereign's favor. Royalty had set the seal of its approval upon his "pretension," and the suppliant of last year was the successful suitor of this. To the sincere welcome of the few who had ever been his steadfast friends Colon now saw added the flattery of many who, without knowing or caring anything about his plans, recognized only that he had the queen's confidence, and smiled on him accordingly. But with him such approaches were thrown away; for he remembered how for year after year the very same individuals had ignored his earnest arguments or scoffed at his urgent pleadings, and he valued their present protestations of friendship at exactly what they were worth, — nothing.

Cheered and encouraged by the certainty of his near success, and sustained by the devotion of his real friends, — who, if scant in number, were both faithful and influential, — Colon saw the days pass without either restiveness or misgiving.

In the almost daily assaults and forays which took place around the besieged city, either to weaken the Moors or to repulse their sallies, he several times took part, and proved himself to be as brave a soldier as he was a skilful and intrepid sailor. He had no love of fighting for its own sake, and his whole life showed that he was sparing of men's blood even under circumstances when, according to the morals of his time, he would have been applauded for shedding it; but to him a Moor was a limb of Satan, and it was a Christian's duty to fight him wherever he was found. So, having had plenty of experience in his younger days, he offered his services now; and his long arm and practised muscles made the Moorish helmet upon which his sword fell ring again.

Thus, with constant discussion and consideration of his great project among his friends, and occasional conferences with their Majesties or some one deputed by them, as to the practical details of its accomplishment, Colon passed the time waiting for his day to come. "Time and I against the world," the Spaniards say; and at length he heard the hour sound when his great work was to be consummated. On the second day of January, 1492, Muley Boabdil the Moor delivered to King Ferdinand the keys of the city which had for so long resisted the Spanish arms, and after saluting the queen, started with his suite toward the distant sierra, where, as the legends say, he turned to take a last look at the beautiful capital he loved so well. Few passages in history are more pathetic, none is more worthily told, than this turning of the exiled king to gaze for the last time on the land of his fathers and the home of his faith. And yet even the eloquence of an Irving should fail with us of the New World in arousing any feeling of regret over the unfortunate monarch's woes; for "The Last Sigh of the Moor" dispersed forever the mists which had shrouded our half of the earth since the day of its creation.

The queen kept punctually her promise to Colon, notwithstanding the thousand and one matters requiring the royal decision. The disposition to be made of the conquered

Moors; the establishment of an administration, civil, military, and ecclesiastic, for the new province; the rewards for those who had distinguished themselves in the campaign; the financial and other measures to be considered in view of the cessation of the long war, — all these, with the constant requirements of the rest of her kingdom, were enough to excuse the queen from adding to her cares the expedition planned by Colon. What possible consideration could a Stanley or a Nordenskjold have hoped for had he laid his plans for a journey across Africa or a voyage to the North Pole before the Emperor William the very week that Paris fell? Yet in the midst of just such a season of busy excitement and triumphant confusion did Queen Isabella recall her pledge to the Genoese navigator, and take from her manifold other duties the time to consider his petition and appoint a commission of her officers to agree with him upon the details of his enterprise.

These negotiations progressed but slowly, despite the well-known sympathy of the queen. In the first place, yielding to the fanatic zeal of their priestly advisers, the Spanish monarchs had decided to expel from their kingdoms all the Jews who were settled therein, to the number of several hundred thousand, and send them after the Moors; and the practical method of carrying out this measure called for much discussion and consideration on the part of their Majesties' counsellors. In the second place, the commissioners considered that Colon's demands were extravagant, and even impudent. He asked to be made admiral of their Majesties in the western ocean, with sole authority over the lands he might discover therein, and receive besides one tenth of all the profits arising from whatever discoveries he might make. Until now most of the members of the commission, and especially its chief, Fernando de Talavera, had disputed the feasibility of Colon's plans, and looked upon them as the dream of a visionary. But once he had the audacity to aspire to the high dignity of an admiral of Castile, with all of its elaborate privileges and honors, it was clear that he must be taught to know his place; and the question of the discovery of a new road to Asia became a matter of no importance in comparison with the colossal presumption of this foreign sailor. This much did the worthy prelate, Talavera, say to Colon in no very gentle words. Having himself just been promoted to be Archbishop of Granada, the idea of any other mortal aspiring to an equally high office in another branch of the royal service seemed to him especially absurd.

"I say not, most reverend sir," was Colon's reply, "that I am wholly worthy of so great an honor at their Majesties' hands; but this I do affirm, and must maintain, that in order honorably to represent their Majesties before the potentates of Asia, and to preserve a proper discipline in the new lands I shall discover, and to have that weight of authority without which the expedition I propose must surely end in disaster and distress, I must be clothed with a fitting dignity. Since this enterprise is to be conducted by means of ships and upon the sea, I conceive the most expedient form for this authority I need to be the office of Admiral for their Highnesses. As for the tithe which I exact from the fruits of my discovery, 't is but justice, and no more; moreover it is dedicated to a holy purpose by my vows, and cannot be abated. I crave your Eminence's pardon, if I speak with unseemly boldness; but from my words I cannot turn back."

There was much discussion in the commission as to this stand of Colon's. His own friends urged him to accept some other title, or make such concession as might be required to secure a prompt adjustment of his contract with the Crown; but while grateful for their interest, he was inflexible.

"I may not alter my position because I must not, honored friend," he answered to Quintanilla, the queen's auditor-general, who pressed him strongly to abate his demands. "With less authority I cannot fitly serve our sovereigns in those distant lands, and with less reward I cannot fulfil the vows I have made to redeem the Holy Sepulchre. If I find for the Crown of Castile the continent of Asia, what I ask is little enough; if I find it not, the Crown loses naught. But this I fear not. It is written that I shall not fail," he added with a grave smile.

What passed between the new archbishop and Queen Isabella we do not know; but when the commission again convened he announced that her Majesty concurred in thinking the claims of Colon excessive, and therefore they could not be granted. This was a hard blow to Colon; but he would not yield a hair-breadth. Taking his leave of the queen's commissioners, he sought out his friends, and bade them farewell. His plans were not yet made, he told them; but he thought he should seek the Court of France as he had started to do the year before.

"What has moved her Majesty to take this view I know not," he said to his friend Fray Diego de Deza; "but this I do know, that her generous aid and sympathy shall ever be borne in my mind, and my children's children shall bless her name. I pray you make my humblest acknowledgments to her Majesty."

With this he set out from the city, intending to return to the little convent at Palos, and there think out new plans in conference with the two good friends who had shown so intelligent and disinterested a sympathy with his aims. But his friends at Court were no less devoted; for no sooner had he left them than Luiz de Santangel hastened to lay before the queen the injustice and unwisdom of losing all the benefits expected from this enterprise for the sake of a point of etiquette which might amount to nothing, and so revived her sympathies that she despatched a messenger to recall Colon with the assurance that her Majesty herself would answer for the acceptance of his conditions.

Three months had passed in these dilatory and provoking discussions. On the 30th of March the edict expelling the Jews was published, and on April 17 the "capitulation," or formal contract, between Colon and the Crown was signed by their Majesties on the bases which he had originally proposed to the King of Portugal and so steadfastly insisted upon in all his long negotiations with the Court of Castile.

The document itself was short enough, considering its weighty matter. Colon had only asked for three ships, pointing out that two of these were already practically available if use were made of the penalty laid upon Palos, and had estimated the whole cost of his undertaking at the moderate sum of a single *cuento,* or one million of maravedies.[1] These the sovereigns had consented to furnish, and there only remained to be executed the agreement as to Colon's reward in the event of his enterprise proving successful. Their Majesties accordingly had instructed Juan de Coloma, one of their principal secretaries, to draw up this contract in proper official form, and present it to them for ratification; and this had now been done. The proposal of Colon being in the nature of a petition, the " capitulation " assumed the character of a reply thereto; and hence it was that the document finally submitted to Ferdinand and Isabella for their approval was couched in the following language : —

"THE matters petitioned for, which Your Highnesses hereby grant and bestow upon Don Cristoval Colon, in partial compensation for what he is about to discover in the Ocean Seas and for the voyage which he is now, with the help of God, about to make therein upon Your Highnesses' service, are those which follow:

"Firstly.[2] Your Highnesses, as Sovereigns (which you are) of the said Ocean Seas, hereby constitute Don Cristoval Colon your Admiral in all those islands and mainlands which by his skill or efforts shall be discovered in the said Ocean Seas, for himself during his lifetime, and, after his death, for his heirs and successors from one to the other forever; with all the dignities and prerogatives pertaining to the said rank, according as Don Alonso Henriquez, Your Highnesses' Admiral of Castile, and his predecessors in the said office were accustomed to exercise it in their several districts."

[1] The accounts, which were closed in August, 1494, give the total cost of this voyage as one million one hundred and forty thousand maravedies, or about twelve thousand three hundred dollars of our money, — truly a profitable speculation for the thrifty Ferdinand! For the source of these funds, consult Note F in the Appendix.

[2] We copy the text of the capitulation as recorded in Navarrete, tomo ii. pag. 7.

The king and queen having given their assent to this clause, the secretary wrote beneath it, —

"This is satisfactory to their Highnesses.
"JUAN DE COLOMA."

"Also. Your Highnesses appoint the said Don Cristoval Colon to be your Viceroy and Governor-General in all of the said islands and mainlands which, as has been said, he shall discover or acquire in those Seas; and permit that, for the proper government of each and all of the same, he shall make choice of three individuals for every office, from among whom Your Highnesses shall choose and select that one who shall be best for your service; and thus shall be the better ruled all those countries which Our Lord may allow him to find and acquire for the benefit of Your Highnesses."

Again the royal assent was given, and the secretary made the minute, —

"This is satisfactory to their Highnesses.
"JUAN DE COLOMA."

"Also. Of all the merchandise of every kind,—whether pearls, precious stones, gold, silver, spices, or other articles of whatever sort, kind, or description they may be, — which shall be purchased, secured by barter, found, acquired, or had in any manner within the limits of the said Admiral's jurisdiction, Your Highnesses hereby bestow upon Don Cristoval Colon, as a gratuity, the tenth part of everything; and desire that he enjoy it and use it for himself, the costs of acquisition being first deducted. That is to say; of all that shall remain clear and free after paying the expenses, he shall take the one-tenth part for himself to do with it as he will, and the other nine parts shall remain for Your Highnesses."

This was certainly a broad and ample return to make to any man, however great his services, considering that the object of Colon's search was nothing less than the whole continent of Asia; but their Majesties showed no stint in their liberality, and agreed to this clause without remonstrance, — perhaps because it cost them no pangs to give away what was not theirs.

"This is satisfactory to their Highnesses," wrote Juan de Coloma again, and signed his name.

"Also. The said petitioner enquires whether, if any dispute should arise in the place where such commerce and trading shall be carried on, either on account of the merchandise which he may bring from the said islands and mainlands to be discovered and acquired by him, as before said, or on account of goods taken from merchants here to be exchanged for the products of the said countries, it shall pertain to his prerogatives as Admiral to decide such dispute? And he begs that it may please Your Highnesses that provision should be made for this now, so that he, or his lieutenant, and not any other judge, shall determine such causes."

This was asking a good deal of the jealous monarchs of Spain, for nothing was considered more absolutely a prerogative of royalty than the administration of justice. But even at this the king and queen did not recoil.

"This is satisfactory to their Highnesses," the secretary was directed to write, "provided that it pertains to the said rank of Admiral according to what was practised by the Admiral Don Alonso Henriquez and his predecessors in their respective districts, and provided it is just." And to this he signed his name.

"Also. In all the ships which shall be fitted out for the said business and commerce, whenever and wherever and as often as they shall be despatched, the said Don Cristoval Colon may, if he shall so desire, contribute and pay the one-eighth part of all that shall be expended in their preparation, and shall then also receive and enjoy the one-eighth part of all the profit resulting from the voyages of such ships."

To this stipulation Colon attached a particular importance. One of the chief reproaches of those who had opposed his project, both in Portugal and Spain, had been that it was all a reckless speculation on his part; that he ventured nothing, and would be in any event the gainer. If he discovered Asia, they observed, great dignities and emoluments would be his; but even if he failed in his effort, he would have secured the command of a royal squadron with all its rank and perquisites, and this, they argued, was in itself a great inducement to the needy foreign adventurer. They failed to consider that he contributed the utmost any man has, — his life and all that it embraced; but critics of this class never do imagine that any (other) man's life can be worth anything to himself. Colon was quick to realize this; and to testify his faith in the practical results of his undertaking and the sincerity of his proposals, he insisted on being allowed to take an eighth share in the enterprise, as a purely commercial venture.[1]

To this the Spanish sovereigns had made no objection, — an additional proof of how little they realized the possibilities of this strange partnership. "This is satisfactory to their Highnesses," the secretary was told to write; and to this affixed his signature.

These were the only clauses in the contract between the Crown of Spain and the Genoese captain who undertook to find for it a western route to the Indies, and found instead a western world. The secretary read them again to the king and queen, and, with the royal sanction, added the formal certificate of their approval: —

"The aforesaid petitions are granted and conceded, with the replies of Your Highnesses at the end of each paragraph, this seventeenth day of April in the year of the Birth of Our Saviour Jesus Christ One thousand four hundred and ninety-two, in this city of Santa Fé, in the Plain of Granada."

The king and queen now attached their signatures to the contract, and returned it to their officer. "By order of the King and Queen, JUAN DE COLOMA," attested the secretary; and then the parchment was handed to Juan Roiz de Calcena, another of the royal secretaries to be registered in the chancellery.

And now the deed was done; the treaty of partition made. It was neither an intricate nor a prolix instrument. Colon was to have rank, dignities, authority, emoluments, and a tithe of all that his discoveries produced, even should he not avail himself of his option to take an eighth share in

[1] His friend, Las Casas, is very explicit in his statement of Columbus's motive in making this stipulation.

the profits of the adventure besides. The Spanish sovereigns were to have, as they hoped, the glorious mission of converting the vast multitudes of Asia to the Christian religion, and the incidental advantage of diverting the countless treasures of the Orient into the depleted coffers of Castile. The bargain was not an unfair one had it been kept in good faith. But the vagueness of its conditions proved fatal to Colon's just claims, and though he was persistent in insisting to his dying day that his rank applied to all the Spanish discoveries in America, and his interests combined amounted to "nearly twenty-five per cent" of *all* that Spain had received or ever should receive from the New World, Ferdinand found it an easy task to interpret the "capitulation" to suit his own more royal, if less loyal, views and necessities.

Of this, fortunately for him, Colon had no anticipation. Happy in the realization of his high hopes, and burning with a desire to crown expectation with achievement, he threw himself into the work of arranging the numberless details called for by the extraordinary nature of his projected journey. The next two weeks were full of busy preparation at the royal Court; for now Colon's counsel and suggestion carried weight, and his views were solicited upon every measure contemplated. On the other hand, the orders and decrees issued in quick succession by Ferdinand and Isabella during the latter days of April give clear evidence of the earnestness of their interest, and their firm determination to spare no effort to make the voyage a success, so far as lay in their power. One decree named Colon Admiral of the Ocean Sea, and Viceroy and Governor-general for the Crown of Spain over all the lands he should discover, as the "capitulation" provided; although, as was but just, he was not to assume these honors until after his discoveries had been made, his office in the mean time being that of Captain-general of the fleet he was authorized to equip. Another decree directed the authorities of the whole coast of Andalusia to furnish to him three ships with which to make the voyage, and also all the provisions and supplies — timber, powder, arms, dried meat, fish, biscuit, wine, and oil — which he might need; and to supply him with all the ship-carpenters, calkers, riggers, and other artisans he should require for putting his vessels in proper condition. Another ordered the officials of the Crown throughout the same seaboard to find for Colon the pilots, shipmasters, and mariners he needed for his squadron; and in case of their refusing to serve, to compel them to accompany him. Still another decree, which was issued at Colon's personal request, guaranteed to those who sailed with him that they should not, while absent with him or immediately upon their return, be sued or sentenced in the courts of Spain for any offence or crime previously committed, — a precaution very necessary, as he explained, when men were wanted for a long cruise; as during their absence at sea they might be prosecuted for all sorts of claims, just and unjust, and condemned without a chance of being heard. Another royal order excepted from inland taxes and duties all the materials and supplies taken by Colon; while others yet assured to those who supplied the expedition either with the ships or their equipment and provisions, as well as to their officers and crews, that they should be paid full value for their property or services at the current market-rates. It was not intended to confiscate the vessels or supplies, or oblige the sailors to serve for nothing; but knowing the opposition likely to arise among the ignorant inhabitants of the seaports against trusting their property and precious selves to a voyage into unknown waters, the sovereigns used their arbitrary powers over the lives and property of their subjects, to enable Colon to secure what he needed by force, if he could not obtain it by fair trade and argument.

To all these mandates was added one other, the most notable of all, which called upon the parish of Palos, by name, to deliver to Colon, as he might select, the two ships whose services were due to the Crown, and with them the equipments and crews he should judge necessary. Thus, although the whole province of Andalusia was nominally obliged to find the three ships destined for the voyage, this particular port was compelled to furnish two of them in virtue of the sentence under which it lay.

In all this work of preparation and arrangement Colon took a keen delight, and his knowledge and experience are evident in the care and completeness with which all the details are planned. As yet his destination had not been made public, partly to avoid the difficulties which would come from alarming those whom it was desired to enlist in the undertaking, but chiefly to conceal for as long as possible the plans of the Spanish monarchs from their adventurous rival of Portugal. The decrees merely stated that Cristoval Colon was going "to certain parts of the ocean on a mission concerning the interests of the Crown." What these "certain parts" were was scarcely more plainly set forth in the several letters of credence which, at his request, were given him by their Majesties, addressed to the Great and Mighty Khan of Asia, and other lesser potentates, of whom so little was known that their names and realms were left in blank!

By the first week in May all his work, so far as it lay at the Court, was finished, and Colon was ready to proceed to the coast and begin the work of collecting his ships and their crews, and fitting them out for his long voyage. But before leaving, the queen added an unmistakable evidence of her personal sympathy and confidence by appointing young Diego Colon a page to her son, Prince Juan; thereby relieving his father of all anxiety on the boy's account, and testifying her esteem for him by bestowing on his son an honor eagerly sought by the nobles of the kingdom for their own children.

Deeply sensible of the cordial support and distinguished honor done him by their Majesties, Colon took his leave of them and of his faithful friends at Court; and, followed by many an earnest wish and devout prayer for his complete success, left Granada on the 12th of May, and made his way with all speed toward the sea-coast and the little convent of La Rabida.

VI.

"I, THE KING!" AND "I, THE QUEEN!"

AGAIN the three friends are gathered together in the good superior's room in the little convent on the hill; but in what different circumstances! — the friar and the physician, proud in the consciousness of having brought about a notable work through their acuteness and earnest faith; the wearied stranger, now a noble of Spain, and High Admiral if his voyage but confirms his confident hopes, holding their Majesties' commission with full powers to procure all he needs for making the attempt; the young lad in the garden below, a page to the prince, with an income which many a grown man of those times would envy.

On the massive table before them, instead of the single dingy map over which they had pored six months before, now lay a number of fresh and imposing parchments, abounding in capitals and flourishes, and having great seals attached. The superior laid down the one he had been reading and turned to Colon, —

"It will doubtless be your wish, Señor Cristoval, that these be published without loss of time. Have you thought how we may best serve you in the matter?"

"I have thought, Father," Colon replied, "that the surest way will be for his Reverence, the curate of the parish, to give notice, as is customary, that letters have arrived from their Majesties, and summon his flock on an appointed day to hear them read. In this both you and our friend the Señor Garcia can much assist me; for the sooner it is done, the sooner can we set to work."

"If you will go with me, Señor Captain," the younger man said, giving Colon his new title half playfully, "I will gladly call on my cousin Francisco Fernandes, their Majesties' notary in our parish, and ask him to arrange the matter with Fray Martin, our priest. We are now at Monday, and if he give notice to-morrow, their Majesties' commands can be read to the people on Wednesday, if so it please you."

"Nay, the quicker the better, my friend," said Colon. "I fear the hardest part of our task is but beginning."

The superior nodded his head emphatically.

"Money you have, and decrees you have and to spare, good Señor Cristoval; but unless a miracle befall these oaken-headed mariners of ours, 't will be no easy thing to get your ships equipped and their crews upon them. Yet must this come to pass, if not one day, then another; for the orders of their Majesties must be obeyed. This, too, our mutinous neighbors know full well, but they must needs grumble and rebel until the latest moment."

"Since God has filled their Highnesses' hearts with the spirit of this enterprise, I fear no other resistance that can be brought against it by men," said Colon. "Beyond dispute it will be far better if we do not have to use harshness in obtaining our fleet; for an unwilling crew is hard to handle once they lose the sight of land."

In the afternoon Colon and the physician visited the notary of the village, and showing him the royal decree addressed to the inhabitants of Palos, requested him to ask the parish priest to summon his people to hear it read on the second morning following. The notary, standing hat in hand in presence of his sovereigns' signatures, promised readily to have this done; and also, in answer to the physician's injunctions, to say nothing of the tenor of the document except to Fray Martin.

The next day, when Garcia Fernandez paid his usual visit to the convent, he was able to say to Colon and the superior that the curate of the village church had duly given notice of the arrival of certain letters from their Majesties, and called upon all of his parishioners, as they were good subjects, to come to the church on the following day and hear the documents read aloud. The same notice, the physician added, would be given at the evening service.

This second warning was, indeed, superfluous; for by noon of Tuesday every soul in the district, from the fishermen on the bay beyond Saltes, to the laborers in the vineyards away up around Moguer, had heard that a message had come from Court and was to be read at church next day. What it was no one knew for certain; but few doubted that it had something to do with that old sentence of Council which had been hanging for so long above their heads. And as they spoke of this, every man who owned a plank in a ship vowed beneath his breath that it should be his neighbor's vessel and not his own that should be chosen for whatever service was stipulated.

On that Wednesday morning, the 23d of April in the year of Grace 1492, the little church of St. George of Palos was crowded to a degree which would have delighted its worthy priest had he not known that curiosity and not piety had been the attracting influence. There were assembled all the dignitaries of the village, its alcaldes and regidors, and the clerk of the Council for that district, and the alcaides, and the notary Francisco, each in his most imposing costume; and there were the Pinzons, the wealthiest inhabitants of the neighborhood, with their families; and there was a great crowd of fishermen and sailors, and hard-featured vineyard hands, — both men and women, — and a slight sprinkling of small landed proprietors or well-to-do ship-owners from the surrounding district, among whom stood out the bullet-pate of Juan Rodriguez of the hard head. Wherever their elders had left room, the bare-legged, brown-skinned urchins of the place packed themselves in, waiting in open-mouthed wonder to see what should happen next.

Colon entered the church accompanied by Fray Antonio and his son Diego, and was soon joined by Garcia Fernandez and his cousin the notary. The morning service was devoutly recited by all present, Colon especially taking part with noticeable earnestness. When the religious offices were over, the curate announced that the señor notary would now read their Highnesses' commands to their loyal subjects of Palos; and a dead silence fell upon the crowded audience. Taking a scroll of parchment from his velvet doublet, — for he had dressed himself in holiday attire, being ever particular as to forms and ceremonies, — Colon opened it and bowed his head in salute of the royal signatures as he handed it to Francisco Fernandes.

Calling to his side the village authorities, and displaying the names of the king and queen and their seals pressed in colored wax, the notary read in a high-pitched voice the following: —

"DON Ferdinand and Doña Isabella, by the Grace of God King and Queen of Castile, of Leon, of Aragon, of Sicily, of Granada, of Toledo, of Valencia, of Galicia, of the Balearic Isles, of Seville, of Sardinia, of Cordova, of Corsica, of Murcia, of Jaen, of the Algarves, of Algecira, of Gibraltar, and of the Canary Islands; Counts of Barcelona; Dukes of Athens and of Neopatria; Counts of Ronsillon and of Cerdania; Marquises of Oristan and of Gociano;

"To you, Diego Rodriguez Prieto, and to all other persons, your friends and neighbors of the town of Palos, and to each one of you, health and happiness!

"Well do you know that for certain acts done and committed by you all in disobedience of Our commands, you were condemned by Our Council to serve Us for twelve months with two vessels, armed at your own cost and expense, whenever and wherever you should be by Us commanded, upon certain penalties, as is set forth more at length in the before-mentioned sentence which was rendered against you."

As the notary reached this point and stopped to take breath, Diego Prieto shifted uneasily from one leg to the other, looking extremely uncomfortable the while.

"And now," the notary continued to read, "inasmuch as We have commanded Cristoval Colon that he should go with a fleet of three ships to certain parts of the Ocean Sea upon sundry affairs which relate to Our service, and We desire that he take with him the two vessels with which you are bound, in the said manner, to serve Us, We therefore order you that within the ten days first following the day on which you are summoned by this Letter, without making any petition to Us, or consulting with Us, or waiting for anything, or needing any further Letter from Us about the matter, you have equipped and put in order the said two armed vessels, as you are bound to do in virtue of the said sentence, ready to sail with the said Cristoval Colon wherever We may order him to go."

When the notary read this paragraph, loud murmurs arose from all over the church. Those who knew Colon by sight were pointing him out to those who did not, and both from men and women were to be heard exclamations of protest and dissatisfaction.

"In their Majesties' name, silence!" shouted the notary. "We are here to listen to their Highnesses' commands, like good and loyal subjects; not to pass censure upon them."

"And upon the completion of the said period," he resumed reading, "you shall depart with him and thenceforth sail with him wherever and whenever he, on Our part, shall say and direct. And We have ordered him to advance to you, for those of you who go upon the said cruise, four months' wages at the rates which are paid to the sailors from other ports who are also to go with him in your two ships and in the third ship which We order him to take; which wages are to be the same as are paid along your coast to men who go to sea in armed vessels. And, having thus set out, you are to follow the course which he, on Our behalf, shall lay down for you, and you are to obey his commands and follow his orders and directions; provided, however, that neither you, nor the said Cristoval Colon, nor any of the others who should go on the said vessels, shall go to the Mine of Guinea, nor to the district thereabouts, which belong to the Very Noble King of Portugal, Our Brother, since it is Our desire to respect and cause to be respected the treaty We have made on this point with the said King."

As these last sentences did not interest the audience particularly, the hum of conversation again broke out, although somewhat less indignantly than before. Clearly the mention of full wages for all who shipped on this cruise, and four months' pay in advance, had brought about some change of mind, especially among the sea-faring men present. It was one thing to be driven against their wills to go on a voyage of which they knew nothing, and another to be offered full wages and a handsome sum down! Altogether the rugged mariners of Palos began to think rather less unfavorably of this stranger and his cruise.

Again commanding attention, the notary continued to read through to the end of the document: —

"And when you shall bring a certificate signed by the said Captain that he is satisfied with your service with the said two armed vessels, We shall consider you to be freed from the said penalty which by the sentence of Our Council was imposed upon you, and from now until that time and from that time until now We shall consider that We have been well and fully served by you in the matter of the said vessels for the whole time and in the manner demanded of you by Our said Council. With notice to you, however, which We now give, that if you should not do as herein commanded, or in the execution hereof should make any excuse or delay, We shall order to be executed upon you and upon every one of you, and upon your property, all the pains and penalties which were laid upon you in the said sentence. And let none of you do otherwise than as herein commanded, upon pain of Our displeasure and a fine of ten thousand maravedies from each of you to be paid to Our Treasury; under which penalty We also command whatever Public Notary shall be called for the purpose, that he give a written certificate wherever he may publish this Letter, so that We may know how Our mandates have been obeyed."

The notary, on reading this clause, drew himself up with much importance, and looked severely about him before concluding.

"Given in Our city of Granada on the thirtieth day of April, in the Year of Our Lord one thousand four hundred and ninety-two."

Here the reader paused to draw a long breath.

"I, the King!" he shouted.

Then after another slight pause, —

"I, the Queen!" in equally loud tones.

In the hush which followed the enunciation of these two

august names, the notary rattled off the "tail-piece" of the weighty document: —

"Signed by their Majesties and sealed in colored wax on paper. I, Juan de Coloma, Secretary of the King and Queen, our sovereigns, have caused this to be written out at their Highnesses' orders. Compared, registered, and entered at the Royal Chancellery, and signed by the respective officials. No fees to be paid. May God save their Majesties!"

What all this last part meant, his hearers could not tell, for he jumbled it all together in one sentence; but when they heard the familiar invocation for their Majesties, even the dullest knew that the ceremony was over, and the crowd began to leave the church, anxious to get outside and talk the whole matter over.

Colon turned to Diego Prieto, as the chief magistrate of the village, and said with every evidence of respect, —

"Will your Worship have the goodness to see that their Highnesses' commands are executed, Señor Alcalde? I would beg that all possible speed be used, and for my own part will gladly be of every help I may."

"Surely, worthy captain, surely," the alcalde answered deferentially. "Their Majesties' commands shall be honored, and that with diligence. But I know not, at the very moment, which ships will best suit your purpose, Señor."

"We will confer as to that more at your leisure, good sir, if so it please you," Colon replied. "Meanwhile I must ask our honored friend the notary to draw up a certificate for me, setting forth that their Majesties' letter was duly read, and get your Worships all to sign it."

"That shall be done, Señor Captain," said Francisco, stiffly. Then turning to the village officials about him, he explained: "'T is in the body of the document that so it is to be done, Señores, and I must look carefully to it."

As Colon, accompanied by his friends and Diego Prieto, came out of the church, he found the greater part of the audience separated into groups about the entrance, eagerly discussing the morning's incident. It was apparent that the larger number still regarded the proposed voyage with disfavor; but whether this was because no destination was named, or because Colon was a stranger and the cruise was considered as a punishment, it was not easy to say. Both the superior and Garcia Fernandez looked grave as they noted the vigorous gestures and heard the loud voices of the groups around them.

As they came out of the building, old Juan Rodriguez left the knot of men where he was standing, and came up to Colon with an awkward salutation.

"How then, Master?" he asked in his heavy-weather tones; "is the cruise in truth to be so long a one? Some of our old women here are saying your Worship will never come back."

"If thou wilt go with me, Juan Rodriguez," Colon said promptly, "thou shall not only come back, please God, but bring thy cap full of golden ducats as well."

"Nay, Master, that I cannot do, the worse for me!" he grumbled. "The vineyard would go to waste, and my old woman will never let me haul a rope again; the saints forgive me for tying to her! But if I cannot go myself I will send some one to take my place," the old fellow said with vigor.

"Well, Comrade," said Colon, laughing, "if thou canst not join me, thou canst in any case bring me some good, stout lads to make the voyage. Thou knowest the kind I like, old friend."

"That can I do, and with a good will, Master," Juan replied, turning to rejoin his neighbors.

One of the latter was declaring, with much emphasis, that none but madmen would sail on a voyage which was going to lead no one knew whither. As for him, he pronounced, all the alcaldes in Andalusia could not force him to go on this one.

"I mind not sailing in Christian seas," the speaker added, as if to save his courage; "but for these voyages to the coasts of Africa and into oceans we know not of, I want none of them."

"*Ola*, Neighbor," said the doughty Juan, as he came up, "'t were better to hold thy peace than thus to tattle like an old nurse. As for voyages, yonder captain knows more of the sea when asleep at night than thou dost at midday with thine eyes wide open; and as for strange oceans, why, one drop of salt water is just like another. 'T is only when thou gettest too much within thee that it does thee any harm. If it is this that scares thee, 't were wise to stay at home and card wool. If thou but keepest close enough to thy house, thou canst never drown."

Having thus turned the laugh on the fault-finder, the old sailor began to extol Colon, and speak about the voyage with an appearance of knowledge he was very far from possessing.

It required no prophet to foretell that trouble was brewing for the new Captain-general; and as Colon and his party made their way back to La Rabida, they debated earnestly the means to be adopted to convert their parchment decrees into serviceable ships and crews.[1]

---

[1] The circumstances attending the reading of the fateful decree are derived from the notarial certificate prepared at the time, and copied in Navarrete, tomo ii. pag. 13.

VII.

THE HEAVY HAND OF JUAN DE PEÑALOSA.

WITHIN twenty-four hours it became clear that a stubborn resistance would be made to the royal commands, and that, so far from helping forward Colon's voyage in any way, the good people of Palos and Moguer intended to embarrass him by every means in their power. When he came to consult with Diego Prieto and the other authorities, Colon found himself opposed by that dead weight of passive resistance which the Spaniards and Portuguese of the less intelligent classes can still exert with such exasperating stolidity. He did not see fit to explain to all he met that his intention was to sail to the remotest bounds of the western ocean, for that would merely have made matters a hundredfold worse; but he gave out, in answer to all inquiries, that he was bound on a voyage of discovery, and that those who went with him would find riches and wealth infinitely greater and in much less time than had been the case on any of the voyages made to Guinea or the African islands. But very few were convinced by his representations. The owners of ships, without exception, claimed that their vessels were old, or rotten, or so out of repair that they could not go on a long voyage; or gave some equally ready excuse for keeping them at home. The pilots, captains, and sailors with whom Colon or his friends spoke, gave a variety of reasons for their not going on the voyage, which showed that there was a general understanding throughout the neighborhood that if this foreign ship-captain wanted to make discoveries in unknown seas he would have to go elsewhere for the means to do it. A handful of the more adventurous spirits, either stimulated by the love of excitement, or influenced by what they knew of Colon's abilities as a commander, agreed to go "if their shipmates would," and most of the turbulent characters of the vicinity were anxious to sail with him in order to take advantage of the royal exemption from trial and punishment during their absence. But by far the greater number took the ground expressed bluntly by a pilot of a good deal of influence thereabouts, one Juan de Mafra, whom his namesake of the hard head had urged to go, knowing the weight his example would have upon his neighbors.

"Save thou thy breath against the time thy wife scolds thee, Comrade," replied the pilot to Juan Cabezudo, "and talk not to me of gold and pearls and spices. Often enough have I been promised these if I would but join some cruise to pirate against the Moors, or go on a voyage to pass some new cape in Africa; and all that I have to show for my pains is this cut across my skull, and a shaking ague whenever a damp wind blows. Thou canst have my share, and welcome, of all these treasures. As for me, though I do not doubt the Señor Colon is a bold captain and a wise navigator, here I stay in this kingdom of Castile; for I take his tales of new lands to be but an idle dream and a vain hope."[1]

While Diego Prieto and his fellow officials professed to be most anxious to give speedy execution to the royal decrees, it soon became evident to Colon and his friends that the authorities were doing all they could to aid the citizens in evading their obligation. Not only did they accept every flimsy pretext that was offered by the ship-owners or the sailors to escape making the voyage, but they allowed some of the most suitable vessels to leave the port so as to get

---

[1] Yet this same Juan de Mafra accompanied Columbus on his later voyages, and became one of the most famous pilots of the western ocean. His last great adventure was with Magellan, as pilot of the "Santiago"

out of Colon's reach; while, in their talks about the neighborhood, they dwelt lugubriously on the dangers of sailing in unknown waters, and on the hardship of being condemned to so dreadful a fate.

Meantime Colon was working and watching, learning all about the ships of Palos and the adjoining coast, and becoming acquainted with the names and acquirements of the pilots and captains and best-known sailors along the shore. With his friends he visited the adjacent towns and talked with the authorities and chief inhabitants; trying to enlist them in his undertaking, and dwelling on the inducements offered by the voyage. He plainly saw that the ten days within which the parish of Palos should have furnished him with the two ships and crews, according to the decrees, were going to pass without this being done; but he took it patiently, for he had already selected the ships he thought most available for his purpose, and had determined how they and their companies should be secured.

When he had arrived at La Rabida, on this second visit, Fray Antonio had brought him into contact with the Pinzons, of whom both the friar and Garcia Fernandez had so often spoken; and Colon had quickly established friendly relations with the three brothers, using their mutual profession of the sea and their studies of its secrets as a starting-point. He made no mystery of his intended voyage of discovery in conversing with these men after the royal decrees had been read in the church; but until he had carefully surveyed the ground and knew on what materials he could depend, he did not take them into his entire confidence, or make any overtures to them to join him in his enterprise. Once he knew just how the land lay, however, as to the ships and their crews, and had formed his plan of action, he resolved to lay the whole affair, so far as it was needful, before the Pinzons, and invite them to embark with him in the undertaking.

Martin Alonzo Pinzon and his two brothers, Vicente Yañez and Francisco Martin, were by far the most influential residents in all the district about Palos. The oldest had barely passed forty years of age, and the youngest was well under thirty, but as a family they had a standing and weight in the community which caused them to be consulted and listened to by their neighbors for leagues around, whether fishermen, or sailors, or farmers. For not only did the Pinzons own houses in Palos and Moguer, and vineyards and gardens as well, but they were also famous ship-owners and sea-captains, as the superior had told Colon on his first visit, and had made long and successful voyages both in the Mediterranean and along the western coasts of Africa and Europe. They were known far and wide to be bold and fortunate navigators, and were popular with the sailors they commanded; especially Martin Alonzo, the oldest of the brothers, who had great authority with the seafaring men of the locality.

In addition to these elements of importance, the Pinzons were bound by ties of relationship, more or less close, to half the inhabitants of the district; and in a Spanish neighborhood these bonds are even yet carefully remembered and willingly acknowledged. Not only does the rural Spaniard's own family down to the remotest ramifications have in some measure a claim upon his consideration; but the family of his wife has one as well, and the families of his brothers and sisters, and of his wife's brothers and sisters, and of the brothers and sisters of the wives or husbands of his own brothers and sisters, and of the wives or husbands of his wife's brothers and sisters, and so on and on until the brain refuses to grasp the wire-drawn connection. When to this appalling array of "parents" is added the countless host of "co-parents," caused by the adoption of godfather and godmother into a family, and the consequent recognition of all their families also, it will be easily understood that in a quiet country where changes were rare, a family would be connected in one way or another with everybody about it, and, if wealthy or in any wise better off than its neighbors, would exercise an important influence upon the body of the clan. In such relations did the Pinzon brothers stand to the whole countryside around Palos and

Moguer; and Colon was quick to recognize the wisdom of his two friends in urging him to make an alliance with Martin Alonzo if possible. For his part, Fray Antonio used all his eloquence and skill in interesting the oldest brother in Colon and his plans, — a task in which he was much assisted by the enthusiasm of the young physician, who, as he had already said, was himself related to the family.

On Saturday, the 2d of June, the ten days granted by the royal decrees to the residents of Palos for the preparation of the two ships expired. Not only were the ships not ready, but both owners and crews had flatly refused to lend their aid to any such "fool's quest" as that proposed by Colon. Just where he meant to go, or what he meant to do, they did not know; but he was going off somewhere in the western ocean on a secret expedition, and they simply would not go with him. Any reference to the powers given him by their Majesties, to call in the aid of the law to compel the owners of ships to charter them to him and oblige the crews of the same to sail, was met with what amounted to a direct mutiny against the orders of the sovereigns. Colon determined, therefore, to despatch a messenger to the Court with a letter laying before their Majesties the exact condition of affairs in Palos and its vicinity, and asking for such further powers as might enable him to secure obedience to the original commands of the crown. In the mean while he decided to show his whole hand to Martin Alonzo, and try to make an arrangement with him which, when backed up by the royal aid, would enable the squadron to be fitted out without further opposition. If once the Pinzons endorsed the enterprise, Colon reasoned, there would be far less talk about resisting the decrees, and all necessity for using force might be avoided.

Martin Alonzo already knew, both from the orders which had been made public and from what Colon had told him, that the latter had their Majesties' authority for what he did, and that he was going to look for land in the west. But now Colon laid before him his commission as Admiral and the conditions of his agreement with the Crown, and frankly invited Pinzon and his brothers to join him in the enterprise. He explained his grounds for expecting to find Asia in the west, and offered to give the brothers a share in the profits of the undertaking, besides liberal salaries for themselves and the pilots, or other skilful mariners, they might induce to accompany them. He was too prudent a man to let Martin Alonzo fancy that his help was indispensable. If he would aid him, Colon said, so much the better for both, for it would bring wealth and honors to Pinzon and enable Colon to escape the use of force in fitting out his expedition. But if Pinzon did not see his way clear to joining him, Colon would still carry out his undertaking, using their Majesties' authority for the purpose, and employing force where solicitations and offers of reward would not avail.

To Martin Alonzo, particularly, the proposal was alluring. Like other intelligent and thoughtful seamen of the period, he had heard vague rumors of land beyond the ocean, and as he sailed along the Atlantic coasts of Africa and Europe had pondered and speculated upon what would be found out yonder, a thousand, or two thousand, or three thousand leagues to sea. Moreover, as the father superior had told Colon, the oldest Pinzon was somewhat of a reading-man; and although the famous book of which Fray Antonio had spoken proved to be no such marvel, when examined, as he had thought, Colon found Martin Alonzo to be a man of judgment and observation, and very ready to agree with himself as to the probability of their finding Asia by sailing with the sun. When he learned that Colon had received the grant of a million maravedies for the expenses of the voyage, and was appointed to the highest marine office in the gift of the Spanish Crown, the existence of that western land became still more probable to Pinzon, and his inclination to have a share in its profits grew daily stronger. To him the gold and pearls and spices, the silks and gems and slaves, of these distant regions were no fictions. Had he not seen all these and other treasures in his voyages to the eastern ports of the Mediterranean? And did not these riches always and everywhere come somewhere from the East, ever from the East? True, this stranger navigator proposed to sail westward; but was he not still seeking only a shorter route to the Indies than by the Red Sea and the Gulf of Ganges? And would not this discovery fill their ships with wealth unheard of, and make them all hidalgos? Thus Martin Alonzo argued, first to himself and afterward to his brothers; until one hot summer's day he came to Colon and told him that if they could agree on terms he and his brothers would use their influence and resources to supply him with ships and crews, and would themselves go with him on the voyage.

He reached this conclusion none too soon for his own peace of mind; for on one of the last days of June a stranger, who was evidently "a somebody" from the state in which he travelled, rode through Moguer and on to Palos, where he inquired for "the worshipful Señor Colon, the Captain of their Majesties' fleet there fitting out." Some of his hearers were inclined to make merry over the idea of Colon having a "fleet;" but others felt rather uncomfortable on noticing the new-comer's air of authority, and directed him, with many protestations of service, to the convent of La Rabida. Here he was received by Colon and the superior with evident delight, for he was no other than Juan de Peñalosa, gentleman-in-waiting of their Majesties' own household; and he came provided with imperative orders to aid Colon in every manner possible to start on his voyage as quickly as he could get away. The better to accomplish this he was commissioned to call upon all the authorities of the Crown, not only civil but military, if it should prove necessary, in order to enforce the royal decrees without further discussion or delay.

Accompanied by Colon, with the superior, Garcia Fernandez, and Martin Alonzo to give more dignity to the incident, early the next day the royal messenger went to the village and made known his orders to Diego Prieto and his fellow-officials. Great was the discomfiture of these worthies on learning that not only was their indifference to the royal commands known to the sovereigns, but that the latter had sent down an officer of their personal suite to see that the good people of Palos now did under direct compulsion what they should have more wisely done from loyalty.

"May it please your Excellency," the poor alcalde said, in a huge flutter at the thought that there was really no earthly excuse for him and his associates to offer, "we have labored diligently as loyal subjects and officers of their Majesties to execute their Majesties' sacred commands. But all our best ships are away on cruises, and those that remain we have carefully examined, and feel not justified in sending them on so long a voyage as that the worshipful Señor Colon proposes to make; for his Worship says he may be gone a year. As for our men, your Excellency, the wars have taken away a great part, and others are at sea, so it has not been as easy as it might seem to gather together so many seamen as the Señor Colon needs; and I hope we know too well our duties as faithful officers of the Crown to send any but our best and most practised seamen upon their Majesties' service."

Here the other officials solemnly bobbed their heads, and looked as wise as so many owls.

"Nevertheless, your Excellency," concluded Diego Prieto, feeling that he was making rather a neat speech, after all, "both I and my colleagues will redouble our efforts to comply with their Majesties' commands, and will send all along the coast to search out fitting ships for the Señor Colon. In this will we endeavor to prove our zeal for their Majesties, and humbly hope that your Excellency will likewise be satisfied that whatever delay has occurred has been occasioned by difficulties and embarrassments we could not surmount in the short time at our disposal, and is not due to any want of devotion or loyalty to our gracious sovereigns or their royal commands."

"Your Worship need have no fear of being misconstrued, Señor Alcalde," said Juan de Peñalosa, dryly. "Their Majesties are quite as much assured of your anxiety to do them service in this business of the Señor Colon as am I.

Nor will it be necessary for you to make so long and laborious a search for the vessels required, Señor Alcalde, for his Honor the Captain has found three ships here in Palos which, he affirms, will properly answer his needs. Since he is satisfied, good sir, who has to sail in them, 't is not for you or me, under your favor, to find fault with them."

"Surely not, your Excellency," murmured Diego, "I am the more rejoiced that his Worship will have no further to seek."

"As to the men required," continued Peñalosa, without noticing the remark, "their Majesties' orders are that those who refuse to go with the Señor Captain when called upon shall be taken in charge by the justices and other officers of the peace of this district, and compelled to sail; and whoever shall refuse to furnish the Captain with the supplies and materials of which he stands in need shall be treated in like manner. And the more to relieve your Worship, Señor, of the embarrassment and difficulty of executing these commands, their Majesties have appointed my good friend and comrade the Señor de Cepada, who is also of their immediate household, to take command of the fortress of this loyal port of Palos, with strict injunction to assist the civil authorities in executing the royal decrees.

"Your arduous labors being thus far lightened, worthy sirs," Peñalosa added sarcastically, turning from Diego Prieto to the other officials, "we may hope, I make so bold, that the owners of the vessels which the Señor Colon has chosen for his voyage shall be apprised forthwith by your Worships of the honor done them, and all haste be made in preparing them for sea. The Señor Captain will pay full prices for everything, whether ships or stores or men, so there is no good cause for refusing to serve him. But should resistance be attempted for other than good cause, why, then, Señors, loath as I would be to have to do it, my directions are most positive to hold your Worships' and your Worships' property responsible for any delay that may occur."

The faces of the alcalde and his companions grew longer

and longer, as Peñalosa's lecture continued. When he ceased they stood speechless before him, too dismayed to answer a word. Their ships to be seized and turned over to Colon, despite all their elaborate excuses! Themselves and their neighbors to be forced to go with him, whether they wanted or no! A new commandant sent down to their fort to enforce these high-handed orders, and they to be arrested and their goods confiscated if any further delay ensued! All this was a sad shock to the easy-going officials, who had counted on wearing out Colon's patience by their persistent delays, and on finding some plausible excuse with which to amuse the Crown in the mean time. But there was no doubt about the reality of their present danger. There stood their Majesties' messenger, sent down expressly by the queen to put a stop to their shilly-shallying; and in those days a monarch seldom let much time elapse between making a threat and carrying it into execution.

The silence was broken by Martin Alonzo, addressing Diego Prieto.

"Señor Alcalde," he said, "I beg that your Worship will take note that I have engaged to find and equip two vessels for the Señor Colon, and to go with him on this voyage with the crews that are necessary. There is thus much less for your Worships to do; and if I can aid you further in finding what yet is wanted, I pray you to make it known to me."

This announcement caused even more of a sensation among the authorities than the declaration of Peñalosa; for not only did it greatly simplify their labors, but it also showed them that there was more in this enterprise of the stranger captain's than any of them had fancied. They were well aware that the Pinzons were not in the habit of "working for the bishop," as they called anything done from mere sentiment; and if the three brothers had agreed to go with Colon it was clear that something besides glory was coming from the voyage. They therefore crowded around Martin Alonzo, eager to know the reasons for his joining Colon; but these he kept closely to himself. He and his brothers were going on the cruise, he said, and were contributing their property and urging their friends and relatives to ship with them. They knew what they knew; and if others wanted to share in the profits, all they had to do was to join too. With this the gathering broke up; Colon and his party going down to the port, and Diego Prieto and his associates remaining behind to talk the matter over and concert measures for at length complying with their sovereigns' orders.

Years afterward, when both Colon and Martin Alonzo were in their graves, the children of the latter claimed that had it not been for his assistance, Colon would never have discovered the new world, and this view has passed to some extent into history. What "might have been" is never easy of denial; but for our part we are satisfied that with his million of maravedies to pay his way and the emphatic decrees of the Crown to support him, Colon would have made his voyage if all the Pinzons in Spain had opposed his going.[1] Be that as it may, there can be no doubt that the co-operation of Martin Alonzo and his brothers was of the greatest value to Colon, and facilitated in every way the fitting out of the expedition. This alone, it seems to us, is cause enough for honoring them, without seeking to extol their merits at the cost of their leader's.

Partly influenced, no doubt, by the action of the Pinzons, but still more by the knowledge of Peñalosa's mission, the owners of a third vessel consented, though with an ill grace, to charter her to Colon. The little squadron was not selected at hap-hazard, nor was it composed of inferior and dangerously small craft. In the choice of his ships and in all the other details of his equipment the commander acted with forethought and deliberation. Two of them, the

[1] "I hold it for certain," said one of the Royal Council, when questioned in after years upon this point, "that if the Admiral Colon had not dared to make that voyage, and had not found the Indies, they would even yet be awaiting a discoverer." Dr. Maldonado was one of the councillors who opposed the project of Colon, and cannot be accused of partiality. His statement was a direct denial of the claim advanced by the Pinzons, and is to us conclusive. For the part actually taken by the Pinzon brothers, see Note G in the Appendix.

"Pinta" and "Niña," were stout coasting-vessels of light draught, of the kind he thought best adapted for exploring purposes; the third, the "Santa Maria," was a heavier ship of greater size, which he chose to serve as a kind of floating fort and headquarters. In making his selection, as in many of his acts on this voyage, Colon was guided by his long experience on many coasts, and especially by what he had learned by sailing with the Portuguese along the western shores of Africa. It detracts neither from his fame nor courage that, instead of venturing to cross an unknown sea in crazy skiffs, as some would have us think, he used his judgment and experience in choosing the vessels on which the safety of his crews and the success of his endeavor must necessarily depend.

The month of July passed rapidly in the thousand and one duties connected with the outfit of such an expedition; for, like a good and prudent sailor-man, Colon himself attended to everything which might affect the results of his voyage. The ships were careened on the river-bank near Palos, and cleaned, calked, and tallowed down. The rigging and sails were overhauled and strengthened, or renewed. Provisions, ammunition and supplies sufficient for a year's cruise away from any chance of replenishing were gathered together from the country round about as far as Seville. Pilots, ship-masters, and seamen were sought out by Colon or Martin Alonzo, and induced to ship for the cruise on the promise of good pay and the hope of a fortune. Some few men-at-arms, too, were chosen, for there would doubtless be blows exchanged before the fleet saw Spain again. A number of landsmen were needed as well; calkers and riggers, carpenters and coopers, and such other artisans as might be wanted about the vessels or their stores on so long a voyage. Finally, there was the small detachment of civil aids, always assigned to a royal squadron to watch the operations on their Majesties' behalf, — a secretary, notary, and treasurer, or comptroller.

The coming and going of all this company, and the stir of their various occupations, turned the little seaport into a busy town during the weeks of preparation. The excitement rose as the ships approached a state of readiness, and both incentives to go and appeals for holding back multiplied among the crews. Many of those who had engaged themselves attempted to draw out at the last hour, and some of those who had declined would now be glad to ship on any terms. Colon himself caught some of the calkers leaving several of the seams in the ships open, so that they would spring a leak on reaching the sea and have to put back to port for repairs. Still others of his people took French leave and hid themselves away to avoid the departure, while yet a greater number watched religiously for the chance to follow so laudable an example. The difference between a *grumete* of Columbus's time and a modern Jack Tar was more in the name and clothes than in the character of the men.

Working early and late, punishing the ill-disposed, and encouraging the feeble-hearted, Colon saw his little fleet approaching day by day nearer to completion. By the first of August he was able to announce to their Majesties that he had ready "three vessels very suitable for the intended service, well furnished with a great plenty of supplies of all kinds, and manned with a large force of sea-going folk."[1]

[1] See the opening sentences of his Diary.

VIII.

THE SEA-BREEZE OUTSIDE THE BAR.

AUGUST is a warm month in the South of Spain, and the nights are short; so it was no hardship for the sturdy sailor-folk and vine-dressers of Palos to be up and stirring long before daybreak on Friday, the 3d of that month, in the year of Our Lord 1492. Out in the stream of the river Tinto lay the "Santa Maria" and the two caravels, — the "Pinta" and the "Niña." Between the shore and the little fleet still plied a few small boats, although the crews had gone on board their several vessels the day before. All hands had confessed and been shriven of their sins, as was the custom of sea-faring men as well as soldiers in those days, — Colon to his devoted friend and helper, the superior of La Rabida; the others to the curate of St. George's church in the village. On the banks were now gathered the inhabitants of the little town, together with many from Moguer, their farewells taken and wishes sped for a prosperous voyage and a quick return; and among the crowd was many a tear-stained face and broken voice, for God and the Saints only knew whether those who sailed on yonder ships would ever see their native shores again.

Almost up to the last hour, Garcia Fernandez had hoped he might accompany the bold and skilful man he had grown so to admire and revere, but it had proved impossible.

"Now the Saints protect you, noble friend!" he had said, as, throwing his arms about Colon, he gave him a hearty Spanish embrace. "I would give five years of my life could

I but make this voyage with you. But, granted that I am alive when you return, naught in heaven or earth shall keep me from joining you when next you sail."

"I would that you could go with us, Garcia," Colon replied; "and your promise shall not be forgotten when we again set out. If it please God, we shall be here again within the year."[1]

To old Juan de Cabezudo and the village priest, Fray Martin Sanchez, Colon had intrusted his son Diego, despite the lad's protests and entreaties to be allowed to accompany his father. The old sailor came up to bid farewell to the Captain, with a suspicious glitter in his half-closed eyes.

"Have no fear for the boy, Master!" he said; "he shall get safe to your good lady in Cordova if Juan Rodriguez has to carry him in his arms. Sinner that I am," he exclaimed in a sudden burst of regret, "that I should be left to tend the children when your Worship sails on so brave a cruise!" And he turned away almost angry with Colon for his own fault in not having gone.

Fray Antonio embraced his friend, the tears running down the faces of both.

"God and His angels have you and all who go with you in their holy keeping, Son Cristoval!" said the good priest, his voice shaking with emotion. "Bear you always in mind that those who love you are daily praying for your welfare, and counting the weary hours to your return."

Colon was scarcely less moved. "I am the least of all His servants, dear friend," he answered. "In His hands we are, and He shall not fail us."

The light mists of early morning were still hanging over the water, as those on shore saw the dim sails slowly hoisted on the shadowy vessels out in the channel, and heard the creaking of the blocks as the sailors hauled them home. Down the river was still gently blowing the cool *terral*, the wind which draws by night from the mountains toward the

---

[1] It has often been asserted that the young physician sailed with Columbus on this voyage; but the Garcia Fernandez who shipped on the "Pinta" as steward was another and much older man.

sea. Aided by this and the ebb tide, the ships gathered way, and slowly stood down stream toward the broad estuary where the Odiel joins the Tinto a league below the town. As they widened the distance between them and those who were left behind, the crowd melted away and turned back to the village church, once more to offer their prayers and make their vows for the safety of those who had gone.

It was broad daylight when the fleet reached the Saltes bar, over which lay the course to the wide Atlantic. The land-breeze had fallen as the sun rose higher, and now at eight o'clock was barely giving them steerage-way. Out beyond the bar the breeze was coming in from the open sea, blowing fresh and strong from that wondrous western ocean. As the ships plunged through the rollers on the shallower bar, the sails filled to the steady gale, and the three bows were headed due south, to clear the Spanish coast and then lay direct for the distant Canaries.

"In the name of Our Lord Jesus Christ," their commander had undertaken his desperate adventure; and as the flat shores of Andalusia drifted from his sight, even his stout heart must have felt that more than mortal skill and courage would be sorely wanted before he saw their level beaches again.

We know already that Colon's studies had led him to believe that the shortest route to the mainland of Asia and the islands lying to the east of it was to be found by sailing due west from the Canaries, and it was for this reason that he had laid his course for that group on leaving the mouth of the Tinto. Moreover these islands formed the frontier possessions of Spain in the Atlantic Ocean, and by touching at them on his voyage, he would be able to replenish his stock of water and provisions, and to some degree break the dread which so many of his sailors had of sailing away into the remote west. The islands had not then been so long discovered that a voyage to them was as yet thought lightly of. Those of his people who had not before ventured so far out on the Atlantic would, he hoped, take heart and lose some of their fears on hearing their own tongue spoken, and seeing the world to be so much the same in that distant archipelago which they had been accustomed to regard as the very confines of the earth.

Colon was too experienced a commander not to realize the possibilities of mutiny and disorder among the motley assemblage which manned his squadron, once they were finally cut off from that part of the world with which they were familiar. Too large a proportion of his crews had shipped with him in a half-hearted way, — either over-persuaded by the Pinzons, or in dread of being pressed into the service by Peñalosa, — for him to have any great confidence in their fidelity and perseverance. With this in view, he had arranged with Martin Alonzo to divide up the doubtful men in such manner that they would all be under a strong control. He himself commanded the "Santa Maria," on which were chiefly placed men from Palos itself, a grumbling and discontented lot in large part. With him also sailed the officers of the Crown, attached to every royal expedition, whom he had selected from those of his own acquaintance who had volunteered to accompany him. A nephew of his faithful friend the superior of La Rabida, Rodrigo de Escovedo, by name, filled the office of royal notary, and was charged with the duty of keeping for their Majesties' inspection a formal record of all the incidents of the voyage. Diego de Arana, a brother of the lady whom Colon considered and treated as his second wife,[1] served as *alguacil*, or justice, of the fleet. Rodrigo Sanchez, of Segovia, in whom he had much confidence, was commissioner, or inspector-general, for the Crown; and Pedro de Gutierrez, one of the queen's own household officers, acted as a sort of general aide. With these to assist him and lend him countenance, Colon was satisfied that he could restrain any attempt at insubordination on his own ship. In command of the "Pinta" he had placed Martin Alonzo, with his

---

[1] Colon in at least one letter refers to Doña Beatriz as his "wife." In his will, however, he leaves her a legacy under her maiden name, adding, "And this I do for the discharge of my conscience. The reason therefor it is not right to mention here."

brother Francisco, as lieutenant, having grave reasons for doubting not only the loyalty of many of her crew, but being still more suspicious of her owners, — two turbulent fellows named Rascon and Quintero, who sailed on her as well. Vicente Yañez Pinzon was captain of the "Niña;" and it is a pleasure to note that from first to last of the long and adventurous voyage this "little girl," as the name signifies, gave Colon neither anxiety nor trouble, and in the hour of his greatest need was the means of saving him and all the company on the flagship. In the crews were sailors from all the maritime districts of Spain, besides Genoese and Frenchmen, Basques and Portuguese, men from the Balearic Islands, a converted Jew, one Englishman, and a single native of the Emerald Isle, — as ill-assorted a company as ever manned a modern man-of-war.

The fresh breeze held good all day, and by sundown Colon was clear of the great bay which lies between Cape St. Vincent and Gibraltar. Signalling his two companions, he changed his course to southwest, and stood straight for the Canaries. Saturday and Sunday found the fleet holding steadily on its way, and making a regular five or six miles an hour. To its leader the fair weather and rapid progress were an earnest of the success he never doubted would be his; and as the western breeze hummed through the rigging, and his little ship rose and fell with the long Atlantic swell, his mind was filled with thoughts and speculations about the ocean which lay between him and the lands he so surely believed lay behind the quivering horizon. There was no lack of work, however, either for him or his crews on these first days upon salt-water, in getting ship and cargo in proper shape for the service that was ahead; and Colon was a man to see that both his own and his lieutenants' vessels were put in right condition. So far all was going well, and he encouraged his officers to dispel, by all means in their power, the foolish dread and doubt which existed in the minds of so many of the men.

On Monday the wind freshened, and the day broke over a gray and boisterous waste of waters. As Colon watched with some anxiety from the high poop-deck of the "Santa Maria" the behavior of his two smaller vessels, he saw the "Pinta" come up into the wind and then fall off, a rolling hulk, in the trough of the sea. Steering for her, he hailed Martin Alonzo and asked what was amiss. The steering-gear had given way and the rudder been partially unshipped by the violence of the waves, the "Pinta's" captain replied.

"Have no fear for us, your Worship," Pinzon cheerily added, knowing well the thought that was in his commander's mind; "we can rig up a makeshift to carry us into port, and the 'Pinta' shall not see Palos until our voyage is done."

The heavy seas prevented Colon from lending any aid to his companion; but he stood by until the skilful master of the disabled vessel had improvised a substitute for the damaged rudder.

"'T is well Martin Alonzo is on board the ship," Colon said to his aides, as they watched the smaller craft tossing and pitching a cable's length away. "I greatly doubt if her rascally owners did not aid the waves in their work of wrecking the rudder there. They are mutinous dogs at best, and gave me many a ruffle ere we sailed. Had they their own way, I warrant, they would find in this early mischance a good excuse for putting back to Spain."

Martin Alonzo was a man fruitful in resource, however, and of an iron will, and before the day was old had signalled the Captain that all was well; and the fleet pursued its way, greatly to the chagrin of the worthy Rascon and Quintero and such of the crews as had hoped the "accident" might lead to a return to Palos for repairs — and desertion.

The next day, Tuesday, the temporary steering apparatus gave way again on the "Pinta," and the squadron had to heave to a second time and wait until it was repaired. These delays and the necessity of sailing cautiously on account of the weakness of the rude arrangement contrived by Martin Alonzo, much impaired the progress of the fleet, and brought it down to a scant three miles an hour. Colon fretted under the detention, and determined that on reaching the Canaries he would endeavor to get another vessel to take the "Pinta's" place. This decision was still further confirmed on the next morning, when Martin Alonzo announced that his ship had sprung a leak over night, in addition to her previous disaster. The report of this new mishap also served to increase the apprehensions of the disaffected among the three crews, which were not relieved by a dispute arising among the pilots as to their precise whereabouts in that vast expanse of ocean. Fearful of leaving the beaten track, and haunted by dread of what might be encountered at every league of unvisited water, the sailors now began to curse the day they started on such a madman's cruise. But Colon, with his more perfect knowledge of navigation and more accurate observation, satisfied the pilots that their course was still a right one, and the fears of the ignorant men in part subsided.

The following Sunday, the 12th of August, proved the correctness of his calculations, and greatly served to revive confidence in their leader among the fickle seamen; for they came within sight of the Peak of Teneriffe and the principal island of the Archipelago, called for distinction the Great Canary. The lofty summit of Teneriffe was at that time an active crater; and Colon's log-book notes that as they approached it they saw "a great flame issuing from the mountain on the island, which is excessively high, in a marvellous manner." Such of his mariners as had not seen a burning mountain before were much impressed by the sight of this huge volume of fire and smoke rising apparently from out of the sea; but their shipmates who had seen Ætna and Stromboli when sailing in the Mediterranean laughed at them for simpletons, and made merry over their fears. Leaving Martin Alonzo at anchor at the larger island, since the "Pinta" could not safely navigate without repairs, Colon continued on to the neighboring island of Gomera in search of the vessel he wanted to supply her place. Failing to find such an one, he detailed a few men to remain behind and collect a store of fresh provisions and firewood, while he sailed back at once to Martin Alonzo. On joining him all hands set to work to careen the "Pinta" on the beach and put her in thorough condition for the hard work ahead. Taught by the recent mishaps to mistrust her owners, Colon and the Pinzons personally superintended the workmen engaged in calking the ship and replacing the rudder. Then, to improve her sailing qualities, they changed her rig from the lateen-sails of the Spanish coasting-vessels to the square sails better adapted for deep-sea voyages. All this was done, the log-book tells us, only " at the expense of great labor and efforts on the part of the commander, of Martin Alonzo, and all the others;" but when it was completed Colon felt repaid for the delay, for the "Pinta" proved thereafter the best sailer of the three.

It was not until the third Sunday, September 2, that this overhauling was completed and the fleet was able to make for Gomera, where was then the chief port of the islands. Here, while the ships were taking in fresh water and supplies, many of the men were necessarily on shore, and from the inhabitants they heard repeated accounts of the land which had been seen on unusually clear days lying afar in the west. No one had as yet been able to discover it by sailing toward it, it was true; but none the less did the residents of Gomera and all who had been in those waters believe firmly in its existence. To Colon the tale was, as we know, no novelty, and he was satisfied that even if such a land did in reality exist, it would be found to be only some unvisited island; but the story had a good effect upon his sailors, for it led them to look upon the ocean as less likely to be so dreadful a wilderness as it was represented, and to hope to find land from time to time, as they sailed away from the world they knew.

On the third day after reaching Gomera, news was brought to Colon which caused him to complete hastily his fitting out and get under way without further delay. A caravel arrived from the adjoining island of Ferro, the westernmost of the Canary group, lying some seventy miles from where he was at anchor, and reported that three Portuguese vessels were cruising in that vicinity without any apparent motive. Spain and Portugal were at complete peace, and there was nothing to attract a foreign squadron to those shores; so the islanders who brought the news were at a loss to account for the presence of the strangers. Colon, however, inspired by his deep-grounded distrust of all that was Portuguese, was quick to fathom the object of this new arrival, and realized that it was full of menace for himself and his expedition.

"Look you, Señor Rodrigo," he said to the inspector, as soon as he heard the report confirmed, " had these ships of the Portuguese king come frankly into port either here or at Ferro, we might have naught to fear, since they would assuredly be bound to or coming from the settlements of that Crown on the Guinea coasts. But since they are lying off the westernmost of these islands and in the very track we should pursue, I cannot doubt that they come to arrest our endeavor and take us prisoners to Lisbon. His Majesty of Portugal has ever been jealous of our gracious sovereign's success at sea, and on the knowledge of our voyage and our intent to touch these islands has doubtless despatched these ships to intercept us. This, too, we owe to the owners of the 'Pinta,'" he added with bitterness.

His officers saw no reason to question the correctness of this view, for both from the Court and from Palos the Portuguese king might have learned the destination of the ships during the time they were fitting out, and had ample leisure to despatch a fleet for their capture, did he so desire. There was but one opinion among Colon's lieutenants, and that was that sail should be made at once and the doubtful cruisers evaded at all costs. Their leader, as was his wont, took the matter calmly, and looked confidently for Divine Providence to deliver him in safety from the threatened catastrophe; but Martin Alonzo was more vehement in his expressions.

"May God forbid, Señor Colon," he said with emphasis, "that the fleet of our great monarchs should turn back at the bidding of any one! We have left our homes to find these new lands of Asia, and with His help we shall do it. Let us steer our course, Señor, and hold our own against all who would check us."

"Well said, Señor Martin," Colon replied; "and if we keep well together, and sail to the south of Ferro, the Portuguese captain shall have but sorry news to take to his king when next he sees the Tagus."

At daybreak on the following morning, the 6th of September, Colon left Gomera and stood westward. His anxieties were far from over, though, for all that day and the next and the third day, until after midnight, they drifted in a dead calm between that island and Teneriffe, consoled only by the reflection that where they could make no progress their envious rivals could make none. Before dawn on the 8th, a strong breeze set in from the northwest; and Colon laid his course due west, according to his unvarying intention to follow the parallel of the Canary Islands in his voyage. As the stately peak sank behind the horizon astern of them, the fears of the more timid among the crews revived, and they were inclined to bemoan their cruel fate in being thus compelled to plunge into the terrors and mysteries of that dreaded western sea; but the stouter hearts and clearer heads among them still laughed down their complaints, and looked forward with eagerness to the wealth and adventures in store.

These men who sailed with Columbus were not the fools and tearful cowards they have sometimes been painted. Like the men of all ages, they were no better than the times they lived in, and theirs were the days of ignorance and of superstition in all that related to the unknown. When the prows of their ships pointed toward the west from Gomera, not only were they leaving astern their own familiar shores of Europe, but also those of Africa and the Cape Verde Islands, of Madeira, the Canaries, and Azores, — all that they had ever heard of as being the very farthest verge of the world they lived in. Columbus himself had never been able to convince many of the so-called wise men of his time that the earth was round, and that by pursuing a given course it might be encircled.[1] What wonder, then, that ignorant seamen from the little creeks and bays of Southern Spain — and much more the landsmen, who formed so large a part of the company — should fear lest some day, by going too rashly westward, they should come to the end of all things and fall over into Space? Their credulity had been fed on wild tales of bottomless whirlpools, of mighty monsters who made but a mouthful of ships and men, and of blazing zones where vessels and crews were burned to coals by the heat of the too close sun. Had we been there, good reader, no doubt our hearts would have sunk as low as the lowest, when the smoky pennant of Teneriffe was lost to sight. As our tale proceeds, we shall find these same men, though at times grumbling and quarrelsome, as becomes all sailors, doing many a deed of daring and high courage, and showing themselves to be in this as well true sons of the sea; whose heads were none the less cool, nor their hands the less ready, when face to face with imminent danger, because their tongues were hung somewhat slack, and they saw according to their lights.

Meanwhile the little fleet was running before a good stiff breeze, and, passing within sight of the highlands of Ferro, soon left the King of Portugal's cruisers hull down below the eastern horizon.

[1] In later years he argued that it was *pear-shaped* rather than round.

IX.

IN THE PATH OF THE SUN.

FOR exactly four weeks to the day, the fleet held its way due west, following persistently the same parallel of latitude. The result completely justified Colon's expectations that he should thereby find the safest and best course, for during all that time they enjoyed fair weather and made steady progress. Once or twice, as we shall see, they were indeed driven slightly off their track, but never for more than a few hours; and in that perservering determination to follow out what he believed to be the true route, no less than in the amazing confirmation of his careful computations later on, we may discern both the evidence of the great navigator's genius and the cause of his success.

At the outset, on losing sight of Ferro, a heavy-head sea assailed the little squadron, whose round and tubby bows offered too ample a surface to any opposing waves; but this difficulty did not last long. On the second day there was a slight return of disaffection among the discontented portion of the crews. Although strictly warned to keep the ship's head constantly to the west, the steersmen of the Captain's vessel repeatedly brought her around to a northwest course, and the other two vessels naturally followed the lead thus given them. The perversity with which this was done, despite his reiterated commands, satisfied Colon that either the men were anxious to give the fleet a greater northing, in accordance with the general belief that the farther north they sailed the farther they would be from the terrors they had heard of, or else that they wished to get a glimpse, if possible, of the famous land of which they had been told when in Gomera. Wearied with this continued disobedience, and conscious of the danger of any sign of weakness, Colon rated the guilty men soundly for their fault.

"Mark you, my men!" he said, going up to them and speaking with sternness; "our course lies west and ever west, and thither shall we sail. See you to it that we leave it not again without my orders. I care for no more of this wandering about, and on your shoulders shall fall the penalty if I am not heeded now."

This trick of his sailors gave Colon renewed uneasiness, and led him to anticipate a frequent repetition of their disaffection in one way or another. The better to avoid this, as far as possible, he resolved to make the voyage seem shorter than it really was. Thus each day, on calculating the previous day's run, he noted privately the real distance; but he announced to his pilots and crew a lesser one. In the twenty-four hours, ending at midnight of the 9th, they sailed in reality seventy leagues; but Colon gave out that they had made forty-eight only. His own expectation was, as we have seen, that he should find land about seven hundred and fifty leagues west of the Canaries, and this he had declared without reserve as his conviction; but as this was based on his calculations alone, — since no one really knew as yet whether there was any other side to the world or not, — he provided like a prudent man for being mistaken, and, to prevent his followers from becoming too soon discouraged at a long voyage, led them to suppose it was much shorter than in fact it was. In these days of corrected observations and patent logs such a stratagem seems puerile; but when the working out of a ship's position was a problem of the highest art, it was an easier matter. As the pilots of the three ships never agreed in their own calculations, and all admitted him to be head and shoulders their superior in the science of navigation, Colon had no difficulty in persuading them of the accuracy of his account. This practice stood him in good stead later on; and, happily for all, when the discrepancy between his figures as proclaimed and those of his pilots grew to be suspiciously wide, he fell upon land, and no further management was necessary.

On the fourth day out from Ferro, the "Santa Maria" passed close to a large mast, apparently the wreckage of a ship of considerable burthen. The sailors tried to seize it, but failed in the effort; and the water-logged piece of timber bobbed gradually out of sight in their wake. Even to this day, when the Atlantic Ocean is little more than a lane for shipping in quiet seasons, the sight of a bit of broken spar will stir some flicker of superstitious sentiment in the mind of many a sailor, and the more especially if he be from the South of Europe. To the mariners who lined the bulwarks of Colon's flagship this lonely flotsam, as it drifted uneasily on that unknown sea, spoke loudly of disaster and destruction to those who ventured farther on. The grumblers had a new text to preach from; and the faint-hearted a fresh excuse for their alarm, which all the jeers of their more courageous shipmates, who saw in the mast only a broken log, were unable to allay.

Two days later this superstitious fear found new food to fatten on; for it was whispered through the ship that the needle no longer pointed north. This was so direct a confirmation of all that they had heard of the end of the earth lying in those quarters and of the awful chaos and darkness lying beyond, that even the bolder seamen began to question the wisdom of going any farther. They had sailed now six hundred miles out into the western sea, and found no land; and if they were once to lose the guidance of the compass, what hope remained of their ever repassing in safety the trackless waste that already stretched between them and home? As if to serve for an additional warning, sent direct by Heaven itself, on the second night after this discovery, while it yet formed the absorbing staple of discussion aboard the "Santa Maria," as the crew were grouped about the deck talking in low tones of the dread which filled their minds, or brooding sullenly over the fate which might await them, a huge meteor shot athwart the sky, and plunged with vast confusion into the sea not far away. Terrified by a sight which even on land was looked upon as a portent of evil and distress, the awe-struck sailors now noticed that the long trail of colored fire left by the blazing mass did not disappear at once, as they were wont to see it, but hung wavering and uncertain on the dark curtain of the night, — a ghostly and uncanny sign full of sinister meaning. Such is often the manner of meteoric wakes in the latitudes where now the fleet was sailing; but it was new to Colon's men, and only served to cast their minds into a deeper gloom. What more was wanting, they urged, to prove the folly of farther progress? Had not God Himself lighted that warning beacon which faded so reluctantly from their anxious sight?

Their commander was keenly aware of this growing discontent among his people, and thought long and deeply over a means for overcoming it. To him the fluctuation of the needle — now familiar to every schoolboy as the magnetic variation — was as unknown and mysterious as to any of his crew; for this was the first time he had observed the strange phenomenon [1] Discarding the childish superstitions of his companions, he sought its explanation in natural causes, being an acute and patient investigator; and if the reason he finally gave his men was not absolutely correct, it served to satisfy them, and was at least as plausible as most theories which have since been advanced. Closely watching the compass day and night, and comparing its fluctuations with the polar star, he found that the variation was greatest at night; while in the morning the needle pointed in a true line with the star. He explained to his pilots and crew, therefore, that the irregularity was due to no change on the part of the compass, but to the fact that the star itself described a tiny circle in the twenty-four hours, the needle thus pointing a little away from it at one hour while at another it was true. So specious was this exposition that it not only allayed the

[1] Columbus was not the discoverer of the magnetic variation, as Mr. Irving considered; basing his supposition on Navarrete's assertion. The phenomenon had been observed and commented on by several earlier geographers.

sailors' fears of a catastrophe from this cause, but strengthened their confidence in their captain's sagacity and professional skill. Both this reasoning of Colon and his act in keeping a double reckoning have been of late years unsparingly criticised as unworthy and paltry deceptions, indicative alike of a lack of principle and courage; but we fail to see the justice of such censure. Colon clearly believed the exactness of the conclusion he adopted regarding the needle; for he maintained it in later years by more elaborate arguments. If he was not as wise as we are in this particular, no doubt our grandchildren shall say as much of us in other respects. As to the double reckoning, he was aware that the distance he had to sail was at least problematical, and knew that his men would seize upon the first excuse to turn back should land not be found somewhere near where his charts established it. In his own words, "the mariners were accustomed every day to see land, and on their longest voyages never sailed two hundred leagues without seeing it." His object was not deception, but precaution; and we cannot find any trace of moral obliquity in the transaction. On the contrary, to our mind, in quieting the seamen's dread lest their compasses had played them false, and in providing for the contingencies of a doubtful future as to the distance to be run, Colon crossed in safety his frailest bridge; for what greater fear could possess the ignorant sailors on such a voyage than that both chart and compass were faithless guides?

Nature herself came now to his rescue, and rebuked the timid apprehensions of his crews with signs of hopefulness so plain that even the landsmen on board could read the message. Over the "Niña" had flown two birds which the sailors recognized as living on shore; and on the 16th of September, the ninth day of their westward sailing, the ships began to pass those great patches of floating weed which to this day attract attention in the southern seas when met with for the first time. So fresh and green were these fields of ocean herbage that Colon himself concluded that they must have been swept off the rocks of some not distant island only very recently, and he was urged by his pilots to change his course, and search for it in the direction whence the weed came; but this he declined to do.

"It is not an island that we are seeking," he answered to their representations, "but the mainland of Cathay; and I know we have not gone far enough as yet to reach it. That there are many islands to the eastward of Asia I am well assured, and some of these may now be near. 'T is folly to seek them, however, when we shall so soon reach the continent itself. Let them stand for the present; on our return we can visit them, if so God pleases."

Even the grumblers were contented with his argument, for they had little to complain of just then. The exquisite softness of the tropical air, the steady flow of a favoring breeze, and the perfect beauty of the mornings and evenings reminded even the rough sailors of the loveliest season in distant Andalusia. The sea was as smooth, they said, as the bosom of the Guadalquivir; and to their fanciful taste the very water of the ocean was less salt than that they were familiar with. One day they hauled on board some floating weeds, which in their eyes were of the kind that grew only in the fresh water of rivers, and tangled in the mass they found a living crab, which they gave their captain,—perhaps as a peace-offering. Around their ships they saw playing fish of the sort which they had known at home; and the "Niña's" men captured a tunny-fish,—a kind which many a man on board had caught by the boat-load in the fishing-grounds off Cadiz. The crews were quickly filled with life and hope, every fear forgotten as rapidly as it had come; and each ship tried to pass the others in keen rivalry as to which should first catch sight of land. Where two short days before all had been gloom and despondency, there was now nothing but eagerness and content. Encouraged by the spirit of his men, and confirmed in his faith in the correctness of his course by the increasing mildness of the climate and the favorable signs which multiplied on all sides, Colon felt assured that he was indeed approaching the tropical seas of Asia.

"This is like your month of April in the South of Spain, Señor Rodrigo," he remarked to the inspector, as they looked out over the densely blue sea on one of those perfect evenings; "we only lack the nightingales to make us feel in Seville. Please God that all these happy signs fail not, and may He bring us soon to land."

Colon had given strict commands that under all circumstances the ships should keep together, — an order easy of accomplishment in that summer sea. But on the 18th of the month the "Pinta" crowded all sail, and kept far ahead of the two other vessels until nightfall. When she rejoined them Martin Alonzo brought her up close to the "Santa Maria," and shouted to Colon that a great flock of birds had passed overhead in the morning, and he had felt so sure that land would be found before dark that he had forged ahead. Queen Isabella, at Colon's personal request, had offered a standing reward consisting of an annual pension of ten thousand maravedies for life to whomever should first discover land, and the temptation was great to keep in advance; but the Captain insisted on his orders being obeyed. He himself had seen that day a fog-bank to the north which he thought hung over land, but he would not change his direction by a single point.

"Keep strictly to the course, Señor Martin," he answered to the "Pinta's" hail. "If we spend our time in beating about after every sign of dry land we see, we shall never reach our goal."

The very next day two pelicans alighted on the "Santa Maria," — genuine shore birds, if any are, — and a few drizzling showers fell without any storm of wind. These were considered to be almost certain indications of the near proximity of land, but still Colon would listen to no talk of varying from his westward course. The islands could wait, he repeated over and over again. What he wanted was the continent of Asia; and that lay directly ahead of them, neither to the right hand nor to the left. To compare the pilot's calculations of the distance so far made, he hailed the two other ships and asked their logs. Cristoval Garcia, pilot of the "Pinta," found that they had come four hundred and twenty leagues from Ferro; Pero Alonzo Niño, of the "Santa Maria" reported four hundred and forty-seven; while Sancho Ruiz of the "Nina" thought they had sailed no more than four hundred leagues. Colon noted these all down and kept his own counsel, relying on the wide difference in their several statements to quiet any new apprehension that might arise among the men. They now fell in with a succession of calms and light variable winds which threw them a little toward the northwest, and did not greatly advance their passage. Still the birds were coming on board during the day and flying off, as night approached, toward the southwest, giving clear token that a resting-place of some kind could not be far distant. Among them were three little land-birds which perched in the rigging and sang merrily until sunset, following then in the wake of their larger fellows; and this was thought to be the best of omens. The surface of the sea, too, was now covered with so thick a carpeting of the weed they had met before, that it seemed like a vast meadow stretching about them as far as the eye could reach, and was as green and smooth as one. A great whale came slowly rolling and spouting toward the ships, forcing his clumsy way through the dense vegetation, as though to examine what strange manner of monsters these might be which were invading his domain; and the seamen recalled that the whales they were used to chase in Europe were found not far from shore. All these spoke of a speedy ending to their tedious journey; but, with crass perverseness, the inconsistent and unreasonable among the crews were led, by the very abundance of such hopeful signs and the long succession of perfect weather they were enjoying, to renew their growling and fault-finding. They noted that the wind had held steadily favorable to their westerly course until now, when they seemed to be approaching a region of calms. All the old women's yarns about ships and their companies floating forever and a day in a region of oily stagnation were accordingly revived. Constantly and ceaselessly, by day and by night, the strong easterly breezes had wafted them into this remote and unknown ocean. Now the winds were failing them, and more and more the fleet was becoming becalmed. With no wind to sail with, how should they ever get farther to the west? And with nothing but head winds to the eastward, how should they ever make their way back over that immense expanse to the port from which they sailed? The least their leader could do, they urged, was to shift his course somewhat, and endeavor, by drawing out of that region of mockery and delusion, to reach the land which apparently lay thereabout. If it should prove to be only an island, it would be better than flying in the face of Providence by engulfing themselves farther and farther in that waveless sea.

Colon saw in this new outbreak of discontent a real and imminent peril. He was not much more than half-way across the distance that lay between the Canaries and Asia, according to his estimates; and if his men grew mutinous both at the wonders and the beauties of Nature, as they seemed inclined to do, he feared they might turn upon him, and either compel him to put about and return to Spain, or at least alter his course and go on an idle search for their fancied islands. In either of these events his grand project would be ruined and his hopes turned into bitter failure.

At this juncture again that good fortune which attended him so faithfully upon this first voyage, and in which he devoutly saw the ever-present hand of the Almighty, came to his aid and relieved him from the threatened danger. On the 22d of the month a fresh breeze sprang up from the southwest, and drove them out of their course toward the north. With such a wind the ships could sail for home when it was necessary, and the murmurings on this score died away. "Greatly did I need this head wind," Colon wrote in his log, his mind evidently relieved from a heavy strain, "because my people were growing very mutinous, as they believed no wind ever blew in these seas which would take them back to Spain." Only the next day the remaining ground of their complaint was swept away; for although the sea had only been ruffled by the recent breeze and soon settled down into its habitual quiet, toward afternoon a heavy swell set in, apparently without the aid of any wind, and tossed the ships about as if to take revenge on the complainings of their crews. "Never since the day when Moses brought the children of Israel out of Egypt were waves so welcome," Colon added gratefully in his journal; and he was as much rejoiced as his mariners were discomfited. To them it seemed little less than a miracle that so great a sea should suddenly arise in calm weather, without any sign of a corresponding wind; but their Captain knew that it came from some heavy gale farther off in the ocean, though this he was careful not to explain at the moment.

Throughout the whole of this memorable voyage we find no indication that at any time Colon feared even for a moment for his own safety; nor are we disposed to agree with those who hold that his life was in constant peril from the violence of his crew. That his men were, in large part, a turbulent and ill-conditioned set, there is no doubt; but this is easily understood when we recall that many of them had come with him against their will, that they were traversing a wholly unknown and mysterious ocean which all their lives they had been led to believe was filled with dark and terrible dangers, and that as the weeks passed without their seeing land their hopes of ever finding it grew fainter and fainter and were replaced by fears lest they should never see their homes again. The mere question of food and water was enough to cause them to dread an indefinite continuance of their strange expedition. Where were they to replenish their stores if no land appeared? What was to prevent months and months from passing over their heads while their stock of supplies sank lower and lower? And what would happen if they really lay becalmed, or were driven hither and thither over the face of that limitless sea? . Shut up together on a small ship, with little else to do than talk over their grievances and find fault, as sailors will, with their commander, we can readily understand that a spirit of discontent and insubordination would spring up and strengthen on very little provocation. But from this to open mutiny and defiance there was a wide gulf to cross, and the quickness with which their grumblings were followed by elation at every new sign of hope and expectation of reaching shore proves, we think, that there was no deep-laid scheme to harm their leader or put an end to his plans by outrage. On one occasion, some three weeks later, we shall indeed find his safety threatened by some few of his men; but we do not believe that even then he was in imminent danger, and nothing in his own writings gives color to such a theory. The only dread he ever expresses is lest he might be compelled to change his course to humor his men, and thus miss the goal he had in view.

On the 25th of September the fleet was again becalmed for the greater part of the day, so that the men threw themselves overboard and swam about the ships, playing and larking as seamen will. Colon brought the "Santa Maria" alongside the "Pinta," and held a consultation with Martin Alonzo regarding their prospect of soon reaching the Asiatic coast. At Pinzon's request he had, three days before, sent to him the selfsame map which he had shown to Fray Antonio and Garcia Fernandez at the convent of La Rabida on that summer evening in the past year, and now he wished to know the results of Martin Alonzo's study of its contents. According to his own record, Colon believed that they had come more than six hundred leagues from the Canaries; and on this map he had, as we already know, laid down certain of the eastern islands as lying about in that vicinity. Keeping this record to himself, he now asked his lieutenant's opinion of their situation, knowing his skill and judgment as a navigator and having confidence in his sincerity.

"It seems to me, Señor Captain," Pinzon replied to his questions, "that we cannot now be far from the islands your Worship has laid down on this map. Our course has held good now for over five hundred leagues due west; and though this is not enough to bring us yet to the great island of Cipango here drawn, and much less to the mainland of Asia itself, it may well be that all the tokens of land we have met with in these later days shall point to the neighborhood of the lesser ones your Worship has painted in to the east of that country."

"There are we in accord, Señor Martin," Colon answered, "and I am content to find that you feel so assured. The lesser islands I entered on the chart are not laid down precisely, for we know not their distances from Cipango; but I believe they cannot lie much farther to the west than they are shown, and the currents here may have thrown us somewhat too much to the north. It may be, likewise, that we have not come quite so far as our pilots think, as we have had many calms these last few days, besides the currents."

"Maybe, your Worship, maybe," Martin responded rather doubtfully, "but their reckonings seem to me to be right enough."

Now, Colon knew that the fleet had come at least one hundred leagues farther than the pilots had calculated; but it was doubly important that even the smaller distance should be thought too great, first, in order that the Pinzons and other officers who knew something of navigation should not lose faith in the accuracy of the chart by which they were sailing, as they certainly would in case they thought they had reached the longitude of the islands Colon had pictured and did not find them; and, second, that the men should be kept as long as possible in ignorance of the extent to which the voyage was drawing out. He therefore asked Martin Alonzo to make fast a line to the chart, and, hauling it on board the flagship, he sat down with his own pilots and such of his sailors as understood the matter, and discussed with them their whereabouts. They had all heard the conversation with Pinzon; and Colon, rightly relying on the high opinion they held of his lieutenant's sagacity, pointed out the certainty there was of reaching the longed-for mainland before many days. The worst was past, he argued, and who would be willing to abandon the reward after so long and arduous a journey to secure it?

That very evening, as the sun was setting, and, as so often happens at that hour in the tropics, the horizon lay clear and sharp on every side as though drawn with a ruler between sea and sky, Colon and his commanders, with many of their crews, mounted the high "castles" built in the bows and sterns of their vessels, and strained their eyes to catch, if possible, some glimpse of land against the western sky. Suddenly there came a shout which drew all eyes toward that ship.

"The prize, Señor Captain, the prize!" called out Martin Alonzo. "To me falls the reward. Yonder is land, due southwest as the compass shows."

At first Colon saw nothing of the discovery reported; but hearing many of the "Pinta's" crew shouting out confirmation of their commander's statement, and the "Niña's" men affirming the same from the masthead and yards to which they had swarmed at the first cry from the sister-ship, he watched the horizon still more closely until to his sight, too, there seemed to be a faint, low blot far away off the port bow.

"God's blessing rest upon you, Martin Alonzo!" called out Colon, on seeing this. "Yours is our sovereigns' reward, but to Him be the praise. Let us give Him thanks."

Then falling on his knees, surrounded by his officers and crew, he solemnly intoned the noble chant "Gloria in Excelsis," followed devoutly by those around him, Martin Alonzo and his brother Vicente Yañez setting a like example to the men on the "Pinta" and the "Niña."

What a picture must the three small ships have presented at that moment, as they slowly rolled to the long swell of that lonely ocean; while the tropical night closed down upon them, and the soft breath of the trade-wind carried the solemn words of those rough and boisterous men out into the west toward the land they sought!

X.

WHAT THE MOON DISCLOSED.

THAT night few eyes were closed and few tongues at rest on board the little squadron; for no one doubted that the morning would see the end of the wearisome voyage. The new country they were approaching, its people, riches, towns, and cities, — all these and a hundred other speculations furnished an inexhaustible text for the garrulity of the excited mariners. Happy were those men who had made the cruise to Africa, or even to the eastern shores of the Mediterranean. They were listened to by their less travelled messmates as almost divine oracles, while they spun their yarns about the strange things they had seen and heard on those wonderful coasts, of the wild and marvellous peoples they had met, and of the treasures which came from the still remoter East. It is doubtful whether on the three vessels a single soul, from Colon down to the youngest ship-boy, had any other thought than that they were at last within touch of the fabulous wealth of the Orient.

According to the Captain's estimate they were about twenty or twenty-five leagues from the land when darkness fell upon them, and he ordered all sails set and the course changed from west to southwest as night set in. The wind, which had failed them entirely the greater part of the day, or only blown in fitful puffs, now sprang up strong and fresh, and carried them swiftly toward their destination. When day broke they had nearly covered the supposed distance, and all hands sought some point of vantage from which to catch the first sight of the promised land. No sign or vestige of it was to be seen; on all sides spread the boundless ocean, as smooth and smiling as any inland sheet, and over its scarce ruffled surface the morning breeze was bearing them cheerily onward, as though in wanton mockery. Thinking they might have steered too far to the south, Colon now led the way again due west until after midday; but seeing still no sign of the land, he changed the course once more to the southwest, in the hope of finding the vanished shore. It was all in vain; as the evening came on, even Martin Alonzo had to confess that they must have been deceived by some cloud or distant haze the day before, and, in the eagerness of their hopes, taken a mere shadow for solid earth.

Great as was this disappointment, it did not affect the sailors as unfavorably as Colon had feared. So many of them had seen that hazy outline in the southwest, that they would not believe themselves mistaken, and the conviction grew up among them that, after all, they would soon reach land. No doubt the fact which they had learned the day before, that Martin Alonzo and all the pilots believed with Colon in the existence of islands thereabout, led them to argue that if they had missed one they would find another; and then the captain himself had shown a willingness at last to steer for land even when it lay off that endless western course. But Colon had no idea of thrashing idly over the surface of the ocean, notwithstanding his momentary deviation; for as soon as he was satisfied that they all had been mistaken he headed for the west, and maintained steadily that direction day after day. For another week nothing occurred to break the monotony of the voyage; the winds were favorable and the sea smooth, so they made rapid headway. Now and then some land-bird would alight on the ships, or a lumbering pelican swoop down to rest on their yards, and once a little flock of sparrows settled in the rigging; but otherwise no new sign of land appeared. The sailors amused themselves with snaring the birds and catching dolphins; but in the absence of any novelty, the old complaining spirit revived. On the 29th a frigate-bird visited the "Santa Maria," and this somewhat encouraged them; for the pilots and other seamen who had made the Guinea voyage had seen these birds in the Cape Verde Islands, and agreed that every night they returned on shore to sleep. Still the everlasting monotony of this summer sailing began to tell again on the men, and they growled out that the birds did them no good, since the land they came from never appeared.

On the first day of October, Pedro Alonzo, the pilot of the flagship, came to Colon in some perturbation, and showed him that according to the reckoning of himself and his colleagues, the fleet had sailed now five hundred and seventy-eight leagues from the Canaries, and were in the very place where, according to the captain's chart, the islands should be found. Colon knew perfectly well that they not only had come that far, but were more than seven hundred leagues west of Ferro; but of this he said nothing to his pilot, and only agreed with him, as with Pinzon before, that the islands were not laid down with exactness and might be still more or less distant. It would be a desperate matter, indeed, were the pilots to reject the guidance of the chart; but by the 3d, Colon himself became anxious lest they might have, in fact, passed through the islands he expected to find, and thus his whole system of computation be at fault. For the first time in three weeks no birds were seen; and this he feared was an indication that the islands lay astern of him, having been sailed past unperceived. He said nothing of this apprehension to any of his officers, however, consoling himself with the reflection that even if they had missed the islands they would be so much the nearer to Asia itself; but none the less was he perturbed and harassed in mind as the limit he had marked for his voyage was approached with no further evidence of land appearing. Once more he was favored by fortune at his moment of discouragement; for on the next day large flocks of the smaller land-birds reappeared, as well as their old visitors, the pelicans, flying still into the west and southwest, as though their nesting-place was there.

Always keeping directly westward, the fleet was now making more rapid average progress than at any time since leaving Palos, Colon's observations showing fifty, sixty, and sometimes seventy leagues a day. Believing firmly that any morning they might now fall upon land, he ordered the smaller vessels to join the flagship every evening before sunset and every morning at sunrise, so that all might thus search the horizon together in the clear atmosphere of those favorable hours for some indication of the expected shores. They had now even passed the nine hundred leagues where, according to his calculation, the great island of Cipango was to be found, and were each day drawing nearer to the spot where, if his chart were to be believed, the continent of Asia was to be met with; so he looked almost from hour to hour for a glimpse of the lands "where the spices grew." Whichever ship should first descry land was to hoist a flag to her mainmast-head and fire a gun as signal, whereupon the others were to join the flagship and sail in company for the coast. It behooved the fleet of their Majesties of Spain to enter the ports of the Orient with becoming state!

As the "Pinta" joined the "Santa Maria" on the evening of the 6th of October, Colon hailed Martin Alonzo and asked whether he had any news for the day.

"Not I, Señor Captain," the other replied, "save some floating sea-grass and a few vagabond birds. Saving your wiser judgment, it would seem to me that now were a proper time to change our course and steer more toward the south. We have already come more than eight hundred leagues to the west, where the islands should be, and as yet have seen no land."

Colon thought deeply before answering. He was aware that they had come more nearly a thousand leagues than eight hundred, and knew only too well how restive the sailors were becoming at his persistent pursuit of the western track.

"In good time, Martin Alonzo," he said at length, "we shall make the change. Let us hold our course a little longer, and then turn southward as you propose. The chart says that Cipango lies dead ahead of us, and we must be close to it now. If we steer southwest too soon, we may miss both it and the mainland too, and have a weary journey for our pains. By sailing the nearer to it, we shall run the lesser risk."

"What your Worship says is well said for me, Señor Captain," Pinzon answered readily. "Whether it be a day or a year, I follow your Worship's orders. But something in my heart tells me we shall touch the coast before long."

Colon had shown his usual shrewdness in speaking of the danger of missing Cipango altogether by steering off his course. The sailors hearing this felt satisfied that their leader knew them to be close to the island, and were thus the more anxious that he should do nothing that might cause them to lose it; while his ready promise to Martin Alonzo to change his direction as soon as it appeared safe tended still more to relieve their minds.

The next morning as the sun was rising, a gun was fired from the "Niña," and the flag run up to her masthead gave notice that her commander, Vicente Yañez, believed the land to be in sight. Immediately all three ships crowded sail and pressed forward in anxious rivalry to discover whether the longed-for shores were indeed at hand; but as the day wore on, the horizon showed again its familiar line unbroken by any object, and it became evident that once more the hope had fathered the delusion, and they were once more chasing a phantom. This repetition of their recent disappointment told more heavily on the temper of the crews, and they broke out into fresh complaints and murmurings. Without doubt this influenced in some measure Colon's decision to change his course without further postponement; but what had greater weight with him was that immense flocks of birds, far more than any before seen, were passing overhead all day, coming always from the northward and flying as regularly toward the southwest. Colon reflected that although the fleet was sailing under summer skies and through the balmiest of airs, farther north cold weather was commencing by these first October days; and he therefore judged that these unusual flights of birds were migrating from the colder climate to their winter quarters in the genial South. This was a shrewd deduction, and was the direct result of his study and observation; for, as he unassumingly tells us, he "had noticed that most of the islands which the Portuguese had discovered had been shown to them by the birds." So when the "Pinta" and "Niña" joined the flagship before sunset as usual, he hailed the former and told Martin Alonzo of the conclusion he had reached.

"In that am I of one mind with your Worship, Señor Captain," shouted back Pinzon. "All this day have I been watching these birds, and they are not holding one course without good cause. If we follow in their wake, we shall surely come to where they are bound."

"We will do so, Señor Martin," Colon answered; "and the more willingly that there is no sign of the "Niña's" land in the west. Lay your course southwest for the night, and take heed that you and Vicente Yañez keep close to me. We will sail that way for a few days, and see if the birds guide well."

This order was received with delight by all the seamen; and when the bows headed away from the setting sun and the fleet stood on the more southerly passage, they forgot their fancied grievances and felt new hopes swell in their hearts.[1]

For several days smooth seas, blue skies, and fair winds still accompanied them, but yet no land appeared. The birds continued to pass overhead by day, and at night could be heard chattering and calling as they swept by in the darkness. Some which alighted on the vessels were caught by the sailors and found to be plainly field-birds, of a kind which could not possibly find rest on the water. Colon himself noticed that the grasses and weeds which floated past his ship were singularly fresh and green, and fancied that the

---

[1] In recording the changes made in the squadron's course, and the conversations between Columbus and Martin Alonzo, we have followed the evidence given by some of the sailors in the great lawsuit of Diego Colon against the Crown.

air was sweet with the fragrance of flowers, — as was, indeed, quite possible; for between the tropics one can often distinguish the perfume of the forests at a great distance from land. But after they had sailed four days on their new course and still saw nothing but sea and sky where they had counted so surely on finding earth and trees, the mutinous element among the flagship's crew burst into loud and unrestrained complaints. They could no longer stand this foolhardy cruising to gratify a dreamer's fancies, they declared. Westward they had sailed at first for four long weeks, and now to the southwest they were making at the rate of over seventy leagues a day; and yet nothing met their sight but water and clouds, and clouds and water. It was little short of sheer suicide to push farther on into that world of delusion. The more crafty among these discontents insinuated also to their simpler shipmates that they were being sacrificed to satisfy the heartless ambition of a foreign adventurer; that Colon was staking his own life and theirs as well on a desperate chance: if he succeeded by any miracle in finding land, he would be made a great lord and gain great rewards; but if he failed they all would pay for his madness with their lives. Had not this enterprise been condemned by all the learned and able doctors by whom it was examined, and did not their own present experience confirm all the objections of those wise men? They had already sailed infinitely farther than any seamen had hitherto dared to venture, and nothing in their duty as good Spaniards to the Crown, obliged them to continue on until they came to the end of the world, with the certainty of eventually perishing staring them in the face. These murmurings and menaces which were at the beginning confined to only a few of the crew and indulged in by them beneath their breath, gradually gathered strength as they passed from mouth to mouth, until a large part of the ship's company became tainted with the infection of disloyalty. Seeing this, the most desperate of the would-be mutineers went a step farther, and hinted at the desirability of " losing " their commander. Suppose he were to fall overboard during the night, while taking the altitude of the Polar Star with his astrolabe? Who would be the worse off for his disappearance? At best he was a foreigner, and no one was likely to probe very deeply to ascertain the circumstances of his removal. Few were willing to give their assent to this scheme, to their credit be it said, although its facile practicability was evident to all. The great majority were content with the milder measures proposed, and confined themselves to demanding an immediate return to Spain. They accordingly sought out their Captain and laid their grievances before him; they had had enough of this phantom-chasing, they now declared, and boldly required that he should put about and give the signal for home.

Colon was a kind and patient commander, thoughtful of his men, and both from consideration and from policy anxious to humor them whenever it was possible. But there was one thing he would not listen to, and that was any talk of turning back. Going forward to where the crew were gathered, when apprised of their demands, he addressed them with frankness and a keen appreciation of the delicacy of his position. He showed them the chart, and explained again at length his grounds for expecting daily and hourly to catch a sight of land, — if not of the mainland of Asia, at least of Cipango or some of the other great islands adjacent to it. He appealed to his pilots and the more experienced seamen before him as to whether they had not repeatedly met with unfailing signs of the nearness of land, and whether it was not merely a question of a few days more or less when they must surely reach a coast. Dwelling at large upon the riches and treasures of the Indies, — their rivers with sands of gold, their forests of spice-trees, their wealthy and populous cities, their stores of pearls and precious gems, — he asked his men whether they were now willing to abandon all the vast reward which there awaited them, after having suffered the weariness and hardships of so long a voyage to find them? Surely, he added, it would be a wiser and more sensible proceeding if they would bear patiently a few days longer with the tedium and privations of their journey, rather than lose all this wealth and plenty, which were almost within their grasp, and face empty-handed the long and perilous voyage back to Spain, only to be jeered and mocked at when they reached their homes at last. Having thus patiently and earnestly argued with his people from the standpoint of their own well-being and advantage, Colon now added a final word on his own account. Drawing himself up proudly and changing his tone of friendly discussion for one of command, he concluded by saying, —

"I am the Captain-General of this fleet and the Ambassador of our royal sovereigns to the courts of Asia, my men. Under their Highnesses' orders we set out for the Indies across this western sea, and to the Indies we are going, with God's help and blessing. Look you to it that we have no more of this; for, grumbling or no grumbling, we are going to find the land we have come so far to seek." Then, turning on his heel, he walked aft to his cabin.[1]

Partly influenced by their leader's arguments and partly abashed by the courage and determination shown by him, the crew once more ceased their open complaining. If it still continued, it was carried on privately among themselves, and Colon heard no more of it. This was on the 10th of October. The next day all was changed.

On Thursday, the 11th of the month, they held still to the southwest course, and ran into a heavy sea, the waves being higher than any they had seen since leaving the Canaries. The land-birds still flew past, always keeping the same direction; but the sailors had almost ceased to heed them, — they had proven false prophets. When later in the day, however, the "Santa Maria's" crew saw a green rush float by their ship, they could not doubt that it had come from shore. Some leaned over the vessel's side eagerly searching for other tokens, while more yet kept a keen lookout along the horizon ahead for the first faint looming of the

---

[1] We have followed both the diary and the account given by Las Casas of the so-called "mutiny." Las Casas apparently wrote from information furnished by Columbus himself.

land. Before long the "Pinta's" men saw plainly drifting past, almost within their reach, a fresh canestalk and a stick of wood; and shortly after drew on board, in quick succession, another stalk, a bunch of weeds which could only have grown on dry land, and a bit of plank. This latter, with a second piece of wood which seemed to have been cut with some tool, satisfied the most sceptical that they were indeed approaching the shores of an inhabited country; and when, toward afternoon, the "Niña's" sailors announced triumphantly that they had seen in the water a bough freshly broken from a tree and covered still with blossoms; the men forgot all past anxieties, and were filled only with the enthusiasm of near success.

At nightfall, after careful deliberation, Colon decided to head west again, satisfied that the shortest way to land would lie in that quarter. Pedro Alonzo, his pilot, in view of these signs of close proximity to shore, had advised him to lie to for the night, and not to sail ahead in the stiff breeze that then was blowing; but the other pilots protested against such action, and urged that the fleet keep straight on, trusting to their lookouts to warn them in time of any threatened danger. Mindful of the excited and impatient temper of his men, Colon inclined to the latter opinion, and gave his orders accordingly. He laid especial injunctions upon the two Pinzons to keep their vessels near his own and maintain a scrupulously careful watch ahead, and promised to whatever sailor should first sight land a silken doublet in addition to the royal bounty. Notwithstanding these precautions, his commands were only partially obeyed. The wind blew fresh and the sea ran high, so that the "Pinta" and the "Niña," being the better sailors, had a good excuse for keeping somewhat in advance of the flagship, and did not hesitate to make the most of it. As for watching, the eyes of every sailor in the three ships were directed over the tumbling sea in hopes of being the first to catch a glimpse of land, both for the sake of the reward and, being true mariners, for the sake of ending a tiresome cruise. They had been deceived by signs before; but this time they had seen and handled the very fruits of the earth, and knew they had not come from far.

The night should have been one of bright moonlight; but a flying scud obscured the moon at intervals, making the lookout all the more exciting with its alternations of light and darkness. Colon himself had taken his station on the high two-storied "castle" which was built up in the stern of his ship; and from this commanding position his keen eye swept constantly the horizon from north to south, anxiously seeking to discover the faintest trace of a coast ahead. At ten o'clock his quick sight caught a glimmer of light out to sea, which almost instantly disappeared. Fixing his eye on the quarter where it had vanished, he called to Pedro Gutierrez and Rodrigo Sanchez, who were near by, and asked them whether they could not see it as well. Then, raising his voice, he hailed the lookout in the bows, —

"*Olá*, in the prow there! See you not a light yonder off the port bow?"

As the ship rose on a billow, Pedro Gutierrez saw the light plainly, and so told the captain; but Rodrigo Sanchez could not catch sight of it from where he stood. Up from the bows too came an answering hail which left the matter still in doubt, —

"No, Señor Captain, we see no light from here."

Once or twice more, however, the wavering spark showed itself to Colon's intent gaze, and then sank out of sight. A lively discussion sprang up on board as to what the light might be. Some, forgetting they were not in European waters, held that it was a lantern carried on a fisherman's boat, and appearing or vanishing with the motion of the waves. Others thought it might be on one of the other vessels at a distance; but this was voted improbable, for they should be directly ahead. Others still flatly denied that there had been any light; they had not seen any, and therefore there could be none. But Colon felt sure that the light was on land, — a torch carried in some one's hand, or the gleam of a fire wavering about, as his line of vision altered, with the unsteadiness of his ship. Few inclined to this belief, though; and as the tiny flame itself had seemed so feeble and uncertain, he did not feel justified in changing the course for so doubtful an indication, and contented himself with repeating to his sailors his warning to keep their eyes well opened. If the light was indeed on shore, they would come up with the coast at some other point soon enough, he argued.

Sweeping swiftly to the west, — for half a gale was blowing, — the fleet held on its way; the "Pinta" leading, with the "Niña" next, and the flagship last of all. Hour after hour went by without incident of any kind. At midnight the watch was changed, and fresh lookouts took the place of those who had been straining their eyes so far in vain; but still the troubled surface of the ocean was all that met the sight. On board the "Santa Maria" the silence was unbroken, except by the swash of the waves against the ship's hull and the low voices of the sailors as now and then they muttered some remark to one another. Just as the watch was again changing, toward two o'clock, the clouds which had been hiding the moon blew off, and the whole sea for leagues around was bathed in a flood of clear white light. Scarcely had the last shadows swept over the rolling sea when a brilliant flash of fire was seen in the direction of the "Pinta," and the dull roar of a cannon was borne down the wind to the vessels astern. It was the signal for land in sight; and the flagship pressed forward to join her foremost consort. As her impatient sailors neared the "Pinta," they had no need to ask the news; for directly before them, not more than a couple of miles away, lay the low and rounded summits of what were clearly sand-hills, while on the beach below a heavy surf was dashing in lines of snowy foam. At the very moment the moon emerged from the clouds, Juan Rodriguez Bermejo, one of the "Pinta's" seamen from a little village near Seville, had seen the first beams fall on the glittering sand and frothy breakers, and had hurriedly fired a gun, with excited cries of "The land! the land!" Had the moon remained hidden but a few minutes longer, there would have been a shipwreck to report.

As it was, its friendly beams disclosed to the joyful eyes of the little squadron a world till then undreamed.

Giving orders to shorten sail and lie to for the few remaining hours of darkness, Colon humbly gave thanks to the God in whom he had trusted through all his perils and adversities, and waited with such patience as he could summon for daylight to expose the nature of his discovery.

What his thoughts were on that memorable night it would be idle to conjecture; but we know at least that they had nothing to do with the continent we now miscall America. We have the warrant of his own words for supposing that he believed those breakers were beating on the shores of Japan, or of some neighboring island in the Asiatic seas, — perhaps on the very territories of the Great Khan himself. Thus far everything had tended to confirm his conviction that he was on the confines of Asia. Long before he started from Spain we have seen him arguing, with map in hand, that at seven or eight hundred leagues west of the Canaries he would find the easternmost of the islands mentioned by Marco Polo and Mandeville; and in fact at that distance he met with such frequent signs of land that he was justified in supposing himself to be passing near them. At a thousand leagues from Ferro he expected to find Cipango; and now that he had sailed only a little more than this distance he had before his eyes the very land he sought! Whatever we may consider his belief, either as a delusion, a mistaken calculation, or a happy coincidence, no one can ever hope by hostile criticism to diminish the glory of this man's achievement. His voyage was the outcome of profound reflection, patient study, and elaborate mathematical computation. He crossed an ocean since the beginning of history believed to be impassable. He found, as he had expected, a continent where the intellectual world of his time maintained that nothing existed but wildest chaos or a stagnant waste of water. Whether that continent was Asia or another, is immaterial in judging the merit of Colon's discovery. He was looking for land on the other side of the world, and there it was confronting him, despite every obstacle, danger, and discouragement that could be opposed against the faith and courage of a single human will.

One of the claims advanced by the relatives and descendants of Martin Alonzo after Colon's death was that the former was entitled to the chief credit of this discovery, because he had induced his commander to turn from the west to the southwest on the latter days of their ocean voyage. Had he, however, kept constantly on his westward course, his glory would have been only the more; for his first landing would then have been on the mainland of the mighty continent which the world owed to his intrepid perseverance. In more recent times even fair-minded historians have not scrupled to deprive him of the minor distinction of having been the first to discover the land he now had found, and have even gone so far as to accuse him of having used his favor with the Crown after his return from this successful voyage to rob poor Juan Bermejo boy of his glory and his pension, since to Colon himself Ferdinand and Isabella awarded the promised bounty. But these detractors fail to give due weight to these essential facts: First, that the fleet carried a royal notary, whose duty it was to record under oath every incident of interest for the information of the sovereigns; and this official dared not even under Colon's demand, make a false report, which would be denied by nine men out of ten among the crew the moment their feet touched Spanish soil. Second, their decree conferring this reward upon Colon the sovereigns expressly say, "We are certain and *certified* that Don Cristoval Colon was the *first who saw* and discovered those islands," — a phrase plainly intimating that they were acting upon the evidence before them. Finally, during the disputes which arose after Colon's death, to which allusion has been made, the very witnesses brought forward by the Pinzons themselves testified that, though none of the sailors could see the light when Colon hailed them on this memorable night, they had heard him call out and ask them the question; and this to us is conclusive that he did see whether they did or not. To argue the contrary is to endow him with the gift of prophecy.

As to what the light was, we believe it to have been what Colon himself supposed, and that it was on what we call Watting's Island, passed by the squadron as they sped onward to San Salvador. Since, however, like Homer's birthplace, there are no less than seven claimants for the honor of being the Guanahani of the discovery, and each is supported with spirit by an equally competent authority, we shall do no more than record our individual opinion.

All these cavillings and disputations are matters of no import in comparison with the gigantic exploit that was now accomplished. To defend the fame of the great-hearted sailor who was watching anxiously for the light of day would be to prove the undisputed. The whole dictionary cannot be framed into chapter or book which shall state more truthfully the title of his claim to immortality than the rude and well-worn couplet still borne proudly by his remote descendants, —

"On Castile and on Leon
A new world bestowed Colon."

Little did he himself think that night of the ten thousand maravedies or the pretensions of any one to have influenced his actions, we may well believe. If he dwelt at all upon the benefits which he should derive from his present discovery, it is more reasonable to suppose that his one idea was that that patch of sand and broken water had made him Grandee of Spain and Admiral of Castile.[1]

[1] For a discussion of the justice of Columbus's claim to be the first to see land, see Note I in the Appendix. The identity of Guanahani with the modern San Salvador, or Cat Island, is, we believe, established by the facts recorded in Note J.

XI.

UNDER THE BANNER OF THE GREEN CROSS.

THE morning light of Friday, the 12th of October, in the year of Grace one thousand four hundred and ninety-two, disclosed to the eager eyes of Colon and his companions a sight which made more than one of them believe they had reached the borders of the earthly Paradise of Holy Writ. Before them stretched the low but not monotonous coast of what was clearly an island surrounded by a sea of brightest emerald, whose long and regular lines of surf crashed down with sullen roar upon sloping beaches of snow-white sand, throwing high in air great jets of dazzling foam. Beyond the sands a low growth of underbrush led up to the dense tangle of trees and vines which covered the land as far as the eye could see, broken here and there by a clearing, which from the ships seemed carpeted with velvet turf. The level rays of the eastern sun were reflected from the glittering surfaces of a million polished leaves or lost in the cool recesses of the shady woods. Along the outskirts of the forest or rising above its undulating line of swelling tree-tops, the feathery plumes of countless graceful palms were tossing restlessly in the cool sea-breeze. The fresh air of those morning hours was clear as crystal; and each object on shore stood out sharp and distinct, as if in miniature. About the ships delicate flying-fish skimmed lightly from wave to wave, and the tiny barks of purple nautili balanced slowly past; while in the clear depths of the sea beneath them their crews caught glimpses of rainbow-colored fishes and beds of many-hued ocean plants. To the jaded sight of the rugged sailors, wearied with the dense blue gleaming of the thousand leagues of tropical seas over which they had come and the turquoise sky at which they had gazed so steadily, all this varied light and motion spoke of rest and keen enjoyment. To their commander it spoke of destiny fulfilled and duty yet to do.

Colon was no longer a Genoese adventurer in the service of Spain, with the temporary office of Captain-general of a Spanish fleet; he was their Catholic Majesties' High Admiral of the Western Seas and Viceroy and Governor of all the continents and islands which might lie therein, — so at least read the royal commission lying there within the strong-box in his cabin, and Colon was a man tenacious of his rights. No more modest mortal ever drew the breath of life; but he had devoted his manhood to this work, it had been successful, and he rightly judged that he was entitled to the very last honor and advantage which had been promised him for his reward. Had he failed, would he have been spared the very last word of derision and contempt?

He gave orders now that all should make ready for the solemn ceremony of taking possession of the new-found territory for the Spanish Crown, and himself put on a gorgeous uniform of scarlet velvet and silk becoming his new rank. Accompanied by the royal officers, — Rodrigo Sanchez, Rodrigo Escovedo, Pedro Gutierrez, and Diego de Arana, — with his pilots and other principal mariners, Colon entered the large boat of the flagship, and was rowed toward a point on shore where an inlet allowed an easy passage through the surf. Behind him followed the boats from the "Pinta" and "Niña," with Martin Alonzo and Vicente Yañez in their respective crafts, surrounded by their pilots and chief sailors, all in holiday attire. Standing in the stern of his own barge, Colon himself carried the royal standard of Castile; while his two lieutenants each bore the ensign of the expedition, — a white banner embroidered with a large green cross,[1] having the initials of the sovereigns at either extremity of the arms, with a royal crown above each letter. As the keel of his boat grated on the white coral sand of the beach, Colon leaped ashore, and throwing himself upon his knees, kissed the ground, and gave thanks to Almighty God for the measureless blessing that had been vouchsafed him. Quickly following their leader's example, his escort landed and knelt in prayer before they grouped themselves around him. Drawing his sword from its sheath and unfurling the flag he bore, he called upon his lieutenants, the royal officers, and all others present to bear witness that he took possession of that land and of all other continents and islands thereto adjacent for the Crowns of Castile and Aragon in the name of the Holy Trinity. Taking up a handful of earth and breaking a branch off a shrub near by, he declared that the land and all it held were now part of the dominions of their Catholic Majesties, christening it San Salvador, after Our Saviour, under whose especial protection he had placed his ships in setting sail from Palos. Having thus complied with the political requirements of his discovery, he reverently bared his head, and offered up in Latin this short prayer : —

"O Eternal and Omnipotent God, by Thy sacred word didst Thou create earth and sky and sea. May Thy name be blessed and glorified and Thy Majesty be praised that at the hands of Thy humble servant it has been permitted that Thy Holy Name should be known and preached throughout this other part of the world."

Then handing to Rodrigo Escovedo, as notary of the fleet, their Majesties' commission, Colon stood proudly leaning on the royal standard while that document was read. After setting forth the many titles and dignities of the Spanish

---

[1] It is worth noting, as probably more than a coincidence, that the green cross was a chosen emblem of the Holy Office of the Inquisition, and as such was a notable feature in all *autos da fé*. Its use by Columbus would seem to be connected with his favorite idea that his enterprise was in the nature of a crusade against Heathendom.

sovereigns, which formed the preface of all official acts, the notary continued : —

"Inasmuch as you, Cristoval Colon, are setting out by Our command, with certain of Our ships and people, to discover and acquire divers islands and mainlands in the Ocean Sea, and We hope that by the help of God some of the said islands and mainlands shall by your efforts and diligence be discovered and won; and, since you put yourself into this peril upon Our service, it is just that you should be for it rewarded, and We accordingly desire to honor and distinguish you for such service; it is Our grace and will that you, the said Cristoval Colon, as soon as you shall have discovered the said islands and mainlands in the Ocean Sea, or any one of them, shall be Our Admiral and Viceroy and Governor in them; and that you shall always thereafter call and entitle yourself Don Cristoval Colon, and that your sons and successors in the said office and rank shall call themselves Don, and Admiral, and Viceroy and Governor of the same."

Rodrigo Sanchez then went on to read the privileges and duties attached to the high position thus created, and the formal notices to all authorities and dignitaries throughout the Spanish dominions that they should recognize and respect Colon in his new capacity. He continued : —

"And We also command all captains, masters, mates, officers, seamen, and seafaring men in general, Our subjects and people, who now are, or who ever shall be, and each and every one of them, that whenever the said islands and mainlands shall have been discovered and won by you in the Ocean Sea, and you, or whoever you appoint, shall have taken the oath and performed the ceremonies appointed for such cases, they shall receive and obey you for all your lifetime, and after you your sons and successors from successor to successor for ever and ever, as Our Admiral of the Ocean Sea[1] and Viceroy and Governor in the said islands and mainlands which you shall discover and acquire."

Then followed the penalties incurred by whomever should fail to observe the respect and authority to which the new grandee was entitled.

[1] We have taken the title of our narrative from this official designation of Columbus's rank. The "Ocean Sea" was the term given to the Atlantic, as distinguished from the Mediterranean Sea.

"Given in Our city of Granada, on the 30th day of the month of April in the year of the Birth of Our Saviour Jesus Christ one thousand four hundred and ninety-two," concluded the notary.

"I, the King!" he added, bowing his head at the mighty names; "I, the Queen!"

Many a man of those who now stood listening to the proclamation of their Majesties' Viceroy had been in the crowded congregation which had filled St. George's Church only a few months before, in that little seaport town away on the other side of the world, when another notary had read certain other royal decrees commanding his hearers to join the unknown stranger who stood in their midst, and sail under his leadership on what they had all believed was a mad and desperate undertaking. Those decrees, like this one they were hearing, were dated on the 30th of April, and like this one were written in the newly conquered capital of the Moors; but in the circumstances of their publication there was a difference as wide as the ocean which rolled between Palos and the sea-girt island where now they stood. The reckless adventurer of April was the Viceroy of the Indies to-day; the tall, blue-eyed foreign sailor, with his odd Italian accent, at whom they had laughed in the Andalusian town, and sworn at in the forecastle of the "Santa Maria," held now their lives in his hand and represented the sovereigns of Spain! Even the roughest sailor present, as he stood in the shade of those strange trees and looked past that stately form in scarlet across the beach to the distant horizon beyond the idle ships, must have felt the contrast, and wished himself anywhere else than so near this unexpected Admiral.

At the conclusion of the notary's reading Colon took before him the oath of allegiance to the Crown on his accession to these dignities, and then his own officers and those of the sovereigns swore in turn to obey him as their monarchs' lieutenant. As for the lesser fry, they acted no doubt according to their natures; some humbly begging his pardon for past offences, and others holding aloof and taking their chances of the Admiral's humor. But Colon, the formalities concluded, turned his attention to another class of spectators who had been silent and awestruck witnesses of these portentous ceremonies.

Even from aboard the squadron, as soon as the sun had risen, it had been evident that the new land was inhabited; for human forms were seen emerging from the edge of the forest and, after gazing at the ships, running back to its friendly shelter. At such a distance from shore it was impossible to distinguish what manner of people the natives were; and when the boats landed they found no sign of human life beyond a few footprints in the sand. As the rite of taking possession of the territory and the reading of the royal proclamation proceeded, however, the Spaniards observed a number of natives watching them closely from behind the trees and bushes. Seeing that they carried no weapons of any kind, the Admiral (as we must now call him in obedience to the royal mandate) ordered his men to pay no heed to them, but allow them to approach as nearly as they wished. Little by little the natives drew closer to the marvellous beings who had so suddenly visited their shores, lost in amazement at the brilliant colors of their brave apparel, the fluttering glory of their silken flags, and the blinding splendor of their burnished armor. Noticing that the islanders wore no clothing and judging them thereby to be savages, the Admiral held out some of the trinkets and baubles of which he had brought a quantity, taught by his African experience of the value of such trifles among uncivilized races. After a while a few of the bolder spirits came forward and took up the gifts which had been left for them on the ground. Seeing no harm happen to their companions, the others gradually advanced, so that the Spaniards were soon surrounded by a curious and astonished throng. Satisfied of their peaceable disposition, the Admiral now led the way into the woods in search of the town or settlement from which he supposed the islanders had come. Some of his party accompanied him, while others remained behind to rear on the beach the wooden cross which at this and every subsequent landing-place the Spaniards raised with superstitious piety. The Admiral gave the strictest orders against the slightest sign of violence or offence being shown by his people to the natives, and even prohibited them from accepting the little tributes which the savages timidly proffered to the strangers in the apparent belief that they were divine beings. Happily his wise policy was respected, and the rude mariners and men-at-arms were bewildered at finding themselves the objects of humble adoration while they raised the emblem of their own faith.

The Admiral and his escort wandered on, as deeply lost in admiration at what they saw as were the savages who followed them at the appearance of their miraculous visitors. The trees were strange in foliage, flower, fruit, and bark. Between the joints made by bough and trunk sprang great bunches of gorgeously colored blossoms or hung huge sprays of waving green. Trees as tall as the oaks of Spain were covered to the tips of their farthest branches with masses of delicate bloom; while from the very bark of others tiny pink and scarlet blossoms grew like thorns on the bushes at home. At every footstep they crushed down some grass or weed or fern unlike any they had ever seen before. Overhead the tree-tops met in a sun-proof roof, each bound to its neighbor by an endless rope of festooned vines. Now and again a stray sunbeam lighted up the green and red of some brightly plumaged bird as it started at the tread of the new-comers, and in the cool gray shade of the darkest corners flashed the painted wings of gaudy butterflies. Odd insects scuttled out of the way as the Spaniards pursued their path; and more than one hardy seaman crossed himself in mortal terror at the sight of some hideous reptile which he thought must have come from the nether gulfs. It was a land of marvel and enchantment to even the more intelligent of the party, and those of lesser knowledge were ready to see in every novelty the impress of a magic hand.

The Admiral tried to gather, by the use of signs, from the natives who accompanied him some knowledge of a neighboring city, or their ruler's Court; but little progress could be made in such a language. After he had explored the vicinity of the landing-place without discovering any habitations, he turned his steps again toward the boats, not caring to venture unprepared too far into a country offering such admirable opportunities for fatal ambuscades. Making some additional presents to the savages and trying to convince them by signs of his benevolent intentions, he gave the order to row along shore, and the boats coasted for some distance before putting back to the vessels in the offing. What happened later in the afternoon, and what were his impressions regarding the day's experiences in so strange a world, we can best gather from the entry made in his journal before the eventful twenty-four hours had reached their close. The Admiral wrote that evening: —

"I have given to some of these people brightly colored caps and necklaces of glass beads to wear, so that they shall have the greater friendship towards us; for I know that it will be easier to influence them and convert them to our Holy Faith by gentle means rather than by force. Other trifles of little value, too, I gave them, and they became so much attached to us that it was a marvel. After we had left the shore they swam out to the boats where we were, and brought us parrots and balls of cotton thread and javelins, with many other things, which they exchanged with us for what we had, such as beads and hawk-bells. Indeed, they would take anything we offered and give whatever they possessed in return with the greatest readiness. But it seems to me that they are a people very poor in everything. They wear no more clothes than on the day they were born, and all those I saw were young men not more than thirty years old. They are well proportioned, with very handsome figures and good faces. Their hair is as coarse as that in a horse's tail, and is worn short. They wear it down over their eyebrows, except a few long locks which hang behind and are never cut. Some of them were painted black, while others are of the same color as the Canary Islanders, neither black nor white. Others again paint themselves all white, others all red, others still of any color they can find. Some paint only their faces, others the whole body; some around the eyes only, and others their noses alone. They carry no weapons, and know nothing about them; for I showed them a sword and they took hold of it by the edge and cut themselves, not knowing what it was. They have no iron at all; their javelins are merely long sticks without any head; some with a fish's tooth at the end and others with something else. They are all, in general, of a good height, easy in their actions and well made. They have the forehead and the head very wide, more so than any nation I have ever seen, and the eyes very beautiful and not small. I noticed several who had the scars of wounds on their bodies, and asked them by signs what they were; and they showed me how people came there from the other islands which are near, and tried to capture them, and they defended themselves. And I believed when I heard it, and still think, that those people come here from the mainland and try to take them captive. They would make good laborers and seem to have a good disposition, because I observe that they quickly repeat whatever is said to them; and I think they could easily be made good Christians, for they do not seem to have any religion. If it pleases God, I shall take with me from here when I leave half-a-dozen of them for your Majesties, in order that they may learn to speak our language. Not a single animal did I see of any kind on this island except parrots."

Such is Columbus's own record of the first day he passed in the New World, as he wrote it in the diary he kept for the perusal of Ferdinand and Isabella.

The next morning at daybreak the beach was thronged with the copper-colored natives, all staring at the ships and making frantic gestures for the strangers to come on shore. The Admiral, however, decided that he would not land at all this day, but remain on board and get things in readiness for beginning the work of systematic exploration of the new country. He was sure that he had not yet reached Japan, — or Cipango, as he called it, — nor the territory of the Great Khan, and assumed that San Salvador was only one of the lesser islands in the Asiatic seas, since the inhabitants showed no sign of the wealth and power which Marco Polo had ascribed to the people of those more important countries. He proposed, therefore, to examine the island, and then sail away in search of the great heathen kingdoms to which he was accredited as ambassador, and which he was now satisfied lay close at hand. As soon as the islanders saw that the Spaniards did not leave their ships, they determined to go out to the fleet themselves, and accordingly went for their canoes.

as the distance was too great to swim. The Admiral wrote that evening in his journal : —

"They came out to the ships in a kind of small craft like a ship's long-boat, made out of the trunk of a single tree and all of one piece, wonderfully fashioned after the manner of these people. They are so large that some of them held forty or forty-five men; while others were smaller, and some only contained a single man. They row with a flat board like a baker's shovel, and move with extraordinary swiftness. If one of them is upset in the surf, all on board set themselves to swimming, turning the boat right side up and bailing her out with the gourds they carry with them. They brought out to us balls of cotton yarn, and parrots, and javelins, and other trifles of no value which it would take too long to write out, and they would trade all they had for whatever we chose to give them. For my part, I was watching them narrowly, trying to find out whether they had any gold, and I noticed that some of them wore small pieces of it fastened in holes bored through their noses. From their signs I understood that by going to the south or by sailing to the southern end of the island, I should find a king who had large vases made of it and a very great deal. I tried to get them to show me the way, but afterwards discovered that they did not know how to go there. So I have decided to wait until to-morrow afternoon and then set sail toward the southwest; for according to the signs many of them made to me, they meant to say that there was land to the south and to the southwest and to the northwest. It seems, also, that the people living in the northwest come often to fight with the people of this island, and then go towards the southwest in search of gold and precious stones.

"This island of San Salvador is a large one and perfectly level, and is full of very green trees and many springs. It has no mountain at all on it, and in its centre is a wide lake which it is a delight to look upon. The natives are exceedingly peaceable, and are so anxious to have something belonging to us that when they have nothing to give in exchange they are afraid we will not give them anything, and so they pick up whatever they can lay their hands on and plunge overboard to swim to their canoes. But when they have anything they will give it all for whatever we offer them; even taking pieces of broken crockery and fragments of glassware in payment. I have seen them give sixteen balls of cotton yarn for three Portuguese farthings, which only amount to a Spanish blanca, and some of the cotton balls weighed more than twenty-five pounds apiece. I put a stop to this traffic, though, and would not let my men take any more from them; but gave orders that if there was much cotton it should all be gathered together and bought for the Crown. It grows wild in this island; but for want of time I have not been able to learn all about it that I should wish. I am sure that the gold which they wear in their noses is found here too; but in order to lose no more time, I intend to leave here at once and see if I cannot find the island of Cipango.

"Now that night is coming on, all the natives have gone on shore in their boats."

It is interesting to learn from these notes which the great discoverer wrote at the close of the day's labor and excitement, how intimately the two great motives which actuated him were associated in his mind. On the very first day he remarks that the natives are so friendly and simple-minded that he believes they can easily be converted to Christianity; and on the next we find him scanning closely the same people as they come on board his ship to see if he cannot discover some token of gold or gems. To bring the heathen of Asia to a knowledge of the True Faith (under the dominion of the Spanish sovereigns) and to gather together the wealth of the Indies for the conquest of the Holy Sepulchre, — these were the objects ever before the sanguine mind of Columbus to his dying day. In this first flush of enthusiastic anticipations he scarcely heeded the products of the earth which the simple islanders offered as their choicest gifts, and to his careless eye the parcels of "dried leaves" which they repeatedly pressed upon the Spaniards were nothing but "trifles of no value." Yet in after times the tobacco of the West Indies brought a far greater revenue to Spain and her colonies than would the mines of Golconda itself had they fallen to her lot. The gifts the gods provide are not always those we have in view.

Confident that San Salvador was not in itself important enough to waste much time over, at least at the beginning of his discoveries, he was impatient to go on to China and Japan, the Cathay and Cipango which he was so firmly persuaded lay within those seas. When the natives pointed to the southwest and northwest, he fancied they were indicating the whereabouts of the kingdoms he was seeking, and instantly determined to hasten thither. But whoever has tried to carry on a conversation with savages by means of signs, will have learned what very doubtful guides they are ; and in the Admiral's case his wishes proved ill interpreters. The islanders could not possibly have any idea of what was passing in his mind, nor he any better knowledge of what they meant when they pointed in this direction and in that ; led away by his eager expectations, he supposed that both he and they were thinking of the same great realms, and so unhesitatingly prepared to follow the lead they all unconsciously had given him.

XII.

AMONG THE ISLES OF IND.

BEFORE leaving San Salvador, — or Guanahaní, as he learned that the natives called it, — the Admiral determined to make a reconnoissance along the coast, to discover if possible the town where the islanders lived, and make acquaintance with their chief or ruler. As soon as it was light enough on the following morning, the 15th of October, he accordingly ordered out his own barge, and the boats of the two caravels, and proceeded along the northern extremity of the island in order to reach the side which was unseen from the ships. As the Spaniards rowed on, following the beach, the savages ran out from the woods and called to them with gestures as if inviting them to land. The Admiral writes: —

"Some of them offered us water and others food; while others still, when they perceived we did not intend to go on shore, threw themselves into the sea and swam out to us. We thought they asked us whether we came from heaven, and one old man came into my barge and in a loud voice cried out to the men and women ashore: 'Come and see the people who have come down from heaven! Bring them something to eat and drink!'

"A great many now appeared, both men and women, each carrying something and giving thanks to God by prostrating themselves on the ground and raising their hands toward the skies. Afterwards they shouted to us that we should go on shore; but I was afraid to land on account of a great reef of rocks which encircles the island, the entrance through which is very narrow, although there is room enough inside for all the ships in Christendom. To be sure, there are certain shoals inside the reef; but the sea is as quiet as a pond. It was in order to examine all this that I set out this morning, so that I might give an account of it to your Highnesses, and also to find a good site for a fort if any should be required. I came upon a piece of ground on which were six cabins, which is almost an island, but not quite. This could be turned completely into an island in two days; but I do not think it necessary, for these people are very ignorant of weapons, as your Majesties can see from the seven of them which I have caused to be seized, that I might carry them with me and teach them our language and then bring them back. Later on your Highnesses can either send out and remove all these natives to Castile, or hold them captive in the island itself, as may be best; for fifty Spaniards can keep the whole population in subjection and compel them to do whatever is wanted. Close to this little peninsula there are good springs and groves of trees more beautiful than any I have ever seen, and with their leaves as green as the woods of Spain in May and April. After examining that harbor I returned to the ships, and gave orders to make sail."

In taking with him these seven islanders to act as pilots and interpreters, it does not seem that the Admiral had to employ force. He speaks of them almost daily in his diary as serving him with willingness and interest, and it is likely the misguided captives esteemed it a high honor to be associated with such miraculous beings as their visitors. But in proposing to transport the whole population to Spain, or to establish a garrison in the island and make the inhabitants work for the benefit of the Crown, he was suggesting neither more nor less than the enslavement of a hospitable and confiding people. In the same paragraph in which he advances this cold-blooded proposal, the Admiral records that the tribe he would thus kidnap as slaves had thanked their gods for his arrival and offered him freely everything they owned! We must believe, nevertheless, that he was influenced by other than cruel or mercenary motives. His whole career proves him to have been a sincere friend and protector of the defenceless aborigines against the greed and arrogance of his rougher followers. Doubtless the explanation of this apparent contradiction lies in the fact that he believed that the surest way of turning them into Christians would be to place them under the tutelage of Spain, and in his opinion the certainty of their gaining heaven was cheaply bought if they only had to give in exchange the labor of their hands. The correctness of this system of ethics is not wholly evident in these latter days; but the Admiral's subsequent course is uniformly consistent with it. The Moors taken prisoners by the Spaniards were considered as slaves; the Portuguese brought back from every voyage to the Guinea coast large numbers of the African negroes; and in both these instances every effort was put forth to convert the captives to the Christian faith. To one brought up in such a school there was nothing unjust or unprincipled in the suggestion of the Admiral, and if in later years it was repudiated by Isabella and reprehended by Las Casas, he returned to Spain and re-embarked for the "Indies" without a word of censure being raised against his present view. Had he foreseen that within fifty years the entire population of the West Indies would disappear under the theory that they were the lawful prey of their Spanish discoverers, he would have been the first to throw about them the strong protection of the Crown.

No such anticipations disturbed the Admiral's mind that quiet Sunday afternoon as the fleet got under weigh and steered for another large island which was visible on the horizon to the west of San Salvador. Sitting in the shelter of his cabin, he wrote out his diary in the calm enjoyment of his novel surroundings. He continues: —

"So many islands are in sight, that I cannot make up my mind which to visit first. The natives I have brought with me explained by signs that there were so many and so very many that they could not be counted, and they called more than a hundred by name. I have therefore chosen the largest one, and decided to go to it; and this I am doing now. It is, perhaps, five leagues distant from San Salvador, and of the others some are nearer and some farther. They are all level, without any mountains, and are very fertile. They are likewise inhabited, and the people on them seem to make war upon their neighbors, although these I have with me are very simple-hearted and magnificent specimens of manhood."

The island for which the fleet was steering proved to be nearer twenty miles distant than fifteen; so, as they had a strong current setting against them, the Admiral gave orders to shorten sail and not attempt to make an anchorage that evening for fear of reefs and hidden rocks. It was quite noon on the following day when he finally reached the coast; and at first he determined to make no landing, as a still larger island was now visible, lying farther to the west; but he concluded that the additional distance was too great to be covered in the remainder of the day, and so came to anchor about sunset off the western point of the island he had reached. To this he gave the name of Santa Maria de la Concepcion, or to be more brief, Conception, in honor of that feast of the Virgin Mary.

The natives he had brought with him from San Salvador, — or his interpreters, as we may call them for convenience, — although as yet they did not know a word of Spanish, indicated to him by signs that there was plenty of gold in this island, and that the inhabitants wore heavy bracelets and anklets of the precious metal. At least, this is what the Admiral supposed they said. But when he went on shore the next morning at daylight, accompanied by all the boats of the squadron, he found the people to be in the same condition as those of San Salvador, without so much as clothing, much less golden rings upon their limbs. On seeing this he came to the conclusion that the interpreters had only told him such tales to get a chance of going on shore and running away. Nor is it at all improbable; for even a few days passed on board the small ship must have convinced the men of Guanahani that the freedom of their life in forest and canoe was preferable to this enforced contact with the Spanish "angels."

Poor as they were, the people of Conception gave the Spaniards everything that attracted their attention, and let them walk unmolested through their groves. Somewhat chagrined at finding no signs of the gold he had expected, the Admiral did not stay long on shore, but soon returned on board the flagship. When he reached her deck he observed that a large canoe had put out from the beach and was lying alongside the "Niña." The natives manning her had been on board that vessel inspecting the wonders of the white men and exchanging trifles with them, and now they were all taking their places in the canoe and making ready to start for land. Just as they were leaving the ship's side, one of the interpreters, who had been placed on board the "Niña," sprang from the ship into the canoe, and the savages dashed their paddles into the water in a mad spurt for the beach. One of the Spanish boats which was coming off to the ships tried to intercept the canoe; but it was a useless attempt, and by the time they had rowed back to shore the natives were safely hidden in the forest. "They ran like scared chickens," the Admiral writes; for he had mounted to the "castle" in the stern of his ship to watch the outcome of the chase. The Spaniards returned to the squadron towing the big canoe with them; but their commander was not wholly pleased with their proceeding. It was of the first importance, in his judgment, not to frighten or disgust the natives in any way; and this escape of one of his interpreters and the patent failure of the captors to recover him, gave Colon no little anxiety for the moment. As he stood looking toward the land, reflecting on the incident, he noticed another canoe with a single paddler come out from a different quarter and head for the "Niña," which was anchored farthest inshore. This man had not seen the flight of his countrymen, and so came rapidly toward the caravel, holding up a ball of cotton yarn to be exchanged for whatever the strangers would give. The sailors made signs for him to come on board the vessel; but this he would not do, although he came close to her side. Seeing this, the Admiral called out to the crew to jump overboard and seize the canoe-man and bring him with his craft aboard the flagship. This they did in a twinkling, enjoying the sport; and before the poor savage knew well what had happened, he found himself before the tall white "god." Making every effort to show his unwilling guest that he had nothing to fear, the Admiral placed on the savage's head a gaudy sailor's bonnet, and tied about his arms some strings of beads, while from his ears he hung a pair of tiny bells. Surprised and delighted with this bewildering generosity, the prisoner humbly offered to the celestial being before him the ball of cotton to which he had stubbornly clung the while; but this was declined, with many signs of gratitude by Colon. After showing him some of the marvels of the ship, the Admiral put him back into his canoe, still grasping the ball of cotton, and had his own men tow both it and the larger one back to the beach, where they left him with the two boats. As soon as the natives who were hiding among the trees saw the Spaniards returning to their ships, they flocked down on the sands and surrounded the lucky cotton-peddler with gestures of astonishment and admiration at the wonderful riches he now possessed. The latter gesticulated freely, pointing to the vessels and then to the trinkets on his person, and held up the ball of yarn in triumph, as much as to say that all that glory had cost him nothing.

"I sent this man back on shore and gave him these presents," the Admiral explains, "because I wanted the natives to think that we are good people, and that the other man (the interpreter) had only run away from us because he was our prisoner for having done some damage to us; and so they all might have a kindly opinion of us, and should not make trouble if your Highnesses should send anybody to this island again. After all, everything I gave him was not worth four maravedies." Plainly it was a good investment of five cents, for nothing that the fugitive interpreter could now say about the strangers would be believed by the people of Conception. Had not the white men sent back their boats unharmed, and loaded their fellow-countryman with magnificent presents, and all this without accepting payment? The poor San Salvadorian would find few to credit him when he tried to make his hearers believe that the Spaniards were only men like themselves.

As soon as his party returned from putting the savage ashore, the Admiral made sail for the larger island he had seen to the west. It was only ten o'clock in the morning, and he hoped to reach it early in the evening, as it did not appear to be more than thirty miles away; but light winds and adverse currents consumed the whole day, and the fleet did not approach its shores until after dark. Like the prudent sailor he was, the Admiral would not come too closely to an unknown coast in the night, so the squadron stood on and off alongshore until daylight.

They were about half-way between Conception and the new island, when they overtook a single savage in one of the small canoes, paddling quietly along over that wide stretch of open sea as though it were a landlocked lagoon, and evidently bound for the same shores as themselves. When the flagship came up, he made signs, asking to be taken up and carried with them; so the Admiral ordered both him and his canoe to be taken in. In the latter the sailors found a piece of mandioca bread, the size of a fist; a gourd of fresh water; a bunch of the precious dried leaves, of which the Spaniards had received so many at San Salvador;[1] and a lump of the red clay with which the savages painted themselves. The Admiral directed that these trifles should be left just as they were, and had the man brought into his cabin. He, nowise abashed, showed Colon a little basket in which were carefully preserved a string of beads and two *blancas*, or Spanish coins of copper; making signs that he had paddled from San Salvador to Conception, and was now bound for the island ahead, apparently carrying the news of the white men's arrival, and taking their presents to show what treasures they had brought. The Admiral gave orders that their passenger should be treated with the utmost kindness, and caused bread, honey, and wine to be served to him as an improve-

---

[1] This the first mention of tobacco occurs in the diary of Columbus under date of October 15; although, as appears from the allusion, his quick eye had discerned the value attached to the plant by the natives of Guanahani, on the very day of his landing. In recording the contents of the canoe referred to in the text above, Columbus writes: "and a few dry leaves, which must be something much prized by them [the natives]; *for they had already brought me some in San Salvador*, as a present."

ment upon mandioca and water. When the island was neared in the evening, he gave him fresh presents, and put him overboard in the canoe to paddle ashore at once. "And this I did," he writes after doing so, "so that he may give good reports of us, in order that when others come here for your Majesties, they shall be received with honor, and the natives shall freely give them whatever they possess, if it please God." Had the Spaniards and their imitators always acted with such prudence, the early history of America would have been less blood-stained than it so unhappily is.

In the present instance the wisdom of such a policy was immediately apparent. Shortly after the savage had reached land, several canoes put off to the vessels as they lay hove to near the shore, bringing with them water and such articles as they had to barter; and this they kept up all night long. The Admiral gave orders that all who came should be fed and presented with some trifle of beads or bells, in consequence of which the natives were hugely delighted. Early in the morning the ships came to anchor near a village on the beach, and a party of men were sent ashore to get a supply of water. On seeing them land, the inhabitants ran to meet them, and vied with one another in showing the strangers where the best springs were, and in carrying their water-casks down to the boats, — seeming proud when allowed to do anything for the visitors. When the boats returned to the ships, the Admiral hoisted sail and started to explore the coast. This island was so much larger than either San Salvador or Conception, that he thought it worthy to be named after the King of Spain, and so called it Fernandina.[1] The people were of the same race as those of the other islands; but they seemed more fearless and somewhat more advanced in their way of life, weaving their cotton into coarse cloth, and wearing aprons of this material about their waists. They were keener traders also; for the Admiral remarks that when they brought their trifles on board

[1] This island has been identified with the modern Exuma. Conception still retains the name given it by Columbus.

the ships "they knew how to bargain and dispute about the payments, which the others did not do." The interpreters had given him to understand that beyond this island was still another, with a great city called *Samoet*, where was great store of gold. Not only did the inhabitants wear it around their arms and ankles, but also in their noses and ears and about their necks. When he questioned the natives of Fernandina about this city, they made signs as if to confirm the story, and all on board the fleet were impatient to reach the scene of so great wealth. That this was a mistake of the Spaniards, the fruit of their absorbing desire to find the promised abundance of the coveted gold, it is scarcely necessary to say; for Samoet was later found to be only the native name for Fernandina. At present the Admiral knew nothing of this. "These islands are very green and fertile, and blessed with a delightful climate," he entered this day in his diary; "but I do not wish to delay in my search for as many islands as possible, and examining them to find gold. Since these natives make such signs that it is worn by the people of the other islands on their legs and arms,— and I am sure it is gold they speak of, for I have shown them some of it which I have, — I cannot fail, with the help of Our Lord, to find the place where it grows." With this object in view he determined to coast along Fernandina for a while, and then steer for the famous isle of Samoet. It was his intention to sail around the southern end of the former island; but Martin Alonzo came alongside, as the ships were getting under weigh, and told him that one of the interpreters who had been assigned to the "Pinta," insisted by his signs that the quickest way to reach the land of gold was by the northern end of Fernandina; so the fleet sailed in that direction.

Coasting leisurely along, they came to a sheltered harbor, which so attracted the Admiral's sailor-eye that he decided to explore and sound it. Taking all the small boats of the fleet, he examined it carefully, and then went on shore, fascinated by the beauty of the situation. A group of natives had gathered to see the Spaniards land; and when the sailors indicated that they wished to fill their water-casks, offered to show them the way to the springs. The Admiral and his party remained behind to admire the astonishing richness and variety of the strange vegetation which surrounded them, finding at every step some new occasion for delight and admiration. On returning to the flagship, the Admiral wrote : —

"While the men were away getting the water, I wandered among the trees, which were the most beautiful things to look at that I ever saw. They are very different from those we are accustomed to, and many of them have several kinds of branches springing from a single trunk, — one branch of one sort and another of another, so that it is the greatest marvel in the world to see them. One branch will have leaves like a cane-stalk, and another like a gum-tree and so on, half a dozen kinds on one trunk. These are not grafted, for one can tell when a graft is made; but they grow wild in this manner. and the people pay no attention to them. The fishes also are entirely different from ours; some are like cocks, of the most beautiful colors imaginable, — blue, red, yellow. and every other color; and some painted in a thousand fashions. The colors are so perfect that there is not a man among us who is not astonished at them, and does not delight in seeing them. Off the islands there are also whales; but on land I saw no animals of any kind except lizards and parrots, although one of the sailors told me he had seen a large snake."

What the Admiral took for different kinds of branches and leaves growing on the same tree were clearly the orchids, vines, and countless parasites which cover the trees of a tropical forest wherever a bough or a knot or any roughness of the bark offers them lodging-place. Where the situation was favorable we have counted a hundred and fifty of these intruders on a single very large trunk; to all appearance part and parcel of the parent stem, and yet each differing entirely from the others in leaf and flower. To one who had never heard of anything of the kind before, it is not singular that the trees seemed to be the work of miracle.

The seamen, on returning from the springs, told the Admiral that the natives had led them inland to a village and filled their casks. The houses were well made, in the shape of a tent, with openings in the roof for ventilation, and were kept very clean and neat inside; having suspended from their walls a kind of net which the people used in place of beds.[1] They also reported that they had seen dogs in the village which did not bark; and these, as the Admiral notes, were the first animals thus far encountered.

One of the seamen said that they had met a savage who had a flat piece of gold, like the half of a Spanish doubloon, hanging from his nose, on which were stamped some letters which he could not distinguish. In an instant the Admiral was aroused; that piece of gold with the mysterious letters might furnish him with a clew to where they were, and be the means of their finding their way to the cities of the Grand Khan.

"How is it," he asked sharply of the men, "that you failed to bring me that golden coin? Know you not that I would give all the savages might ask to have those letters in my hand and learn whence they had come?"

"If it please your Nobility," the man replied respectfully, "we offered all we had to get it for your Worship; but the savage refused to part with it for all we had to offer, and made signs that he dared not let us have it. Your Worship has forbidden us to take aught by violence, or easily might we have obtained the piece, for we were armed and they were naked."

"In that you acted rightly," the Admiral answered, anxious to maintain the spirit of discipline; "yet gladly would I have paid dear for the trinket. Another time bring such a man to me or to the other captains, and let us see if we cannot deal with him."

Colon was greatly annoyed at losing this bit of gold, and shows as much in his diary; but it is very doubtful if it would have been of any service to him. What the sailors thought were letters was probably nothing more than the rude ornamental lines which some of the tribes on the mainland cut

---

[1] These were called *hamacs* by the natives; whence our term for them. In Brazil they still go by the name of *redes*, or nets.

on their golden ornaments, as well as on their pottery and other handiwork. We have seen that they travelled from one island to another, and this nose-jewel may have come from a quarter where the people were more skilled in the arts than on the lesser islands; so the matter was not so important, in all likelihood, as the Admiral esteemed it. His attention, however, was fixed on this one metal for the present, and he passes by with a bare mention the abundance of a grain which apparently was sowed and gathered throughout the year. Cotton, tobacco, and corn — the three products which have contributed most to establish the gigantic commerce of the continent he discovered — were classed by the great navigator as trifles of no especial value.

Taking their course again along the coast, the fleet sailed on until a thick haze with heavy showers of rain obliged them to put off to a safer distance from land, and thus they kept on all that afternoon and night. The next morning they stood in again near shore, and coasted on around the island. They made no landing that day; but when evening drew on came to anchor as a measure of precaution. On the following day, the 19th of October, the fleet left the island of Fernandina and put out to sea, heading eastward in search of that famous Samoet of which such alluring tales were told. A few hours after sailing they came in sight of another large island, and by noon had reached its coast. This, the interpreters explained to the Admiral, was Samoet itself, and he named it Isabella[1] in honor of his royal patroness. Following along its shores, he reached toward evening a noble harbor surrounded by wide beaches of sand, and here he anchored for the night. There were no indications of a town visible, much less of so great a city as he was looking for; but the interpreters insisted by their gestures that not far off was a great city where dwelt the king who had such stores of gold. The Admiral was beginning to grow somewhat suspicious of these repeated tales of kings and treasures, although his anxiety to find them would

[1] The island now known as Isla Larga.

not permit him to disbelieve wholly the stories of his interpreters. He wrote on the afternoon of his arrival: —

"In the morning I am going alongshore until I can see and talk with this king, who, according to what they tell me with their signs, is lord over all these islands hereabouts, and is properly clothed, and wears much gold about his person. Nevertheless I do not put entire faith in what they tell me, not only because I cannot understand well what they say, but because I see that they themselves are so poor in gold that however little this king might have it would seem to them like a great deal.

"This cape, which I call Beautiful, I take to be an island apart from Saomet, and conceive that there are others yet between; but I do not attempt to examine everything in detail, for I could not hope to do it in fifty years, and I wish to see and discover the most that is possible, so as to return to your Highnesses in April, God willing. It is true, however, that if I find any place where there are gold and spices in plenty I shall remain until I have collected all I can; and thus it is that I do not do otherwise than sail on until I come to such a place."

No doubt crossed the Admiral's mind that he was cruising among the islands of the Eastern Indies off the Asiatic coast; and from the time he discovered Fernandina we find him constantly calling the natives "Indians,"[1] as day by day he enters in his journal the incidents of his explorations.

[1] Columbus first uses the term on the 17th of October, — "All these Indians I am taking with me."

XIII.

IN SEARCH OF FAR CATHAY.

"THIS cape where I have come to anchor I have called Cape Beautiful," the Admiral wrote that night, "for so it is; and I did not anchor before, as I saw it from a great distance so green and lovely that I came hither. But such are all the other lands on these islands, and everything about them; so that I do not know in which direction to steer first, for my eyes never weary of seeing these beautiful forests which differ so greatly from our own." The next morning, as soon as the sun was up, the fleet weighed anchor and stood along the coast in search of the city of the king. Point after point was passed, and beach after beach, but no vestiges of town or capital appeared. At night the two smaller vessels anchored, being able to run in close to shore by reason of their lighter draught; but the flagship was hove to at a safer distance from land, as running a greater risk from rocks and shoals. The next day, Sunday the 21st, they all made sail together and coasted along until they reached a favorable harbor, where they came to anchor again. After breakfast the Admiral and his lieutenants went ashore and visited a village which was near at hand. The savages fled at the approach of the Spaniards, and the latter examined the houses at their leisure. Their commander repeated his stringent orders that nothing should be disturbed. "I would not let them take so much as the value of a pin," he writes. In his eyes this island was yet more beautiful than any they had seen; and he refers again and again to the immense size of the trees, and the fact that everything was fresh and green, with the flowers all in bloom, although at this season winter was setting in in Europe. Some of the birds sang so enchantingly that no one wanted to return to the boats; while the parrots and others of gay plumage seemed countless in number and variety. In the midst of the forests several charming lakes were discovered, their placid surfaces framed in circles of densest green. As they strolled along the banks, the men started up a wonderful reptile, like the basilisk of fable, which took to the water, where it was followed and speared to death. So extraordinary a beast was this that the Admiral directed that the hide should be kept to be taken to the Spanish sovereigns as a curiosity. From his description their quarry seems to have been a large iguana, — truly a startling apparition when seen for the first time. Some of the men found also the aloes plant, which they told Colon was of much value in Spain for medicinal purposes; so he directed them to gather a large quantity and take it on board the ships. Certain of the trees, as well, he thought looked like spice-trees, but he did not venture to gather their fruits, as he knew little of such matters. As the party continued on their way, the natives — or the Indians, as we may call them on the Admiral's authority — appeared in groups, watching distrustfully the progress of these miraculous white beings. To one who came up boldly to the Spaniards a present of beads and other trinkets was given, and at his demonstrations of delight the others drew near with confidence. The better to establish amity, Colon gave them each some gift, making signs that his men wished water for drinking; so they quickly provided themselves with gourds, and showed themselves anxious to gratify their visitors.

As yet there was no sign of gold or king, and the Admiral decided to sail around this island, as he had done at Fernandina, in search of the city where both were to be found. His interpreters now made him understand that to the south of Isabella was another and very much larger country which they called *Cuba*, which contained ten great rivers and was so extensive "that they could not paddle around it in twenty days;" and he decided to make sail in that direction as soon as he had finished his exploration of the present island. The Admiral writes: —

"Although my Indians call it Cuba, I believe, from the signs they make, that this must be Cipango. They say that in that place are to be found many ships and merchants, and very great, and near it is another large island, which they call *Bohio;* but this and the others which they say lie between here and Cuba I can visit as I sail thither. According to whether I find plenty of gold and spices, I shall then determine what to do. But at all events I am decided to go to the mainland and visit the city of Quimsay, and deliver the letters of your Majesties to the Grand Khan and ask him for a reply, and return to Spain."

Well might his friend and historian, Las Casas, note on the margin of the Admiral's diary, "All this is gibberish to me!" So fixed in Colon's mind was this one prevailing idea of his being near the continent of Asia, that not even the new disappointment he had just suffered, in finding the people of Saomet naked and treasureless like all whom he had met, could shake his conviction that the great island he had heard of called Cuba was Japan itself, and that China and India — the kingdoms of the Khan — must lie not far away. Whatever we may think of his geography, we cannot but envy his faith and perseverance.

As for his interpreters, they were doubtless doing all in their power to gratify him. They saw the Spaniards evidently anxious to go from island to island, and so pointed out the direction of one after another without having any idea of what their masters really wanted. If a piece of gold was shown to them, they would nod their heads and point toward another island. When they had reached this, and the Spaniards had explored it and made new signs that they wanted "more," the Indians would nod their heads again and point somewhere else. Savages who were unable to count as high as ten could have no very definite conception of what constituted much or little; the gold was no great treasure to them, and when they had showed a few men wearing it in their ears or noses they felt that they had done all that was desired of them. What could these white people want with that yellow stuff, anyhow? It was soft and good for nothing, and no brighter than the polished armor and weapons of which the strangers had such a plenty; without taking into count their fabulous wealth of other still richer things, such as beads and bells and needles! And so, no doubt, these poor interpreters fancied they were doing admirably, and continued with their simple process of answering the questions they did not understand. Now that they were at Saomet they pointed southward and said, "Cuba;" and Colon, thinking it sounded like "Cipango," read ships and merchants and countless wealth in the signs they made. For all he knew, they might have been telling him how many canoes had taken part in the last foray executed by the natives of the great island against their neighbors.

"All last night and all to-day have I been waiting here at anchor," the Admiral wrote on the day following his arrival in Isabella, "to see whether this king or any of his people would bring me gold or anything else of value." But these islanders were like the others, naked and poor, painted in all the colors of the rainbow, and offering nothing more valuable for exchange than javelins and cotton. When the sailors would give them a bit of broken glass or a fragment of a cracked pot, the Indians would hand it from one to another as though it were some divine treasure. Now and again a savage appeared with a little scrap of beaten gold stuck through a hole in his nose or ear, and this he very willingly exchanged for a tiny bell or a few colored beads; "but it was at best so little that it was almost nothing," the admiral writes in some disgust. The winds were light and contrary, and the ships could not leave their present berth. The sailors went ashore again for water and to gather more aloes, and Martin Alonzo killed another iguana; but nothing occurred to be recorded. All day long, too, the rain poured down in torrents; and in the midst of their discomfort the sailors remarked that the air was warm even then, and were surprised that it did not grow chilly. On the morning following, finding that the wind died away and a dead calm set in, the Admiral abandoned his intention of sailing around Isabella, and decided to head direct for Cuba as soon as a breeze sprang up. He wrote: —

"I have made up my mind not to sail around this island as I had intended, in order to search for the city and have intercourse with this king or lord, since that would delay me a great deal and I perceive that there is no mine of gold in this country. Besides, to sail around these islands many kinds of wind are necessary, and the wind will not always blow the way men want Moreover, it is not worth while to remain here longer, as I am going to where there is commerce to be had on a large scale and to find a country which will be very profitable. For all that, I believe that this island might prove lucrative enough in spices; but I know nothing about these, for which I am more grieved than I can say."

Here we find the Admiral clearly in doubt as to which was the best course to pursue, with his own feeling plainly in favor of abandoning the lesser advantage for what he hoped should prove a greater. The winds decided the matter for him; for at midnight a fresh breeze was blowing, and, hoisting all sail, he stood away to the southwest in search of what he was satisfied must be Japan.

The wet season in those latitudes had by this time set in, and the rainstorms were frequent and violent, while the winds were uncertain and fitful. The Admiral persisted in his attempts to get from his interpreters some intelligent knowledge of the great island for which he was bound, and was more and more convinced that it was indeed Cipango. "I am sure," he writes, "from the signs made not only by my own Indians but by the people of all these other islands that this must be that Cipango of which such marvellous tales are told; and from the globes and maps of the world which I have seen in Europe I know that it must be somewhere in this neighborhood." His impatience to catch a sight of the famous country increased as the ships lay idly on the quiet waters of the Bahama Sea in the dead calms which now befell them; and whenever a favorable breeze sprang up he crowded on every inch of canvas that his sticks would hold, detailing in his journal with a true sailor's delight all the sails he spread upon masts and yards to give his vessel the greater speed. On the 25th of October he came upon a group of seven or eight little islands surrounded by such wide-stretching shoals that he called them the Isles of Sands,[1] and here he anchored overnight. His Indians now represented that from here to Cuba was only a voyage of a day and a half in their canoes, and he was correspondingly elated at the news. From their gestures he gathered that the country he was approaching was very extensive indeed, and rich in gold and pearls. Beyond all doubt, he repeats, this is Cipango. Setting sail on the morning of the 26th, the fleet kept on steadily all that day and night and the next day. Toward evening of the 27th they came in sight of land, which the interpreters said was the country they were seeking, and the Admiral steered direct for the coast. On the morning of the 28th they were off the mouth of a large river, and into it the vessels steered and came to anchor.

"So beautiful a country I have never seen," the Admiral writes; and in saying this he does no discredit to his experience, — for the western end of that noble island as viewed from the sea in the earlier hours of daylight is truly a vision of rarest loveliness. The keen eye of the great discoverer wandered past glittering beaches of whitest sand, over the undulating surface of luxuriant forests, to where broad slopes of brightest emerald led gently upward in ever-mounting terraces to the verdure-covered foothills and frowning precipices of the gloomy sierras farther inland. The light mists of morning which veiled the lower levels were slowly dissipated as the sun gained strength, and along the forbidding faces of the loftier ranges the rising vapors were blown in softly rolling clouds, save where here and there embosomed in some steep and sheltered valley, they hung smooth and motionless. The contrast between the brightness which flooded the sea and sand and sunlit woods

---

[1] Presumably the cays of the Great Bahama Bank.

and the shadows of the mighty rocks and deep gorges of the distant mountains grew quickly less as the morning advanced; but even the full glare of broad daylight could not wholly dispel the purple shades which lingered in the far recesses of the rugged interior. The scene recalled to Colon's mind the majestic beauty of the Sicilian coasts and the familiar grandeur of the noblest scenery in the sierras of Granada; although, he hastens to add, the landscape before his eyes was by far the fairest that mortal sight had ever rested upon. Anxious to know more of a land which offered such a vision of delight, he quickly embarked in his barge and went on shore. Close down to the river's edge came the dense forest of the tropics, — a riotous confusion of buttressed trunks and festooned vines, twisted roots and thorny undergrowth, of blossoming boughs and swaying orchids, — all mirrored in the polished surface of the stream below. The splashing of the sailors' oars alarmed a multitude of gayly painted birds which gleamed in the sunlight as they swept into the shelter of the woods, while from all quarters came the chatter and music of a thousand unseen others. The Admiral landed at the river's mouth, and took possession of the country with due formality, calling it Juana, after the young Prince Royal of Spain. A few canoes had put out from shore as the fleet came to anchor; but when they saw the boats manned and headed for the beach, the frightened natives paddled back and sought safety in their pathless forest. Near the landing-place the Spaniards found two huts, which from their contents must have belonged to fishermen, for they contained nets and lines made from the fibre of palm-trees, hooks of bone, rude harpoons, and other fishing-gear. The huts had one apartment only, but were of unusual size; and from the number of fires smouldering about the floor the Spaniards concluded that several families lived together under a single roof. The only living thing visible was a dumb dog of singular appearance, and the sailors would have carried it off except for the Admiral's orders that everything should be left untouched. Going back to the barge, he had his men row him for some distance up the river, scrutinizing closely all he saw, and enjoying with keen appreciation the prodigal beauty of his surroundings. "It was such a delight to behold all that freshness and those wonderful forests with their multitude of birds," he writes, "that I could with difficulty turn back to go on board the ships." He noted several plants and wild-flowers like those of Europe, and remarked that in several places, even along the seashore, the grass grew long and fresh close down to the water's edge; from which he concluded that no furious tempests could ever rage there, for otherwise the beaches would everywhere be swept bare of vegetation. The palms, too, he observed, were far more sightly than those of Southern Europe and the African coasts, as here their trunks were clean and straight, and not cumbered with the ugly growth of dead fibre which disfigured those of the older world. Fascinated with his morning's experience, he reluctantly gave orders to row back to the ships. He was fully persuaded that he had at length reached Cipango. In the bald and scarred faces of the remoter mountains he believed lay hidden mines of gold, and on the beach near the fishers' cabins he had seen large piles of mussel-shells. What could be clearer than that these were the source from which were drawn the famous pearls of the Orient? When he showed them to the Indians on the "Santa Maria" they made signs that people came from ten days' distance off to seek them. To the Admiral's eager mind this obviously meant that China was only that far away; the ships of the Great Khan, of course, came hither to get these pearls and other treasures, and took them back to the kingdom of Cathay. A rash conclusion to draw from a few empty shells and a range of distant mountains, you will say; but we must bear in mind the extraordinary coincidence that Colon had found this great island and its lesser neighbors very nearly where the charts showed him Japan should lie, and that the wonderful novelty of everything about him showed conclusively that he had reached a new and marvellous region. As he had no dream of any other land than Asia in this direction, it is not singular that he should have taken Cuba for the great Asiatic island, and looked confidently to find within a few days' sail the eastern continent itself. Firm in this belief, and impatient to reach the capital of the country and meet its king, he now weighed anchor and sailed westward along the coast. Just as he had named after Our Saviour the first land he touched at on this cruise, so now he called by the same all-powerful name the first landing he had made, as he supposed, on the wondrous shores of Cipango.

The next day, as the squadron sailed along the coast as near the land as it seemed prudent to go, they came upon another and larger river, which offered an ideal harbor. Coming to anchor within its mouth, the Admiral took his barge and rowed up it some distance before going on shore. Finding that the salt water entered it as far as he had gone, he called the stream the River of the Tides, and noted with pleasure its suitableness for a naval station. He had taken with him one of his interpreters, as a village was situated near the river's mouth, and he desired to hold communication with the inhabitants; but as the boat drew near the beach, the natives fled to the woods, and all efforts to find them were unavailing. The houses in this settlement were the largest and best built that the Spaniards had thus far seen; and this confirmed the Admiral's conviction that he was drawing steadily nearer to the great cities of the Indies which Marco Polo had described. They were carefully thatched with palm-leaves, clean and tidy within, and arranged with some approach to the regularity of streets. From their contents they too were occupied each by several families, and their residents were engaged in fishing. Besides the dumb dogs already seen, the sailors found many tame birds of odd appearance hopping about the dwellings. What surprised them most was a number of statuettes of women which they saw in the houses carved out of wood, and a quantity of grotesque masques sculptured from the same material. Whether these were meant as idols, or were used in the native sports, the Admiral could not decide; but he argued also, from the presence of these tokens of a higher grade of intelligence, that he was approaching the seat of government, or at least some city of importance. The large skulls of what appeared to be cattle hung on the walls of several of the cabins; and this he thought an additional indication of increasing civilization, for he had seen no signs of flocks and herds before. Cheered by these observations, he returned on board ship with high hopes of reaching the territories of the Khan erelong. In his diary that evening he dwelt on the beauty of all about him, — the profusion of brilliant flowers and gaudy birds, the sweet flavor of the fruits, the stately character of the forest-trees. Even at night, he adds, the delicious perfume from the woods and the ceaseless music of the crickets filled all on the squadron with delight. His crickets were doubtless for the most part katydids and frogs; but at a little distance away the nocturnal concert of those forests is grateful to more exacting ears than the Admiral's were at that period. The climate was all that could be wished, he says, — the days neither hot nor cold, but more temperate than those he had passed on the other islands; and this he ascribes to the vicinity of such lofty mountains. Altogether he was disposed to find something to praise and extol at every turn. Even the waters of the ocean near the mouths of the rivers he thought seemed to be fitted by nature for the growth of the rarest qualities of pearls!

The next day the fleet continued toward the west until they came in sight of a lofty headland which closed the view ahead. As they stood for this, the "Pinta" hailed the flagship, and Martin Alonzo came on board the latter. He was full of a grand discovery he had made regarding the land along which they were coasting. It was not the island of Cipango at all, but the veritable mainland of Asia, — the empire of the Khan.

"Always under your Excellency's wiser judgment, Señor Admiral," he said, feigning a submission he was far from feeling, "I take it to be a thing assured that this country is Asia itself, and not the island of Cipango. The Indian who sails with me as interpreter has made some progress with our tongue, and learned to understand me with much certainty. He makes me know that Cuba is not the name of an island, as your Worship has hitherto conceived, but that of a great city which lies four days' journey from the river which we shall find beyond the lofty cape for which we now are steering. This same heathen plainly says that the king of this country is constantly at war with the Great Khan, who would conquer the land and add it to his dominions. The Khan, my interpreter tells me, is here called *Cami*, which your Worship will see is but the same word altered to their manner of speech, and his capital is called by them *Fava*. Moreover he gave me many other names of towns and cities which I cannot bear in mind. But so great and joyful an intelligence I thought it right to bring without loss of time to your Excellency's knowledge."

This piece of news coincided so exactly with the Admiral's wishes that he was ready enough to accept it for gospel truth. To be sure, he had supposed that Cuba was an island, and that it was beyond a peradventure Cipango, for so his charts gave him cause to believe. But he might easily have misunderstood his Indians as to the first point; and the rough map he sailed by made no pretensions as to the exactness of its distances, so he might easily be nearer Asia than he fancied. Accordingly he adopted without hesitation the views of Martin Alonzo.

"I give you hearty thanks, brave captain," he replied, "for this your love and diligence. The news you bring is indeed of the most welcome. Let us press all sail, and hasten to double the headland, that we may the sooner reach this river of which your Indian tells, and open intercourse with the city of this king."

As the ships drew nearer to the cape, the Admiral reflected deeply over what his lieutenant had laid before him. The more he pondered, the more he was satisfied that he had mistaken the signs of his own interpreters, and that instead of Cuba being an island it was the continent itself. He recalled now that he was about in the latitude where Marco Polo had placed the kingdoms of the great Oriental prince, and judged that the cooler weather he had recently encountered was additional evidence of his nearness to Cathay. Since the king of this country was at war with the Great Khan, it was obvious that the territories of the latter, with all their wealth and treasures, could not be very remote. He therefore determined that as soon as he had passed the cape and anchored in the river beyond, he would send a party to seek the city of which the " Pinta's " Indian had told Martin Alonzo, and that by their hands he would send some of the presents and letters which the Spanish sovereigns had given him to deliver to the potentates of the eastern realms which both they and he supposed would be reached. In casting about for the person who should best fulfil this embassy, he thought of one of his men who had been sent on a somewhat similar mission some years before when on a voyage to the Guinea coast. This man, with some of his Indian interpreters, he therefore resolved to send; if they were successful in finding the king and establishing friendly relations with him, the Admiral would later on endeavor to open communication with the Great Khan himself.

Rejoiced with this solution of his perplexities, Colon watched the grand and beautiful outlines of the Cuban coast slip slowly past his ships, never doubting for a moment now that somewhere beyond the mountains of that wild interior lay the populous cities of the Chinese Kingdom and the fabled riches of Far Cathay. Such robust structures can the imagination rear on the corner-stone of fancy, that he and his lieutenant both had built up the whole continent of Asia, with all its teeming millions, on the airy gestures of a naked savage.

As though to warn them of their error, no sooner did they reach the distant headland than a strong adverse gale drove them back on their course. Seeing that it was hopeless to try to double it until a change of wind occurred, the Admiral led the way back to the safe harbor they had left earlier in the day at the River of the Tides, christening the point he had failed to pass the Cape of Palms, from the great forests of those trees which clothed its outlines from base to summit.[1]

[1] The harbor of San Salvador entered by Columbus on first nearing the Cuban coast is supposed to have been either the modern Caravelas Grandes or the Bay of Nipé. His course along the northern shores of Cuba is not easy to follow in detail upon the charts of to-day; but those interested will find it ably discussed by Mackenzie in the Appendix to Irving's "Columbus," by Becher in his "Landfall of Columbus," by Fox in the United States Coast Survey Reports for 1880, and by Murdock in the "Proceedings of the United States Naval Institute for April, 1884." These are all easily accessible; but the student will wish to examine the arguments of Von Humboldt, Varnhagen, and the other foreign critics as well.

XIV.

THE EMBASSY TO WHOM IT MIGHT CONCERN.

THE next morning, the 1st of November, as the Spaniards rowed toward the shore, the natives again deserted their village and took refuge in the woods, despite the Admiral's precautions on his previous visit to convince them of his kindly intentions. When the sailors had filled their casks with water and were returning to the ships, a single Indian emerged from behind the trees and stood watching their departure. Apparently he was acting as sentinel for his companions; for he maintained stolidly his position, with his eyes fixed on the ships, as if waiting to see what the strangers should do next. After breakfasting the Admiral landed again, taking with him an interpreter to communicate with the solitary native who so persistently was observing their every movement. The interpreter as soon as he came within speaking distance called out that there was no cause for fear; that the white men were not soldiers of the Great Khan, and would do no harm to the people of the village, but would rather make them rich presents, as they had done to the natives of the other islands, whose good friends they were. This, at all events, is the speech the Admiral told his own Indian to make. How much either the savage in the boat or the one on shore knew of the Tartar Emperor of China is problematical; but no doubt the interpreter realized that he was to make friends with the man on the beach, and said as much to him. On hearing his declaration others of the natives left their hiding-places and drew near to the water's edge; so the interpreter leaped overboard and swam ashore, where he was well received by them and conducted into one of the cabins near by. He must soon have convinced them that no harm was intended; for shortly after a number of them came running down to the water, and launching fifteen or twenty of their canoes, paddled out to the boat, which returned to the ship followed by the whole flotilla. The savages, as usual, wished to barter their cotton and other possessions for the trinkets of the Spaniards; but the Admiral forbade his men to take anything at all except gold. This he tried to make the Indians comprehend was the only thing the strangers wanted. So far these people gave no signs of using it. One man alone had a piece of silver hanging from his nose; and the Admiral found consolation in the reflection that there must at least be mines of that metal within reach. Throughout the day the savages kept up a constant intercourse with the fleet, and many of the Spaniards went on shore and strolled through the forest without molestation. From the gestures of his native guests the Admiral understood that their king lived at a distance of four days' journey from the river, and that they had sent to advise him of the arrival of the white men when the ships had anchored there for the first time. In three days more, they affirmed, — or he thought they did, — a large number of merchants would arrive from the capital to establish traffic with the Spaniards. This could only mean to his mind that he was on the borders of Cathay. All the natives of the other islands visited he had already observed were friendly to one another; so evidently they were leagued together to resist the invasions which the Great Khan sent from the mainland to conquer them. Now that he found the people of Cuba of the same race and tongue, he felt confident that their country must be one of the easternmost provinces of Asia adjoining the kingdoms of the Khan, and imagined that in their wars with that powerful prince the natives of the islands came to their assistance, and they also helped the islanders at need; in short, Cuba was now China, and the lesser islands were the

Celebes. The Khan of Tartary was at war with them all, sometimes directing his armies against the Chinese and sometimes against the islands; and all these copper-colored people were allied to repel his assaults on their independence. This was so obvious to the Admiral that he was anxious to make peace with the King of Cuba, and so open a road to the cities of the Khan himself. He writes in his diary: —

"I am certain now that this is in fact the mainland, and that I must be somewhere near the cities of Zayto and Quimsay, which are about one hundred leagues apart. That this is the mainland is proved by the fact that the current of the ocean now comes from a direction contrary to what it formerly did; and yesterday when we were sailing toward the northwest it grew colder as we advanced."

China and Tartary, Japan and the Spice Islands, the cities of the Mongol prince and the treasures of the Indies, — with such splendid phantasies was the mind of Colon filled as he stood on the deck of his flagship watching the canoes freighted with naked savages plying to and fro over the surface of that beautiful harbor on the northern coast of the Pearl of the Antilles. There is something almost painful in the eagerness with which his sanguine mind discarded one illusion only to adopt another more groundless still; but he reasoned from what he esteemed to be mathematical premises. He remarks: —

"I took the altitude here last night with the quadrant, and found that we are twenty-one degrees above the equinoctial line. My calculations also show that we have sailed 1,142 leagues since leaving Ferro; and surely this is the mainland."

Upon further reflection the Admiral determined to send his own messengers in search of the King of Cuba, instead of waiting for the arrival of the merchants promised by the natives; but he altered somewhat his intentions regarding the personnel of the embassy. Of late his Guanahani interpreters had shown signs of restiveness, entreating him to return them to their homes; and he feared that once they found themselves at a distance from the ships with but a single Spaniard, they might desert him altogether. He accordingly chose the sailor, Rodrigo of Xerez, who had acted as ambassador on the Guinea voyage before referred to, and a converted Jew named Luiz de Torres, a man of much education, who spoke Hebrew, Chaldaic, and Arabic, as well as Spanish. Marco Polo, the Venetian, when he was travelling in China two hundred years before, had found numbers of Jews in the territories of the Grand Khan, and the Saracens were known to be neighbors of the Tartar ruler; so the Admiral thought it probable that if his men succeeded in reaching the capital of Cuba, they should find some one who could speak one or the other of Torres's languages. With these two Europeans he sent one of his Guanahani interpreters and a native of the village at the River of Tides to guide them through the country and testify to his compatriots as to the friendly dispositions of the white men. To his envoys the Admiral gave careful and minute instructions. They were to follow their guide to the royal city, provided the journey thither did not require more than three days; under any circumstances he would look for their return on the sixth day. Upon reaching the Court they were to present themselves before the king with becoming reverence, and inform him that the Sovereigns of Spain had sent their Admiral to these shores with a letter and many rich presents for the Cuban king, and that the Admiral solicited an audience with his Majesty in order to deliver these to him. They were to expatiate upon the glory and power of their Catholic Majesties, and to assure the king that the Spanish monarchs only desired to establish relations of friendship with him and his allies. Above all, the messengers were to explain to the king that the Spaniards who had arrived in Cuba had no connection, however remote, with the Khan of Tartary; on the contrary, they would gladly make a league with the king with a view to establishing a profitable and enduring commerce with his people. While on their journey the men were to keep a close watch for any signs of gold or other treasures, and were to bring back a careful report of all they saw, particularly around the royal Court. In order to show the king and his subjects what the white men chiefly desired, the envoys took with them small quantities of gold, spices, and pepper to serve as specimens. They were also well supplied with trinkets for paying their way and making presents, and an abundance of provisions. Having satisfied himself that his wishes were clearly comprehended, the Admiral gave the men his blessing, and they departed on their adventurous errand. Turning at the edge of the forest, they waved a farewell to their companions on the beach, and then following the footsteps of their savage guide, were lost in its depths. It is difficult for us nowadays to restrain a smile at the idea of looking for the Court of a Chinese monarch among the mountains of Cuba; but we cannot fail to admire the easy confidence with which these two men set out to seek for a savage city in the heart of so wild a country, and among a numerous population of whose real character they knew nothing. Whether it was contempt for the natives, or trust in the Saints, or sheer reliance on their own prowess, we cannot tell; one thing is clear, that on this voyage and all later ones the early Spanish discoverers never heeded danger nor counted their foes. They went straight at whatever and whomsoever opposed them, as though their mind could not conceive the thought that they might fail.

The next day, the 3d of the month, was devoted to exploring the river and its banks. The Admiral was much pleased at finding an admirable place for beaching his ships and overhauling their hulls. He rowed on several leagues up the stream, until the summit of a lofty hill showing through the tree-tops suggested the possibility of securing an extensive view of the surrounding country. It was no easy task for him and his companions to make their way to the top of this eminence; but they finally accomplished it, only to discover that no view was possible on account of the dense growth which covered the whole hill. The Admiral did not begrudge the exertion, if we may judge by his record of the excursion; for he declares that at every step he found something new to admire in the bushes and trees about him, and that his eyes never wearied of watching the gorgeous birds darting through the sunlight, and the vivid butterflies floating from shrub to shrub. The fragrant odors of the woods caused him to search on every side for nutmegs, pepper, and other spices, and he offered a reward to whomsoever should be the first to bring a specimen of any of these productions. A great breaking of branches and peeling of bark at once ensued, the seamen in the party eagerly assailing every tree which seemed at all likely to yield any one of the precious condiments. In such pleasant fashion, rowing and sounding on the river, strolling and studying on land, the Admiral and his party passed the day; while on board the ships the sailors found amusement in trying to understand the savages who continued to swarm about the vessels offering whatever they possessed, from the dried leaves they held in such high esteem to their prettily netted "hamacs," in exchange for a few glass beads or a hawk's bell.

The next morning the Admiral took his cross-bow and was rowed up the river to hunt for some of the beautiful birds he had seen the day before. Such splendid plumage was a rarity to him, and he thought that even the mighty Spanish monarchs would think them no mean present. After shooting as many as he could in the cool of the day, he returned to the flagship about ten o'clock, his usual hour for breakfast. Here he found Martin Alonzo awaiting him with another discovery; for this Pinzon was a shrewd and diligent man, ever on the lookout for advantage. This time he held two pieces of a reddish bark in his hand, which he showed to his leader with evident content.

"Here at length is the true bark of cinnamon, your Worship," he exclaimed. "One of my crew, a man of good sense though he is a Portuguese, has brought me this from shore. He says he met an Indian who had two bundles of it, and a quantity of red nuts besides, which my man judged to be spices; but under your Worship's orders he dared not take them from the savage, even by way of barter."

"These men of ours show little wisdom, Señor Captain," the Admiral replied, showing some vexation. "This spice is of the rarest, and of an exalted value in all the marts of

Europe. I thank you for your notice; but we must make our hard-heads know that when they meet with treasures they dare not take they must bring the bearers to us to deal with as is best. We of the command cannot be everywhere and our eyes be on everything at one single moment."

"Your Worship knows the seaman's saying, Señor Admiral," Martin Alonzo answered, "that an order is an order, or else a waste of breath. Nevertheless, I am ever doing what in me lies to get my men to bring to me whatever seems to them of value, and shall continue so to do, as your Worship wishes."

The Admiral was annoyed that this discovery should amount to so little. Cinnamon at that period was one of the most precious objects brought to Europe by the caravans from Asia, and was almost worth its weight in gold. Perhaps some doubt of Martin Alonzo's entire truthfulness may have entered his mind as well; for of late he had noticed a somewhat more independent manner in his lieutenant than he thought was due to himself as representative of the Spanish Crown. But he let this feeling pass, as he had done before; and when the first-mate of the "Pinta" told him that he had found near the landing-place some trees which he believed were cinnamon, the Admiral went with him at once to see if indeed the costly bark grew near at hand. This time, too, he was disappointed; for although the bark was fragrant and had a pungent taste, it clearly was not what the mate had thought. That the pieces secured by Martin Alonzo's sailor were the genuine article there was no doubt; and calling the Indians about him, the Admiral showed them the bark as well as specimens of cloves and pepper, hoping that they might recognize them and indicate where they could be found. From their signs he understood the natives to reply that not far from there, in a southeasterly direction, great quantities of those things could be secured. Encouraged by the success of his experiment, he now showed them a piece of gold and a few pearls, and inquired if they knew where such were to be had. Most of the Indians looked at the articles with stupid curiosity, as if not seeing anything remarkable about them; but some of the older men pointed again to the southeast, and made signs that in a place called *Bohio* a great plenty of these things could be had, the people in that country wearing them as ornaments around their limbs and necks or in their ears or noses. The Admiral also understood them to say that some of the tribes of Bohio had only one eye in the middle of their forehead, while others had heads like dogs. All the enemies whom they captured in battle they beheaded, and after drinking their blood, cooked and ate their bodies. These monsters, he also gathered, had many large ships and much rich merchandise, and were altogether a powerful and wealthy nation. What meaning the Indians really intended to convey by the gestures which the Admiral interpreted in so extraordinary a manner, it would not be safe to conjecture; apparently some reference was being made to the cannibal habits of the Caribs and their huge canoes. To Colon it was patent that they were talking of the Dog-heads and One-eyes of the Asiatic islands described by Mandeville and the Venetian, and he credited even more than he heard. The monsters had no terrors for him, implicitly as he might believe in their existence; to Bohio he intended to sail at the earliest opportunity, unless his messengers should bring him satisfactory news of gold and treasures in the city they were visiting. So far he had met with nothing of real value at the River of Tides. There was an abundance of cotton, to be sure, which seemed to grow wild all the year round; for he noticed the flowers, open balls, and green pods all growing on one tree; and some of the other vegetable productions were good, especially a large root which tasted like chestnuts when roasted, and would be a great boon in Spain;[1] but all these bulky articles were not worth loading his ships with. What he wanted was gold and pearls, or, at the least, spices and silk.

On the morning of the 5th he ordered the vessels to be made ready for beaching; the flagship was to be careened

[1] Probably the *Yucca*.

and calked first, and then the others in succession, so that there would always be two afloat ready for any emergency. While the "Santa Maria" was being warped on the sands, the mate of the "Niña" came up to where the Admiral was watching the operation and saluted him.

"By your Excellency's favor," the man said in some excitement, "I claim a reward."

"A reward for what, good Maestro Diego?" Colon answered. "Hast found the cinnamon forest or a mine of gold? There should be such hereabout, if all signs fail not."

"If your Excellency pleases," Diego replied, "'t is not so good as gold; but 't is better than the bark. If my eyes lied not, I have found the trees which bear the precious mastic gum; but in my haste to get hither I have dropped the piece I gathered for your Worship."

"Thy reward is none the less sure, Diego, if thou canst point out the place. I will ask Don Rodrigo to go with thee and note the fact in due form. Thou art very right in holding that thy news is welcome."

Sending for the royal inspector, the Admiral requested him to accompany Maestro Diego to the spot where he had found the gum and certify to the fact of its existence. So rare and valuable was mastic then esteemed, that its discovery would, the Admiral knew, be considered a matter of much importance by the Spanish sovereigns; and he awaited with interest the report of Don Rodrigo Sanchez. When the latter returned he declared that beyond doubt the trees were of the true mastic kind, and he produced some of the gum and a branch of the foliage as evidence of the fact. These the Admiral carefully preserved for his royal patrons, granting without further discussion the promised reward to the fortunate discoverer. His desire to obtain the largest store possible of gold and gems did not in any wise blind him to the importance of these less valuable productions. His intention was, as we have seen, to return to Spain in April, and he naturally labored to take with him as great an amount of treasure as he could, as the most effectual answer practicable to the cavillings and criticisms with which his project had been assailed. On his return to "the Indies," which he planned should take place without loss of time, he would provide for the trade which he anticipated in the other merchantable articles.

That same evening, as it was growing dark, the crew of the flagship, which was high and dry on the beach, heard some one hailing them from alongside. It proved to be the two envoys, Rodrigo de Xerez and Luiz de Torres, who had returned a day before the limit allowed them. A ladder was quickly lowered, and they clambered on board, accompanied not only by the two Indians who had started with them, but by three others, who were presented to the Admiral as one of the principal chiefs of the city they had visited and his son, with a follower of theirs. When Colon saw that the strangers were naked and treasureless, he knew that he was as far as ever from finding the royal capital he was so anxious to reach; but ordering refreshments to be brought his visitors and making them every sign of welcome and friendship, he called upon his messengers for their report of the journey.

They had travelled, they told him, quite forty miles before they came to the "city" the Indians had described. The road was a narrow path leading almost all the way through dense forests, though here and there they traversed broad savannas carpeted with grass and flowers. Such a variety of new and strange trees and plants they had passed, often covered to the topmost bough with aromatic blossoms, that they could not attempt to recount them. As for the birds, their number and kinds were infinite, — all wholly unlike any they had ever seen in Spain, except some partridges which they saw in a meadow and the nightingales they heard in the woods as they marched along. The first two nights they slept in the forest, not wishing to stop at the little villages of four or five huts which they passed on the way, although the people seemed to be friendly, and showed no fear after their Indian companions had explained who they were. On the third day they reached a town which from the guide's information they knew to be the city to which they were bound. It consisted of only about fifty houses, constructed of canes and palm leaves, like all that they had seen, but very well built, and so large that each house contained at least twenty inhabitants. As they approached the place, the people flocked out to meet them to the number of a thousand or more, and after hearing the interpreter's declaration led them into the largest of these dwellings, the principal men of the town taking them by the arm as a mark of honor. When all the men were gathered within the house, the women were forbidden to enter; and the Spaniards were seated on stools in the midst of the apartment. One after another the savages then pressed forward, kissing the white men's hands and feet, and touching them to see what manner of strange creatures they might be. From their gestures the envoys believed that the Indians supposed they had come down from the skies, — an error which the messengers do not seem to have corrected. After the first excitement had subsided, the savages all squatted on the floor in a circle around the strangers; while the interpreter explained in a long harangue what great and powerful people these white men were, how wonderfully they lived, and what extraordinary treasures they possessed, assuring his hearers that they were the best beings in the world and true friends of the natives, to whom they gave magnificent presents, such as those he wore. He concluded by saying that they must take very good care of these miraculous visitors, and when they returned some of the chief governors of the town must go with them to see the great captain of the white men, and talk with him. This, at all events, is what the two Spaniards supposed their man was saying. The only thing they could be sure of was that he was talking about them, and that they had to sit still and look very important while five or six hundred eyes were staring them out of countenance. When this address was over, Luiz de Torres rose and exerted his eloquence in Hebrew, Arabic, and Chaldean. The savages listened with breathless admiration; and if they made no reply it was doubtless because not a soul present, not even his companion, understood a word of what he was talking about. After a becoming pause — meant probably to testify their approval of the linguistic effort just closed — the Indians all rose and filed solemnly out of the building, and the women took their places. They also went through the same process of adoration, some of the hardier ones pinching the unhappy Spaniards to see if they were flesh and blood despite their singular appearance. When this ordeal was over, the women too sat down in a circle, and the interpreter told them also whatever he could remember or invent concerning their marvellous guests. After a while the men returned in force, and the wearied ambassadors were allowed to wander about the town and examine at their pleasure all that excited their curiosity. They showed the natives the cinnamon and spices they carried with them, and their hosts signified that in that neighborhood these were not to be found; but as the Indians at the river had done, they indicated that off somewhere in the southeast these articles could be obtained in abundance. As for other cities and kingdoms or their treasures, the messengers could learn nothing, and in the town itself was no vestige of king or Court. Some of the men seemed to have more authority than others; but the people were much like all the savages they had thus far seen. They were plainly delighted with the presence of their guests, and showed them unstinted hospitality, setting before them the choicest dishes, pressing them to eat, and insisting that they must not leave them for several days. At night the strangers were lodged in their neatest cabins, and received every attention that it was in the Indians' power to bestow. When they started out the next morning to return to the River of Tides, the natives broke out into extravagant lamentations, more than half the population of the village, men and women alike, endeavoring to accompany the visitors in the conviction that they would lead them right up into the sky above. The Spaniards had to repel the excited multitude, and made signs that none should join them except a single chief, who brought with him his son and a companion, — no doubt for his greater safety. Both in going and coming they had met with many natives passing between their villages; and some of these had smoke escaping from their mouths and nostrils in a truly diabolical fashion. They carried in their hands a "burning stick" and some of the dried leaves the white men had noticed so many times before, and they would put this stick in their mouths and blow out a cloud of smoke, which had a pleasant perfume. The interpreter explained that by so doing they experienced no fatigue when on their journeys; but the whole matter had a heathenish look about it. As they came through the little villages on their way back, the savages showed them much kindness, which they requited by making trifling presents; and now they had arrived unharmed and well at the ships. They ventured to hope that his Excellency the Señor Admiral was contented with the manner in which his orders had been executed.

The men had done their work admirably, and this the Admiral told them; but he was none the less chagrined at the insignificant results of their mission. He had looked for a powerful king and had found but one naked savage the more, for a wealthy city and had found a huddle of huts! However, he was far from letting his disappointment be apparent. Turning to his savage guests who had accompanied the messengers, he loaded them with attentions, giving them a profusion of whatever they seemed most to like in eating and drinking, and making them presents of the trifles which pleased their fancy. From them he learned of other islands and countries in the adjoining seas, the most important of which he understood to be the land in the southeast, and thither he decided to steer as soon as his vessels were overhauled. He was desirous of taking the new-comers with him on the voyage, and even to carry them to Spain to exhibit to the sovereigns as examples of the inhabitants of Cuba; but as the night advanced, the savages became restive, and showed by signs that they wished to go on shore. Anxious not to offend them, the Admiral allowed them to take leave, helping them over the ship's side with all the ceremony imaginable. As they parted from him, they signified that they would return in the morning; but, as he writes with evident regret, "they never showed themselves again."

Thus ended the first diplomatic mission undertaken in the New World. The Admiral had failed to find any trace of the treasures of Cathay; but he had learned what use the Indians made of their "dried leaves." Many a jaded mortal who has tried their remedy for fatigue will bless the memory of the two ambassadors, as the "pleasant perfume" curls upward from his "burning stick"!

XV.

THE EVIL DEED OF MARTIN ALONZO.

THE work of overhauling the three ships was completed by the 7th of November; but a constant succession of contrary winds detained them in the harbor until the 12th. During this delay the Admiral continued to explore the forests of the neighborhood for further indications of valuable barks, gums, or fruits, and in especial tried to obtain a quantity of the gum-mastic discovered by Maestro Diego. In his younger days, when cruising in the Grecian Archipelago, Colon had visited the island of Chios, and observed the manner in which this gum was gathered; for that island had nearly a monopoly of its production. He now turned this experience to practical use by sending his men into the woods with instructions how to tap the trees and collect the flowing sap. They cut into a vast number of the trees with little return in the way of gum, which puzzled the Admiral until he noticed that the trees were in full fruit at the time, and that the sap would not run freely at that season. At the period of blossoming he was satisfied that they would yield countless tons of the fragrant resin, and that a large and profitable commerce could be established. In anticipation of such a traffic, he remarked that the flat summit of a lofty rock near the entrance to the river afforded an admirable site for a fortress. "Thus, if this should prove to be a valuable trade and worth the effort," he writes, " our merchants can come here freely, safe from the intrusion of any other nation. May Our Lord, in whose hands are all successes, arrange all this as shall be best for His glory! One of the Indians made signs to me that this gum-mastic is very good to cure the stomach-ache," he adds with a rather abrupt change of thought.

Charmed as he was with his present surroundings, and clearly as he perceived the value of this port for the purposes of regular commerce in the future, he was impatient to leave it and visit the new land of which the natives had recently spoken. Sometimes they seemed to call it Bohio, and at others *Babeque;* but they always indicated that it was in the southeast, abounded in riches, was very extensive, and contained a numerous and ferocious population. After much misunderstanding and confusion, arising from certain irreconcilable differences between what his informants said at one time and at another, he came to the conclusion that Bohio was the name of that province of Asia lying east and south of Cuba; while Babeque was the island lying farther off to the southeast. On this theory he subsequently acted, although it is not always easy to distinguish one place from the other in following his conjectures regarding them. Babeque was pre-eminently the home of gold. Here the precious metal "grew;" and so lavish was its profusion that the natives of that fortunate country collected it at night by torchlight along the beaches and beat it out with hammers into rods! What was the meaning of the gestures which shaped themselves in the Admiral's mind to this extraordinary interpretation, it is useless to query; but he had seen already so much that was marvellous that this also was incorporated among his beliefs, and the search for Babeque became the leading motive of his immediate actions.

He was beginning to lose some of his early confidence in the sincerity of the natives and the correctness of their declarations, and had more than once doubted whether his own interpreters were entirely frank in their statements to him. The urgency with which they joined the Cubans in lauding the greatness of Babeque aroused a suspicion that there was an ulterior motive behind so much enthusiasm, and he feared that they were planning to lead him to some island nearer to Guanahaní, where they should be able to escape from their masters and make their way home. As a measure of precaution, he therefore resolved to take with him some of the natives of the village at the River of Tides. So on Sunday, the 11th, when a canoe with six young men came alongside, as was the daily habit of the savages, he detained the five who came on board, and sent the one remaining in the boat back to land without his companions. Before the inhabitants fully realized his purpose, he also sent his barge ashore and seized seven women with three children, all of whom he took on his own vessel. This was simply a bald act of kidnapping, undefensible by any sophistry; but the Admiral saw nothing censurable in the proceeding. The end more than justified the means, according to his way of thinking, and he was actuated, he believed, by praiseworthy motives. He writes with perfect candor: —

"I did this because the men will behave better when they reach Spain if they have their wives with them than if they have not. Many times I have seen the natives of Guinea brought to Portugal to learn the language of the Christians; but when they were taken back to act as interpreters, and the Portuguese counted on finding them useful because of the kind treatment shown them and the gifts they had received, they would run away as soon as they reached their native shores and never again appear. But if we have their wives, the men will be anxious to serve us well; and besides the women will teach our own people the language, which is the same in all these islands of India, where the savages understand one another and travel about in their canoes. This is very different from what I have seen in Guinea, where there are a thousand separate languages and no one tribe understands another."

He also argued that he was conferring an inestimable benefit on these poor heathen in enabling them to receive the Christian religion. He remarks: —

"They have no religion at all, and are not even worshippers of idols; but they are very superstitious, and believe that there is a God in heaven and that we came down from there to visit them. They follow us closely in all the prayers we say, and make the sign of the cross after us, so that your Majesties ought to cause them to be converted to Christianity; for I believe that if this beginning is made, in a little while a great multitude of these nations shall be brought into our Holy Faith."

The Admiral's intentions were plainly of the best, and he consistently showed great humanity to all the natives who came in contact with him; but the fact remains that he took these and other savages captive without offence committed by them, and proposed holding the women as hostages for the good behavior of their husbands. Nor was he fortunate in the selection of his prisoners; for the women were not the consorts of the men thus suddenly impounded. That very Sunday evening an incident occurred which emphasized the danger of wrong and injustice being done by acts of violence, under whatever specious plea they may be performed. As the ships were getting under weigh to stand out of the harbor, a canoe came up alongside the flagship propelled by an Indian, some forty years of age, who made signs entreating to be taken on board. On being questioned by the interpreters as to what he wanted, he replied that his wife was one of the seven women kidnapped, and the three children were his also, and he begged to be allowed to accompany them wherever they were going. Truly a pathetic picture that, on the crimson surface of the placid river, framed in its setting of darkening forest and lighted with the gorgeous coloring of the tropical sunset: the lonely Indian in his little dug-out pleading with the mighty strangers on the great ship to be permitted to share the fortunes of his loved ones, whatever might be in store for them or him! Even in those early days the Indian had no rights which the white man was bound to respect; but for our own part we fail to see wherein the devotion and self-sacrifice of the nameless savage were one whit less beautiful than those which have caused the name of Ruth the Moabitess to be remembered for more than twenty centuries. "This greatly pleased me," the Admiral says in his diary; "and now with this man's coming they are all consoled, so that they must all have been his relations." We would rather he had ordered out his barge and sent the plucky native and all his "relations" on shore, with a goodly gift of beads and bells to show his admiration for such unselfish courage.

Sailing out of the River of Tides at early dawn of the 12th, the fleet coasted along eastward toward the country the Indians called Bohio. Though he passed in sight of many broad rivers and spacious ports, the Admiral would make no landing, but kept steadily onward. This he did for two reasons, he tells us: first, because he wished to go with all speed to the island of Babeque, for which the wind was favorable; and second, because he saw no large towns or cities along the coast, and did not care to lose time in examining harbors which could just as well be visited later on. By evening he was in sight of the mountains which, according to his interpreters, divided the "province" of Cuba from that of Bohio, and the ships were hove to to avoid the hidden dangers of the coast. When morning broke, he resumed his eastern course; but, a stiff northerly gale springing up and threatening to drive him on the lee shore, he put well out to sea and made such progress as he could to the eastward. That night, also, he lay to, not venturing to maintain his headway in a sea where the Indians told him there were many islands, and being perplexed with the variable winds; but at daybreak on the 15th he determined to head again for Cuba, or Bohio, as he now supposed the coast nearest him was called, and continue his voyage toward Babeque. When his savage passengers saw the fleet steering again for shore, they were overwhelmed with terror and trembled in every limb. That part of the "mainland" was Bohio, they reiterated, where the inhabitants had but one eye and ate all whom they could seize. Their representations had little effect on the Admiral, however; for just now he was looking for a safe anchorage, and the number of eyes possessed by the Bohioans was a secondary consideration. The weather was unsettled and stormy, and he wished to get at least within reach of shelter. He did not want to be forced to abandon his easterly direction; for he had observed as he had run up into the north and northeast that the air was a good deal cooler, and he feared to encounter the storms of winter should he be carried in that direction. Now that he was on the Asiatic coast, he desired to remain, and thus he led the way again toward land. As he drew near the coast, though, the wind shifted, and he found his only possible course was westward, little as that suited his plans. Scanning carefully the shore as he was driven along, he saw no harbor whose entrance was wholly free from risk of accident under the conditions then prevailing, for the gale was increasing in violence and the sea was running high. After seven or eight hours of this unsatisfactory progress, he spied a broad and quiet channel which promised to lead safely to a harbor. Entering this and following it for several miles, he was delighted at emerging into a wide expanse of unvexed sea, from whose surface rose an infinite number of mountainous islands, whose summits, as he sailed close past their bases, seemed fairly to pierce the skies. On one side this ocean lake, or lake-like ocean, was bounded by the mainland, where rugged sierras pressed down to the very water's edge; on the other, an endless prospect of towering islands and waveless sea stretched away into the distance. The Admiral could find no words to express his admiration and pleasure at the vista thus suddenly opened to his view. If what he had seen before of this wonderful country had so astonished him, what was he to say of this new region? "So many and such lofty islands I have never seen hitherto," he writes. "The world cannot contain any higher mountains than those which are before me along this coast and in this archipelago. Certainly no more beautiful ones exist; for these are free from ice and snow, their heads are covered with verdure and their feet with palms, while they slope so steeply that the largest ships can approach them without the least danger." Some of the highest peaks were so sharp and delicate that he likens them to the point of a diamond; others had flat and even summits like tables; while all were densely clad with vegetation. To his mind it was beyond dispute that these were part of the seven thousand four hundred and forty islands which according to

Marco Polo lay between Cipango and the continent of Asia; and he expected to find them stretching away on all sides beyond the horizon. The combination of mountain and forest which distinguished their topography was evidence to him that they had concealed "great riches and precious stones and spices within them." So fair a paradise, he thought, was entitled to a name of peculiar honor; and so he christened the island-studded ocean "The Sea of Our Lady,"[1] after the Virgin Mary. In closing his description of its attractions, he regrets with evident sincerity that he cannot do it justice, and begs their Majesties that they should not be surprised that he dilates so on its beauties, for he pledges himself that he has not been able to relate the hundredth part of all the perfection upon which his eyes had feasted. It is not easy to determine the exact route of the squadron on these three days; but it would appear from the Admiral's description that he had been carried westward by the currents which set along the northern coast of Cuba, and was now among the groups of islands which lie opposite the southern point of Florida. His biographer and friend, the good Bishop of Chiapas, has noted on the margin of his copy of Colon's diary: "If he had continued toward the north, in two days more beyond doubt he had discovered the mainland of Florida." As he did not, we need not pursue the subject.

Cruising leisurely through Our Lady's Sea, the Admiral on the 15th entered his barge and visited some of the islands, taking possession of them, as was his wont, for the Spanish Crown, and causing crosses to be erected wherever he landed. They all seemed to be inhabited; but as the natives fled at his approach, he was unable to hold intercourse with them. Around their cabins the ground was tilled in plantations of mandioca, yucca, and other vegetables, while in the woods were many fruit and mastic trees. On the following morning he ran in close to the mainland and went on shore with the intention of exploring the

[1] This is supposed to be the island-covered sea which lies to the north and east of Cape Cabrion.

vicinity and setting up the customary emblem of his faith. As though to reward his pious labors, he discovered near by the landing-place two trees growing in such a manner that the one bent athwart the other in the shape of a cross so perfect that no carpenter could make a truer one. Looking upon this as little less than a miracle, the Admiral and his companions knelt in adoration before it; after which he ordered his men to cut the two trunks down and dress them, so that he might tow them to the spacious port which lay near the entrance of Our Lady's Sea, and there re-establish them as a landmark and a signal that the Christians had taken possession of the sea and all within it. When he returned to the flagship, he found the Indians diving overboard, searching in the shallow waters for the conch-shells of which they were so fond. He ordered them to look for pearl-oysters as well, and they brought up a number which had no pearls. The shells were so large and handsome that he hoped in good time pearls would be discovered in abundance, attributing their present failure to the unfavorable season of the year. The following day, the 17th, was passed like its predecessor in exploration and investigation, which more and more confirmed the Admiral's belief that he was penetrating the limits of the Orient. In the little *cotias* which hurried under shelter as the Spaniards approached, he fancied he saw the large rat-shaped rodents described by the travellers to the Indies; and some of the trees around him seemed to bear nutmegs, while now and again the warm air was loaded with a fragrance he took for musk. We cannot otherwise account for his lingering so many days in this one locality, when he himself declares repeatedly his impatience to reach Babeque, than by supposing that he considered that he was in the Chinese Sea and wished to discover for himself, if possible, the marvels and wonders described by the worthy Marco Polo. He lost this day two of the Indians whom he had taken at the River of Tides, and afterward transferred to the "Niña" as being less crowded than the flagship. Taking advantage of the liberty allowed them, they slipped overboard and quietly swam ashore, in rude indifference to the preparations made by the Admiral for their solace in this world and their salvation in the next. Early on Sunday, the 18th, Colon ordered out all the boats with as many men as could be safely spared from the ships, and rowed to the mouth of the port which entered the Cuban mainland near the channel giving access to Our Lady's Sea. Here the great cross was erected on a high hill whose freedom from trees allowed the holy emblem to be seen for many leagues in all directions from the sea. The appropriate offices were said and chanted to the best of the company's ability, and the harbor was named the Port of the Prince. On returning to the ships the Admiral announced that he would re-commence his voyage to Babeque on the following morning. He did not wish to start on this same day, he writes, "because it was Sunday," which is the first intimation we have of any such scruple on his part.

Monday, November 19th, the fleet resumed its course, and worked to the eastward as well as it could with light and variable winds. It was blown so far out of its course that night that on the 20th the Admiral found himself within an easy day's sail of Isabella. The winds were so unfavorable for pursuing his journey to Babeque, and the sea was becoming so angry, that he would gladly have sought the shelter of his earlier discovery; but he reflected that if he did this his Guanahani Indians would unquestionably make their escape. They were already complaining that he had broken faith with them in keeping them so long. Their understanding was, they said, that they were to be released as soon as they had shown the Spaniards where gold was to be found, and this they claimed to have done. Judging from their subsequent behavior, it is more probable that they were frightened at the prospect of visiting the terrible monsters of Bohio and Babeque, and invented the excuse of the Admiral's broken promise; for it is certain that such a pledge could not have been given by means of any imaginable signs. At all events, he was not going to run any risks of losing them just as they were beginning to understand Spanish and become of daily increasing assistance; therefore, instead of heading for Isabella, which was only thirty-five miles off, he put about and made for the Port of the Prince, which was nearly twice the distance. By the time he reached this harbor it was night, and, not caring to risk making an entrance, he once more tacked about and sought the open sea. At daybreak he was forty miles away from the Port, and as the wind changed for the better he resumed his easterly course in the hope of reaching Babeque.

Toward evening, as the breeze served his purpose, he shifted his direction somewhat toward the south, in order to skirt more closely the Cuban coast. He noticed, after changing his course, that the "Pinta" did not follow his lead as promptly as she should have done; but he thought little of this at the moment, as she was the swiftest sailer of the fleet and might be standing on with the intention of overtaking the flagship later. As the night closed in, however, he saw the "Pinta" away off on the horizon, still steering due east with all sails set, and every moment increasing the distance between herself and the two other vessels. Loath to believe that so true a sailor and so brave a man as her captain undoubtedly was would be guilty of so rank an act of disobedience, the Admiral assumed that the distance had misled him, and that the "Pinta" must in reality be heading for him; so he directed that his own ship and the "Niña" should take in part of their canvas and continue their way to the coast under easy sail. He likewise ordered that a bright light should be maintained all night long as a guide to the missing vessel. With these precautions taken, he hoped against hope to hear Martin Alonzo's hail before many hours were past; the more especially as the wind blew strong from the direction of the "Pinta" to where her consorts were slowly forging along. The anxious night passed without incident, nevertheless; and when the Admiral mounted the castle of his ship as soon as the first gray light of morning broke in the eastern sky, both ocean and horizon were bare of ship or sail. There was no longer possibility of doubt or error:

Martin Alonzo had deserted his companions and steered eastward for some purpose of his own.

That Colon should be disturbed and anxious at this foul deed was natural enough, and his anger was equal to his indignation; but both policy and pride demanded that he should not openly attach too great importance to it, or confess himself to have been abandoned in cold blood by his chief lieutenant. That such was the case, and that the motive in Martin Alonzo's mind was a compound of envy and greed, the Admiral did not question. No other solution was admissible. There was no storm raging to separate the ships, nor had any accident befallen the "Pinta" to render her ungovernable. She had ample opportunity to rejoin her sister ships had her captain so desired; for the wind which then prevailed would have brought her to them in three or four hours at the most. That her absence was intentional, he was convinced; and as he reflected upon the matter Martin Alonzo's object gradually grew plain before him. Ever since the proclamation of Colon as Admiral and Viceroy, the captain of the "Pinta" had shown a restive independence which ill befitted his inferior rank. The knowledge that he had been largely instrumental in getting together the fleet which had made this gigantic discovery; the fact that he and his family had contributed a considerable sum of money to the costs of the expedition; the belief that he was as good a navigator and as wise a geographer as this Italian adventurer, and had done as much as he in finding land and securing these rich countries,—all these thoughts had fostered his self-importance, and helped to feed the feeling that he was being unjustly treated, and deserved quite as high a rank and as great a dignity as had been conferred on his commander. These sentiments had led him imperceptibly to assume toward the Admiral a bearing which the latter found it difficult to support. "Many another insolence has he said and done to me," Colon writes in his diary when recording the desertion of his lieutenant. But as two of his ships were commanded by the Pinzons, and the greater part of his crews were Palos men, related to or dependent on the three brothers, the Admiral had disguised his impatience at Martin Alonzo's treatment and smothered his resentment for the sake of his expedition's success. Now he recalled the fact that it was the interpreter assigned to the "Pinta" who had been the first to inform them of the extent and importance of Cuba, and he was convinced that the same man had given her captain some other information about Babeque which had inflamed Pinzon's cupidity to such a degree that he had forgotten the obligations of duty and loyalty, and gone to reap the benefits of the new discovery for himself alone. Instead, however, of making sail in the direction taken by the fugitive "Pinta," the Admiral resolved to complete his examination of the country of Bohio, and then continue on to the island of Babeque. By so doing he would not appear to his men to be distressed by the action of Martin Alonzo, nor would he lose the opportunity of learning the truth regarding this nearer country of which his interpreters had told him such strange tales. His decision was a wise one; but it required a stout heart and a strong will to reach it.

As soon as his own Indians had realized that he was steering again for the Cuban coast, with the palpable intention of resuming his explorations, they lost all control over themselves, and could scarcely speak from sheer distress. They repeated over and over again that the people of Bohio were atrocious monsters, dog-headed and one-eyed; that they were ferocious warriors, possessing superior weapons; that they butchered and devoured all the captives they took in war, and made constant raids into the other countries of Cuba and the adjacent islands, for the sole purpose of securing victims. These inhuman creatures, the interpreters said, belonged to a tribe called *Canibals*, — the name since applied to all man-eating races by their more fastidious fellow-men. But the more his Indians talked, the more the Admiral desired to visit these extraordinary people. If they were well armed, as his interpreters alleged, they must be more advanced in the arts than the other nations he had met; and moreover, according to the Venetian, such a race of one-eyed cynocephali inhabited some of the islands near Cipango, and he wished to see whether these "Canibals" were not the same savages. So he headed straight for a prominent cape on the coast; but light baffling winds and strong currents kept him off shore, and finally drove him so far back to the west that again he found himself near the entrance to Our Lady's Sea. Here a landlocked harbor, which he had not before perceived, offered so desirable an anchorage that he decided to put in there and await a favorable wind for resuming his eastward journey. He remained for three days in this port, exploring its surroundings, and finding that it surpassed any he had yet seen for convenience and situation. The country around was fertile, abounding in palms and other beautiful trees; and a large stream entered the head of the harbor, rushing down from the mountains above with much violence and noise. On the flanks of these mountains grew extensive forests of noble pines and oaks, so tall and straight that they would furnish masts and timbers for all the ships of Spain. Among the pebbles in the bed of the stream he picked up stones which were veined with gold, — "like those I have found in the Tagus," he says, — and others seemed to be ores of iron and silver; all of which, being worn smooth by the water, he inferred must have been brought down by the floods from the range above. The sight of so magnificent a harbor surrounded by so rich a country, and especially the abundance of materials for ship-building, seems to have acted as a partial antidote against his chagrin at Martin Alonzo's disloyalty. He writes on the 25th: —

"It has pleased Our Lord on this voyage to lead me always from what is good to what is better; so that everything I have thus far discovered has been superior to what preceded it, whether it be lands and forests, or harbors and streams, or plants and fruits and flowers, or the people themselves; all of which things are different in each place from what they were in the others."

To this favored spot, when he took formal possession, he gave the name of St. Catherine's Port, having reached it on the eve of the festival of that saint.

XVI.

ALPHA AND OMEGA.

ON the morning of the 26th of November the fleet left St. Catherine's and proceeded eastward along the coast. The magnificent panorama of lofty mountains, luxuriant forests, deep harbors, and crystal streams which unfolded hour by hour filled the Admiral with enthusiasm. "It was a glory to see it all," he writes; and several times he came to anchor and landed in the boats to inspect some notably good port or enter the mouth of a river larger than its fellows. Off to the southeast rose two headlands remarkable for their altitude even in that region of towering summits. One of these peaks, he understood from his interpreters, was on the mainland of Cuba; the other was on the island of Bohio. This information caused him no little perplexity; for the natives seemingly conferred this latter appellation with bewildering impartiality on every fresh district they caught sight of. Originally it was indeed referred to as an island to the southeast; but later it had been a province of Asia adjoining that of Cuba, and on the 13th of this month he had even been shown the chain of mountains separating Bohio from the latter province. Since then he had supposed that he was sailing along the coast of this country, for his interpreters had accounted for their alarm by making him this statement; but now they pointed it out to him as an island still in the remote distance, and left him completely in the dark as to what the region was which he was now exploring. There was little assistance to be had from his Indians just then in determining his locality; for whenever he spoke to them about the coast or its inhabitants they turned pale and shook with fright, although he made light of their tales and tried to laugh away their fears. In this uncertainty he watched the shore attentively for any appearance of towns or cities; but the only signs of population which he found were the remains of fires at some of the landings which he made. He accounted satisfactorily for this absence of settlements by supposing that the population of this province, whatever it was, lived farther inland among the mountains, where they would be secure from the invasion of the ferocious Canibals. For his own part he began to doubt that the latter were the monstrosities they were pictured by the interpreters. Their name, he fancied, gave him a clew both as to their race and nature. *Can*-ibals; what more evident than that they were the warriors of the Khan, that Bohio was part of his dominions whether island or province, and that the fears of the timid and defenceless people of the other islands had exaggerated these resistless soldiers into demons of inhuman shape? For the time being this solution seemed to reconcile at least a part of the perplexing contradictions of his interpreters. Dependent as he was upon exchange of signs for the greater part of his information, the Admiral's conception of any people or place other than these before his eyes was liable to alter widely from day to day; and this gives to the working of his mind an appearance of fickleness which it was far from possessing. He was sure that in good time he should find Cathay and the Court of the Great Khan. He was convinced that Cuba was the mainland of Asia, although his mind was open to correction in favor of its being Japan upon the production of sufficient evidence. As to the other provinces or islands he visited and heard of, his impressions might have to be modified by circumstances; but this did not affect his general ideas as to where he was, or diminish his confidence that sooner or later all would result as he had hoped. Meanwhile the knowledge that he was certainly adding each day fresh territories of richest promise to the dominions of his sovereigns gave him a contentment and satisfaction which served to curb his impatience at not finding immediately the golden treasures he was seeking.

At last, on the 27th, a large village was seen situated near the mouth of a broad stream ; and this the Admiral set out to visit as being the most imposing settlement thus far encountered in his cruise. As the Spaniards approached the shore in their boats, the whole population lined the river-bank, crying out at the top of their voices and brandishing their spears. Some of the sailors who had picked up a few words of the language called to them that they should not be afraid, as the strangers were their friends ; but no sooner had the first few men leaped ashore and started toward the savages than the entire tribe broke for the woods and disappeared. The seamen visited the huts, but found nothing of interest or value therein and upon hearing their report the Admiral ordered the boats to return, and resumed his voyage. Later on in the day they found themselves off the entrance to a deep bay from whose shores an undulating plain of wide extent swept inland to the base of the blue mountains surrounding it on all sides.[1] Winding across its surface could be traced the course of several considerable rivers, while here and there columns of smoke arose, as if marking the sites of towns and villages. Enchanted with the prospect before him, Colon anchored close to the beach and went on shore, to meet the natives if possible and establish friendly relations with them. No Indians could be found, although the condition of the cabins and cultivated grounds which were discovered near by indicated that their owners had left them only recently. Continuing up the river in his barge, the Admiral found at every turn fresh cause for admiration and delight. Even Our Lady's Sea he was forced to admit, exquisitely beautiful as it was, lacked the varied attractions of this favored locality. As he was rowed along he called the attention of his companions re-

[1] The port of Baracoa, near the easternmost extremity of Cuba. It well deserves all the praises lavished by Colon on the beauty of its surroundings.

peatedly to the marvellous vistas which opened in every direction.

"Have mortal eyes ever beheld the like, think you, Señores?" he asked in his delight. "Were I to endeavor to convey to their Majesties even an imperfect idea of these enchanting scenes, a thousand tongues would not suffice to relate their charms, nor would my hand be capable of describing even an inconsiderable part."

These outbursts of pleasure and appreciation, amounting often to positive glee over the natural beauties of the new lands he was visiting, are constantly encountered in Colon's diary. They are, as we have already seen in several instances, often accompanied by a comparison with other landscapes in the older world which had attracted his admiration in earlier years; and not infrequently a shrewd inference is drawn from the differences which distinguish the two localities associated in his mind. That his imaginative faculty should have been so extremely susceptible and yet that in all emergencies he should have been so immediately the man of action and quick resource, is one of the many interesting contradictions in the character of this extraordinary individual. At the present time, as he ascended the river, leisurely inspecting one and the other bank, he remarked a grove of fruit-trees so regular in their growth that he judged it to be a cultivated orchard, and, under a palm-thatched shed hard by, an immense canoe which astonished him by its size. These he took to be evidences that the people of the region were more advanced both in agriculture and the mechanical arts than any before met with, and on returning to his ships he planned to make an earnest attempt to hold communication with them. Fortune favored his design apparently; for a week of bad weather followed, during which the fleet was unable to leave its anchorage. Availing themselves of the opportunity, the Admiral and his men made repeated excursions in the neighborhood, and found every indication of a large and industrious population; but, try as they might, they failed to come upon any of the natives for several days. That the people were there, was evident; but they succeeded in avoiding the white men with singular dexterity. A party of sailors who had gone ashore to wash their clothes and afterward pushed on into the forest, reached a village of some importance situated at a distance from the shore; but as they emerged from the trees, the savages took to flight, and when the Spaniards entered the houses they found no one left. Another day several of the crew arrived at a native settlement only to see the usual exodus take place as they appeared. On this occasion they did succeed in overtaking an old man whose years reduced his speed to that of the armed white men; but after presenting him with some trinkets they let him go, much to the annoyance of the Admiral, who rated them soundly for not bringing their prisoner to where the interpreters could converse with him. Possibly the seamen thought he was no proper companion for good Christians, for in one of the cabins of this same hamlet they found a human head hanging in a basket from a rafter. This they brought to the Admiral, supposing that it was all that remained of the last captive taken by the guileless inhabitants of this happy land. Their commander, however, was not inclined to believe in the existence of man-eaters, and contended that the head was that of a chief or principal man thus preserved as a token of veneration; "because," as he says, "very many people live together in each of these houses, and they must be all relatives descended from the same stock." The subsequent discovery in other towns of a number of these detached polls was a strain upon this charitable theory; but it was doubtless correct, for we are told that such was the habit among some of the West Indian tribes, and we still find it practised among the scattered nomads of the remoter regions of the Amazon and Orinoco. With this first head the Spaniards found also a great cake of wax, which proved a more welcome offering to their leader, — "for where there is wax," he writes, "there must be a thousand other good things." [1]

---

[1] A note by Las Casas on the margin of Colon's diary says that this wax must have come from Yucatan, as there was none in Cuba. There certainly were bees, though, as we shall presently see.

On the fourth day of his enforced stay in this harbor the Admiral despatched a party of eight armed men and two interpreters to scout into the interior and make a fresh effort to establish relations with the natives. This detachment visited several hamlets, and reported that the country was everywhere well cultivated and thickly populated, but that they had failed to have speech with any of the people. The houses were not only deserted, they said, but stripped bare of all their contents. It was obvious that the inhabitants had a mortal terror of the mysterious visitors who had landed upon their coast. At one place the scouts had come suddenly upon a group of four Indians digging over a field with pointed sticks. The instant they observed the Spaniards they dropped their rude implements and darted into the woods at a speed which it was hopeless for their pursuers to attempt. The scouts also reported that on the banks of the river, carefully housed under a palm-thatched roof, they had seen another great canoe, which was over sixty feet long, and would hold one hundred and fifty people. It was hollowed out of a single trunk, and smoothed and finished with astonishing exactness. The description of this huge craft excited the Admiral's professional interest, and on the following day he was gratified by an experience of his own. He had started out with several of his men to explore one of the several streams which flowed into the bay. Some distance above its mouth he reached a small cove, in which were lying five of these immense canoes, carefully drawn up side by side on the beach under the shelter of the dense foliage of the forest. From this spot a path led through the woods, and on following it Colon came to a roomy and well-built shed, under which lay a sixth huge boat, as large as a galley of seventeen benches. This cove seemed to him to be a sort of dockyard where the canoes were launched after being finished in the shed near by; and he was greatly impressed by the skill and intelligence displayed in the making of these vessels. "It was a pleasure to see their workmanship and gracefulness," he writes.

On the same day — the last of his detention in this port — he succeeded finally in meeting the natives, only to learn that they were in no wise different from those hitherto seen. He had climbed to the top of a high hill to get a better view of the country, and there had found a hamlet, whose inhabitants were taken too much by surprise to escape at once. As they started to run, one of the interpreters called out that there was no reason for fear, as the white men were benefactors, not enemies. At this some of them halted, and on being offered a handful of presents were hugely pleased, and shouted to their fleeing companions to come back. The Admiral held out beads and such stuff in exchange for the spears with which all the men were armed; and the readiness with which they surrendered their weapons convinced him that they were not very desperate warriors. Their arms were only long staves of heavy wood hardened in the fire, of the same sort as the tribes of Amazonia still carry. From the way they had all started to run, Colon affirmed that ten Spaniards could put to flight a whole army of such foes. That his estimate of their courage was not unduly contemptuous, was almost immediately proven. There was little in the village to interest the visitors; but in one of the neatest cabins the Admiral observed that instead of a single large apartment the interior was disposed into many small chambers, constructed in a singular fashion, and having suspended from the ceiling over them numbers of shells and other objects. Thinking that this might be a temple or religious house, he made signs asking if it were so, whereupon the Indians clambered up and dislodged some of the ornaments, which they pressed him to accept. He took a part of their gifts as curiosities, and after repeating his expressions of good-will started to return to his boats. On the way he sent two or three men back a short distance to fetch honey from a tree which he had noticed, and with the rest of his party entered the boats and shoved off from the bank. While lying thus waiting for his men, a great throng of the natives suddenly appeared, rushing down to the water's edge close to where the boats were riding. They were painted red all over, wore bunches of feathers plaited into their hair, and carried bundles of light javelins in their hands. One of them waded out to the stern of the Admiral's barge, and made a long harangue. This was lost upon the Spaniards, of course; but they noticed that at intervals the savages on the bank lifted their hands up to the skies and gave a mighty shout. Colon was of the opinion that they were saying how honored they were at the white men's visit, and indicating that the latter must have come from heaven; but his interpreters began to turn a sickly yellow, and trembling from head to foot implored him to row out into deep water, saying that the Indians proposed to kill them all, and were only making a speech before proceeding to do so. Finding that the Admiral would not move, one of the interpreters seized a cross-bow from a sailor and held it up before the crowd on shore, explaining that this was a magical weapon of the strangers, with which they could kill all the people in Cuba; then taking up a sword, he flourished it toward them, declaring that by its means the white men could cut off all their heads at once. At this threat the whole tribe turned to run away; but the Admiral held out beads and other presents, and leaping ashore went boldly to them, motioning that they should give him their weapons in exchange. Pacified by his attitude, they now returned and surrounded both him and the boats, freely parting with all they had in trade for any trifle the Spaniards proffered. So brisk was the traffic that when the sailors had exhausted their beads and gew-gaws they did a thriving business with fragments of bread and bits of a turtle's shell which they broke into scraps. When the honey-seekers rejoined them the Spaniards bade farewell to their now disarmed adversaries, and returned to the ships. The Admiral in particular was surprised at the conduct of the savages, and did not know which to hold in the lower esteem, — the crowd of Indians who had fled at the sight of a sword shaken by the terrified interpreter, or this person himself, who was still shivering from fear, although the savages were out of view and he himself was in a place of safety. "And he was a tall fellow, and muscular withal," Colon writes in evident disgust.

On the morning of December 4 a light wind sprang up from a favoring quarter, and the two vessels left their pleasant anchorage in the beautiful harbor of Puerto Santo (the Holy Port), as the Admiral had named it, — whether from the supposed temple near by or from a kindly remembrance of the distant Portuguese island where his wife's father had been governor in long-past days we cannot know. The wind held fair; and all day long the little squadron held its course eastward along the coast, passing new ports and rivers and steering from cape to cape as long as daylight lasted. Through the night he lay hove to off one of these commanding headlands, anxious to continue his cruise by daylight, so as to examine with care the whole extent of coast. At sunrise on the 5th he resumed his easterly voyage for eight or ten miles toward a steep and lofty promontory which closed the coast-line in that direction. On reaching this point and rounding it, he saw that beyond the coast ran no longer east, but trending for a short distance south, made a sharp turn backward, and stretched on indefinitely to the southwest. This was clearly the end, at least to the east, of the land he had been following. Whether it was the eastern point of Asia or of Japan, he could not satisfactorily determine. The interpreters constantly referred to Cuba as an island; but he had sailed for such an unheard of distance along the coast that he could scarcely believe it to be any other than the proper continent of Asia. Now that he had reached this abrupt termination of the shore, his faith was somewhat shaken as to its being *terra firma*, and he resumed in his diary the use of the name Juana, which he had given to it as an island. In this doubt as to the true character of Cuba he continued during the rest of this voyage and after his return to Spain; but on his second voyage to the Indies in the following year he reached the positive conclusion that it was the veritable Asian mainland, and in this conviction remained to the day of his death.

Meantime, as he debated the problem, the wind was bearing him along the eastern face of the glorious island toward the noble headland we now call Cape Maysi. Whether to pursue the new trend of this same coast and follow it into the south and west, or to make direct for the faint blue outline in the eastern sky where the interpreters again insisted that Bohio lay, was a dilemma which, he records, gave him much concern. To go northeast in search of the once vaunted Babeque was out of the question; for the prevailing winds would not permit. After much deliberation he decided to steer for Bohio, reserving the continuation of his Cuban cruise for another opportunity. Altering his course, therefore, he stood for the land to the east, with all sails set to a favoring gale, and the lofty mountains of the beautiful region he was leaving astern melting little by little into the hazy distance as those ahead gained form and substance.

The cape which lay farthest toward the rising sun on the coast now rapidly dropping below the horizon, he called Alpha and Omega; because it appeared to be the first extremity of the mainland as it was approached from the Old World, and the last to be seen by those who left the New. In the stormy years of his later life Colon must have looked back with heartfelt longing at the weeks of unalloyed delight which followed his advent to the wonderful western world, and yearned to be again drifting with his little vessels along the mountain-crowned coast which he had taken for the empire of Cathay. He wrote in his diary while lying wind-bound in the Holy Port: —

" It is beyond dispute, your Majesties, that where such lands exist there must be an infinite variety of valuable products: but I am not stopping long in any one place, as I desire to visit as many countries as possible, in order to give an account of them to your Highnesses. Besides, I do not know the language of these people, and they do not understand me, nor do I or any one with me understand them. These Indians I am carrying with me as interpreters very often mistake one thing for another, and I cannot trust them, as they have many times tried to run away. Nevertheless, if it pleases Our Lord, I will see as much as I can, and little by little shall go on learning and comprehending what they say; and I will make the people in my service acquire this language, for I have observed that thus far all the natives use the same tongue.

"And I certify to your Majesties that I do not believe that beneath the sun there can be any lands which are superior to these in fertility. in the moderation of heat and cold, or in the abundance of plentiful and wholesome waters. These are not in any respect like the streams on the coast of Guinea, which are all pestilential; for up to the present time, God be praised, out of all my people there is not a single one who has had so much as a headache, — except one old man who suffered from a trouble he has had all his life, and he was well again at the end of two days. And in saying this I speak of all three ships.

"In the interior of this country I believe that great cities are to be found, and a population without number, and many articles of great value, and that both with those countries I have already discovered and the others I hope to find before returning to Castile, all Christendom will establish a commerce, and especially Spain, to whom they must all be subject. And I venture to say that your Highnesses should not permit any foreigner to trade or set his foot here except Catholic Christians, since the object and beginning of this discovery were the spread and glory of the Catholic religion; and that no one should be allowed to come to this part of the world who is not a good Christian."

Such were the estimates Colon had formed of Cuba and the plans he made for its future. Their Majesties were careful enough to see that "no foreigner set his foot" in their new dominions; but as to the other recommendations of the Admiral they were wasted words. Even in those times there was no lack of critics who looked upon the discoverer as a sentimental enthusiast. The gold he found was useful to hire soldiers and buy materials for French or Italian wars. As for the "spread and glory of the Catholic religion," — *paciencia !*

The sun was getting low when the ships drew near enough to the coast of what we now call Hayti for the Admiral to distinguish the grand mountain ranges and broad savannas which make this island only little less fair to the eyes than its lordly neighbor to the west. Steering for the nearest cape, the one we know as Mole St. Nicholas, he reached the coast too late to anchor that night. The purple shadows of the distant summits had already given way to the darker hues of approaching night; and over the level prairies, which but a few moments since were aglow with the gorgeous coloring of sunset, the deepening gloom of the hurried twilight had settled. The "Niña" was able, with much caution, to run in close to shore and make her way to a secure anchorage beneath the headland; but the flagship stood off and on, waiting for the light of day before following her consort's lead. In the morning, as a consequence, she was several leagues away from the point where the "Niña" lay, and the Admiral made haste to rejoin his companion. Going ashore early in the day, he took possession of his new discovery, calling the cape and harbor where he was St. Nicholas, after the saint on whose festival he had reached the land. To the other points and bays which he had seen he gave such names as his fancy or that of his associates dictated, — the cape of the Star, of the Elephant, and so on. The country near his landing-place he found to be well under cultivation. The forests were not so dense as those of Cuba; and among their trees were many he thought resembled those of Spain, while others he believed would be found to produce spices and precious gums. The plain which spread away inland to the foot of the mountains resembled to his fancy the famous *vega* of Cordova in Castile, and the thick turf of grass and flowers with which it was carpeted increased the likeness. The nights, too, were cooler than those of Cuba, and the climate more nearly approximated that of October in Spain. In fact, so strongly was he reminded of the country of his adoption by all he saw in this latest landfall that he christened it Hispaniola, or Little Spain, — a name destined to be as famous for the wealth and surpassing fertility of its territory as for the misery and sufferings of its unhappy population. As yet the natives had only been seen at a distance; but from the swarm of canoes which appeared as the day wore on, the Admiral judged that the country must be thickly inhabited. This opinion was confirmed by the large number of smoke columns visible by daylight and of fires at night, which he descried in the interior, and which he knew not whether to attribute to the existence of villages in the places where they were seen, or to consider as signals lighted by the people near the sea to warn their allies inland of the approach of enemies. His experience in the Moorish war and along the Barbary coast inclined him to accept the latter explanation.

For the next five days the ships sailed leisurely eastward from Cape St. Nicholas, examining the spacious harbors of the northern shores of Hayti (or, rather, of Hispaniola, as we should call it hereafter) and exploring the country adjacent to them. To a large island lying some ten or twelve miles north of the main coast he gave the name of Tortugas, from the shoals of turtles thereabouts encountered, — a spot afterward known to history as the chosen home of the buccaneers and freebooters of the Spanish Main. Each day of his progress increased Colon's impression of the likeness between this lesser Spain and the greater one beyond the Atlantic; and he remarks that even the fish the sailors caught in their nets and the birds they heard singing in the groves were like those of the old country. Wishing to learn something of the natives, he sent six of his stoutest and most intelligent men, whom he armed well, to push a few leagues inland and see what traces they could find of town or hamlet. They reported, on their return, that they had found no village at all, but only a few scattered huts with the vestiges of fires at many places on their route. The whole district was well cultivated, they said, and broad paths traversed it in every direction, so that a large population must be somewhere near.

The Admiral was eager to continue his course along the shores of Hispaniola, in order to learn its character and extent with as little delay as might be; but the winds held him prisoner for several days in a harbor opposite Tortugas, which he had designated as Port Conception on reaching it the 7th of the month. His Indian interpreters, either to terrify him, or because they knew no better themselves, or perhaps from a misconception of their signs and broken Spanish, now perplexed him mightily with their description of his present locality. Bohio was no longer an island, and

Hispaniola was not Bohio at all. The real region of that name was on the southern side of Hispaniola, and was vastly larger than Cuba, — so great, indeed, that the ships could never sail around it. It was from this more remote country, it now seemed, that the Canibals were wont to come to harry the islands and steal the inhabitants. Hispaniola was an island by itself, and was named Aiti or Hayti. As for Babeque, it was somewhere off beyond Tortuga, and was very great and rich. What they meant we cannot hope to ascertain, interesting as it would be to know the extent to which any acquaintance with geography was common among the natives. It is possible that Bohio was the mainland of South America, and the Canibals were the Caribs of Guiana and the Windward Islands; or it may have been Yucatan and Mexico. Any of these could have been, and no doubt were reached by the great canoes of Cuba and the islands. Such boats still make voyages only little less adventurous. Possibly, again, this name may have indicated San Domingo, the eastern portion of Hispaniola, where certainly gold abounded and cannibalism was and still is practised. Babeque may have been Jamaica, or one of the Lesser Antilles, or perhaps, as he had surmised, only a fiction of the simple Indians to get the Admiral to go back nearer to their native Guanahani. At all events, it is apparent that he understood as little what they meant as we do, and, like a wise man, determined to stay where he was and explore the magnificent domain on which he had landed. Later on, he says, he might search for the other regions of which his interpreters spoke so confusedly, if time and the winds should permit.

XVII.

HIS UNCLAD MAJESTY.

ON the 12th of December the Admiral went on shore with his officers, and set up a tall cross at the entrance of Port Conception, "as a token," he writes to his sovereigns, "that your Highnesses hold this country for your own; but chiefly as a memorial of Our Lord Jesus Christ and for the honor of the Christian religion." After this ceremony he again despatched three of his men inland to make another effort to find the natives. These scouts came upon a large body of Indians, and hailed them in such words of their language as they knew; but the whole crowd started off at full speed in mortal terror, so that the Spaniards returned baffled to the shore. On their way back to the ships they overtook a canoe which had come upon the vessels unawares on rounding a point of land hard by. Paralyzed with astonishment at first, the savages had quickly thrown themselves into the water and swum to the beach, leaving one woman behind, who fell into the sailors' hands. When she was brought to the flagship the Admiral was delighted to learn that she spoke the same language as his interpreters, and he directed them to tell her of the strangers' generosity and goodness. After she had lost somewhat of her fright he put a gayly colored robe upon her, — for she was before dressed mainly in smiles and tears, with a bit of gold through her nose for ornament, — and having given her a quantity of trinkets, sent her on shore with an escort of armed men and several of the interpreters.

The woman was by no means anxious to return to her people, for when they reached land she declared that she wished to remain on the ships with the Indian women she had seen there; but at length she started out for her village, with the escort accompanying as a guard of honor. Late at night these men returned to the flagship, and reported that they had found the distance so great that they judged it best not to go too far into the country; but that the woman had continued her journey in high contentment, saying she would tell her people of the kind treatment she had received, and that on another day they would come in numbers to visit the white men.

The next morning the Admiral sent a detachment of nine stout men with an interpreter to push on to the settlement and persuade the inhabitants to hasten their coming. This party found the town to be some ten miles from the sea, situated on the banks of a wide and picturesque stream, which flowed through a vast and fertile plain. To their eyes the luxuriant beauty of this broad expanse surpassed that of the vaunted meadows of Cordova " by as much as day excels the night;" and they quickened their pace on sighting the houses. There were apparently at least a thousand of these in the place, with a population of quite three times as many men, besides the women and children; but no sooner did the little band of Spaniards approach than every living creature in the village started off on a mad stampede. The interpreter pursued them, calling out that the strangers were not Canibals, but friendly beings come down from the skies, bringing rare treasures with them as gifts. The sound of their own speech, with the inducements it conveyed, caused a few of the runaways to halt and then draw slowly near to the visitors. As usual, the example was contagious, and in a moment the Spaniards were surrounded by an awe-struck throng of a thousand or more, all with their hands placed upon their heads in token of submission, and quaking with dread of the possible fate awaiting them. A small expenditure of presents and kind words speedily reassured them, and they then led the visitors into the best houses, where a feast of cassava bread, yuccas, fish, and whatever else the native larder afforded was promptly spread out. The interpreter had heard the Admiral say that he would like to secure some good parrots, and he now said to the savages that the chief or lord of these mysterious white men desired to have some of those gaudy birds. In a twinkling the Indians rushed into their cabins round about, and brought out a perfect flock of painted chatterers, pressing the Spaniards to take them, and refusing to accept any payment. In the midst of this amicable intercourse a loud commotion was heard some distance away; and the visiting party were alarmed to see a great body of savages approaching in orderly array, as though bent on hostile purpose. Happily it proved to be only another troop of friendly natives, escorting in triumph the husband of the woman so kindly treated by the Admiral, who was come to thank these marvellous white people for the attentions shown his wife and the magnificent presents they had given her, — whereby no doubt he had been raised to an envied pitch of affluence among his neighbors. New courtesies and compliments now ensued, so greatly to the delight of the Indians that when the Spaniards at last indicated that they must set out on their return march their savage hosts begged them to remain at least until the next day, promising to give them many beautiful things if they would do so, and saying that runners had been sent up into the mountains to collect the best of all they had for the visitors. On arriving at the ships the scouting party made a graphic report of their experiences to the Admiral, assuring him that not only was the country the richest and most attractive they had ever seen, but the inhabitants were more intelligent and handsomer than the best in the other islands. As for the fruits and forests, birds and flowers, waters and air, the choicest regions of Spain itself could not produce their equals.

Curious to examine for himself the district of which his men had spoken so enthusiastically, the Admiral sailed from Port Conception on the 14th, and after a day of contrary winds, during which he touched at Tortuga, came to anchor on the 15th at the mouth of the river which watered the great plain his party had explored. The current was so strong his seamen could not row against it when he attempted to ascend the stream in his boats, and, after towing them for a short distance along the banks, he was compelled to abandon them altogether and pursue his way on foot. For this reason he failed to reach the large town visited by his scouts; but he had a good view of the broad savanna, and remarked the sites of several important settlements farther inland toward the mountains. He was as much charmed with the region as his men had been, and christened it the Valle del Paraiso (or Vale of Paradise), on account of its abounding fertility and exquisite scenery. The river winding through it he called the Guadalquivir, since it reminded him so much of the one of that name which irrigates the lovely country about Cordova in Old Spain. As for the natives, they fled as soon as they saw the strangers; and this, with the many columns of smoke he observed in the interior, confirmed his former belief that they were accustomed to the incursions of enemies, and had a code of signals for announcing the arrival of invaders upon their shores.

At midnight the ships again set sail, following the coast in search of some principal town where a convenient landing might be made. Toward morning they overhauled a single Indian paddling along in the same direction. The Admiral was attracted by the skill and courage with which the savage handled his frail craft in the heavy sea which was then running, and took both him and his canoe on board. The change was a welcome one to the Indian, for he was feasted on bread and honey, and received many presents besides; so that when the vessels came to anchor in a deep and convenient harbor about five or six leagues from Port Conception, he hurried on shore in his canoe to tell his countrymen a generous tale as to the wonders of the white men. Near the anchorage was a large settlement, which seemed to be but recently built, as the houses all were fresh and new; and soon after the Spaniard's arrival the natives gathered on the beach to the number of five hundred or more. Many of them came out in their canoes to the vessels, and were taken on board and made much of; while the crowd on shore watched the extraordinary crafts which had entered their quiet waters, and eagerly interrogated all of their neighbors who had ventured to visit them.

In a short time the Admiral noticed a young man come down to the beach accompanied by a number of older men. From the honor paid him by the other natives the interpreters declared that he must be the king of that region, and the older companions his counsellors. It was with no small degree of disappointment that Colon saw that the youthful monarch was, save for an elaborate coat of paint, dressed only in the total absence of costume affected by the natives of those islands; but he none the less determined to do his duty to royalty, and accordingly sent Don Rodrigo Escovedo on shore with an interpreter bearing a handsome tribute for his Majesty. Don Rodrigo, as became a dignified Spaniard and an officer of the Crown, discharged his mission with as much state and propriety as though the savage before him wore as many clothes as the Pope of Rome. Bowing low before him, the emissary presented his gifts, and asked the young prince to deign to receive them from the Viceroy of the Indies as representative of their Most Catholic Majesties of Spain. The interpreter explained at greater length to the king that the strangers came from heaven, where their own sovereigns ruled, and were travelling among these islands in search of the yellow metal which the Indians wore in their noses, but the white men wanted for some less apparent purpose. Just now they were anxious to reach the country of Babeque, where, they had been told, a great quantity of this precious material was to be had, and on their way thither had visited Hispaniola, and wished to make friends with the ruler of that beautiful country and take him under their powerful protection. The king received the presents with a self-possession and decorum surprising in one who displayed so scanty a wardrobe, and after consulting with the old men who attended him, replied that he was pleased to hear all the interpreter had said; that the way to Babeque lay to the eastward, and there was indeed much gold in that land; in two or three days the strangers could get there; and if they wanted anything in his country, he would give it to them with very great readiness. With that he took his departure, followed by the old men carrying the presents. "He used very few words," the Admiral writes, as though admiring the reticence of this savage potentate. On the afternoon of the same day the young king returned to the beach with his retinue, and came on board the flagship. The Admiral showed him every token of respect and honor, taking him into his own cabin, and setting before him a plentiful repast of the best the ship afforded. The king only tasted the things offered to him, and then passed them on to his counsellors and those who were with them to dispose of finally. The Admiral tried to explain to him that the sovereigns of Castile were the most powerful princes in the world, and to impress him with an adequate idea of their grandeur and the extent of their dominions. But nothing would convince his guest that the strangers were mortal beings; to him their home was in the skies, and the great monarchs the white chief talked about were the rulers of the celestial regions.

In the morning of the next day, when a party of sailors went on shore to cast their nets they were overwhelmed with attentions and gifts by the natives. Among other things brought by the Indians was a number of unusually long arrows pointed at the ends with sharp bits of hard wood, which they explained had been used by the ferocious Canibals when they last had made a raid on the island. The Spaniards noticed that some of the Indians had what seemed to be holes in the fleshy parts of their bodies over which the skin had grown in ghastly scars, and they inquired how such terrible wounds had been caused. To their amazement they were told that these men had been captured by the Canibals, who had cut out the pieces from their flesh at one time and another and eaten them; evidently intending to devour their prisoners by mouthfuls instead of disposing of them at once. The unfortunate captives had escaped; but the terrible cicatrices of course remained. In recording this story the Admiral laconically adds, "This I do not credit;" and we do not blame him for his lack of faith. The people of this neighborhood possessed no weapons of their own, not even the rude spears which the Spaniards had elsewhere seen. They seemed to have no idea of fighting. When an enemy appeared they ran away and remained in hiding until he had left their coast, — a simple and easy method of resisting all invasion. They wore small ornaments of gold in their ears and noses, — sometimes a tiny grain or nugget, sometimes a thin plate; and these they would gladly surrender for a few beads or the brass tip of a lace-string. One old man, who was apparently a person of authority among them, wore about his neck a plate of thin gold as large as one's hand. When he saw the avidity with which the white men traded for even the smallest pieces of the metal, he went into his cabin and broke his ornament into little fragments; then bringing them out a few at a time, he bartered them off one by one, thus getting far more beads for his piece of gold than if he had exchanged it as a whole. This greatly amused the Admiral, and he remarks that the old chief's cleverness shows that these natives were more intelligent than most he had met. In the afternoon he took an interpreter and went on shore with the royal notary, Escovedo, and Diego de Arana, the alguacil, to collect as much gold as he could from the savages, and learn, if possible, more about the place from which it came. As they were conversing with the old chief who had shown the genius for trade, a large canoe arrived from the island of Tortuga, with a crew of forty or fifty men. As the boat drew near the beach, all the natives present squatted down on the ground as a sign of peace to the new-comers; and as soon as the latter came on shore, they did likewise. This formality over, the old chief rose and made a furious speech to them, ordering them back to the canoe, and telling them to be gone without delay. This the Tortugans did without remonstrance;

the old man following them to the edge of the beach, and splashing water over them to hasten their movements. Not content with this, he picked up some stones and hurled them after the intruders, pressing one into Diego de Arana's hand and urging him to do the same, which the latter prudently refused to do. When the canoe was gone the Admiral learned that in Tortuga there was more gold than among the people of the village, because the smaller island was nearer Babeque, whence the gold was said to come. Evidently the old chief did not want the other islanders to have any share in the good things of the white strangers. All this made the Admiral believe that the mines from which the gold was derived could not be far off, and revived his hopes of soon finding them. In answer to his questions, the old chief explained that the gold country was only four days' journey from where they were, and promised to get the Spaniards a large quantity on the next day. "I do not believe that he can get us much gold," the Admiral writes, "for the mines are not situated here; but I may be able to learn more exactly where they are." Accordingly he decided to wait one day more at his present anchorage, to discover if possible the location of the mines.

The next day, December 18, was the festival of Our Lady of the O,[1] or of the Annunciation, as we call it, — one held in very particular esteem by the maritime nations of Southern Europe. In honor of the occasion the ships were dressed with all their flags, and the officers and crews donned their holiday wardrobes and carried their brightest arms. From time to time salutes were fired from the small cannon of the vessels, and the Spaniards remarked with satisfaction the wonder and consternation which the discharge of the artillery caused among the natives who thronged the beach. Early in the forenoon, in the midst of these pious and politic rejoicings, the young king made his appearance, carried in a litter on the shoulders of four bearers, and followed by an escort of two hundred of his subjects. With him came

[1] So called from a ring of rocks, near Segovia, where a chapel was built dedicated to the Virgin.

his counsellors as before, and also his brother and his little son, the latter borne on the shoulders of a stalwart Indian. Entering one of the large canoes, the king came directly on board the flagship, and ran quickly aft to the cabin where the Admiral was at breakfast. Colon would have risen as he saw his guest enter; but the king sat down by his side, making signs that he should not rise or disturb himself in any wise. The scene that followed cannot be better told than in the Admiral's own words: —

"I thought that the king would like to eat some of our dishes, and directed that he should be served at once. When he entered the cabin he had made signs to all his people that they should remain outside; and this they did with the greatest promptness and obedience in the world, all sitting down on the deck except two old men whom I took to be his counsellor and tutor. These entered the cabin and sat down at the king's feet. When I set the dishes before him he took only a little taste as we do for ceremony, and then he sent them to his people, all of whom ate a little. The same he did with the wine, touching his lips to it and then giving it to the others. All this he did with a wonderful dignity, using very few words, and those, as far as I could judge, appropriate and full of sense. The old men at his feet watched his lips and spoke with him, repeating all he said with a very great respect. After having eaten, one of his attendants brought him a belt, made very much like those of Spain, but in a different kind of work, which he took and then handed to me, with two pieces of gold beaten very thin. I believe they find but little of this metal in these parts, although I am sure they live near to where it grows, and that there is an abundance of it. I noticed that the king was attracted by a coverlet which was spread over my bed; and this I gave to him, with some really handsome amber beads I wore around my neck, and a pair of red shoes and a jar of orange water. With these presents he was so delighted that it was a pleasure to watch him, and he and his counsellors showed great regret that they could not talk with me nor I with them. Nevertheless, I understood that he told me that in case I had need of anything, the whole country was at my service. I sent for a rosary of mine to which, as a token, I had attached a golden *excelente*[1] on

---

[1] An old Spanish coin worth about fifteen dollars. Las Casas says that he had seen and handled this very coin and rosary after Columbus's death, — apparently in San Domingo.

which are stamped the likenesses of your Majesties, and this I showed to him; telling him that your Highnesses, as I had said the other day, ruled over the best portion of the whole world, and that no greater princes were in existence. I also showed him the Royal Standard and the banners of the Green Cross, and all this he admired mightily. He said to his counsellors that your Highnesses must surely be great rulers, since you had sent me so far from heaven without any fear; and many other things he said which I could not understand, but it was clear that all he saw astonished him."

When it began to grow late the king took his leave and started for shore, the Admiral showing him all the honors due a royal prince, and firing a salute as he left the flagship. On reaching land the king mounted again into his litter; his little son was perched on the shoulders of one of the chief men, and the train moved away on the road to the town where he lived, which was some twelve or fifteen miles off. Meantime his brother had come on board the flagship to make his own visit, and was treated with much respect, although no such distinguished honors were shown to him as had been lavished on the king. After satisfying his curiosity and receiving a number of presents, he also returned on shore and set out after the royal party. Some of the Spaniards who were wandering about in the village and its neighborhood met the cortège later in the day, as it was proceeding inland, and reported the details of the spectacle to the Admiral. In advance, they said, marched several of the native chiefs, each carrying one of the presents received by the king; one bore the bedquilt, another one red shoe, a third its mate, a fourth the jar of orange water, and so on. Behind these came the litter of the king, followed by part of the escort; then, after an interval, came the king's son, mounted on a chieftain's shoulders and accompanied by another detachment; then, some distance in the rear, the king's brother, walking along supported on either side, as a mark of dignity, by a chief holding an arm. The sailors also said that wherever they had gone they had found that the king had issued orders that they were to be feasted and treated with much honor by the natives; all of which gratified the Admiral exceedingly, as indicating that his prudent and considerate treatment of the Indians had borne the desired fruit.

One only regret marred his pleasure on this busy day. Among the old men, or counsellors, who had accompanied the king was a certain venerable chief who showed himself to be much more communicative than his royal master. This ancient told the Admiral that within a hundred leagues or so of Hispaniola were many islands where gold existed in dazzling abundance, one of them even being composed of solid gold! The natives of those islands, this veracious informant explained, obtained the metal by sifting it from the sands about them, and then melted it into bars or made a variety of figures with it, such as birds, animals, and so on; all of which he drew with his finger for the Admiral's better comprehension. On hearing of such a bewildering plenty of the coveted gold, the Admiral was sorely tempted to hold the old man captive and get him to serve as guide to those alluring regions; but he reflected that the seizure of a person so near the king would surely provoke the whole population, and so dismissed the idea from his mind. "If I only knew how to talk with him," the Admiral regretfully writes, "I would have asked him to go with me; and this I am sure he would have done, so friendly did he show himself to me and all the other Christians." As it was, he resolved to seek these newly mentioned countries as soon as he had finished examining the island where he was; and with this decision he dismissed the old counsellor, all unconscious of the dangerous distinction proposed for him. If we might hazard the conjecture, the old man may have been talking confusedly of the gold deposits of the mainland; for we know that the Chiriqui Indians of Darien had great quantities of treasure, and worked their gold into such figures as he described to the Admiral.

The Spaniards closed their day with an act of devotion befitting the festival they celebrated. Going on shore with a large company from both ships, the Admiral set up a great cross in the open square around which the chief houses of the village were built. Seeing the white men engaged in the work, the natives flocked to their assistance and aided them in every way they could; and when, the work completed, the Spaniards knelt down to worship the sacred emblem, the savages all followed their example, imitating exactly their motions and gestures, vastly to the satisfaction of the Admiral, who saw in their humility the augury of an easy conversion. So kind had been their reception of the Spaniards, and so gentle were their manners in every way, that he called this harbor the Puerto de Paz, or Port of Peace. He says, speaking of the natives in general:—

"All that they possess and think that we should like to have, these people bring to us; and this with a spirit so willing and contented that it is a marvel to see. Nor must any one say that this is because what they have is of little value; for whatever they own they give freely, without distinction of value,—pieces of gold as readily as gourds of water; and it is always easy to tell when a thing is given with a willing heart."[1]

Thirty years afterward there was not a corporal's guard of these "savages" alive. The "Christians" had starved and flogged and worked and tortured the whole race off the face of their noble island. There is no moral to such a tale: it is all the other way.

[1] Las Casas records an interesting custom of Columbus: "When any gold or other precious objects were brought him by any one, he entered into his oratory and knelt down, asking the bystanders to do likewise, and saying, 'Let us give thanks to Our Lord, who has made us worthy to discover such great treasures.'"

XVIII.

A GLOOMY CHRISTMAS.

WHILE sailing along the shores of Cuba and among the islands of Our Lady's Sea, the Admiral seems to have laid aside for the moment his eagerness to find at all costs the golden wealth of these fancied Indies, and abandoned himself to the mere delight of living amid such peaceful and enchanting scenes. Once arrived among the people of Hispaniola, however, the sight of their glittering ornaments, meagre and trifling as they seem to have been, revived all the ardor of his earlier intentions, and he was now as keen to reach the source of gold — or " the place where the gold grows," as he sometimes terms it — as he was when first he noticed the precious metal in the noses of the Indians of Guanahaní.

Leaving the Port of Peace on the night of the 18th of December, he was driven about in the channel between Tortuga and the main island until the evening of the 20th. Continuing then his coasting to the eastward with a favoring breeze, he passed several capes and harbors, and at sunset of that day anchored in a noble bay lying between lofty headlands and sheltered toward the sea by a little island. This being the vigil of St. Thomas, he christened the islet by that name and the port as well, while he called the bay the Sea of the Port of St. Thomas, so great was its extent and so many the islands scattered over its surface.[1] Here also a vast and fertile plain spread inland from the

[1] Now known as the Bay of Acul.

harbor to where the mountain-ranges formed a towering barrier about it on three sides. To the Spanish sailors these sierras appeared to be even loftier than the Peak of Teneriffe, although, unlike that awesome mount, they were covered to their summits with dense forests of gigantic trees. From the ships many settlements could be seen dotting the plain in the distance, while columns of smoke in the direction of the mountains bespoke the presence of others yet more remote. In this bay the vessels anchored and were soon visited by a canoe-load of Indians, who were treated with kindness and dismissed with gifts as usual.

On the following morning the Admiral took the small boats and went on shore. Two men who had been sent to a neighboring height to look for the nearest village reported that a little farther along the shore was a large town situated only a short distance back from the water. Thither the boats were rowed, and at their approach the natives gathered in crowds upon the beach, and indicated by their gestures where a landing should be made. They exhibited a good deal of trepidation, however, when the strangers drew near their waiting-place, and it was only after the interpreters had made their usual declarations and exhibited their offerings that the savages came down to the water's edge and mingled freely with the Spaniards. Their numbers increased at every moment; and as the new-comers arrived upon the scene they renewed the signs of welcome and astonishment with which the earlier arrivals had greeted their visitors. No sooner were the white men well on dry land than the natives brought them plentiful gifts of bread and other eatables, together with fresh water, both in gourds and in earthenware jars somewhat after the fashion of those used in Spain. This was the first pottery the Admiral had thus far encountered, and he remarks the incident as showing the advancing scale of civilization in these people. Like the inhabitants at the Port of Peace, they were gentle and liberal, possessing no weapons and handsome of face and figure. The Admiral sent a small party inland to visit the town while he and his companions remained at the landing and conversed with the crowd there as well as they could. During this intercourse a canoe arrived from another part of the bay, with a request from the chief of that district that the Admiral would visit him also. As soon as his scouts returned from their excursion, he prepared to comply with this request; but upon seeing him about to leave them the natives on the beach near by raised a hideous lamentation and entreated him not to abandon them. Making his peace as best he might, he rowed along the shore to this second settlement, closely accompanied by the canoe of the messengers, who seemed fearful lest he should not visit their ruler. His arrival was clearly expected; for on reaching the point of land where this chief's village was situated, the Admiral was received by him and a large throng of his tribesmen with loud acclamations of friendship and affection. Moreover, a large supply of their choicest foods had been prepared; and as soon as the boats approached the beach, the chief sent the banquet down to his visitors, making his own people sit on the ground apart meanwhile. Seeing that the white strangers accepted his hospitality, he sent men to fetch more food and parrots and whatever else they held in estimation, while himself with his following drew near the Spaniards and pressed their offerings upon them. When the Admiral, after distributing a generous portion of trinkets among these amiable savages, indicated that he must return to his ships, there was a general outcry of regret and protestation from the crowd, in the midst of which he rowed away still followed by some of his more ardent admirers in their canoes.

His arrival at the vessels was the signal for a fresh outbreak of enthusiasm on the part of the population adjacent to the anchorage, and the ships were overrun by the people from shore. The number of canoes was not sufficient to furnish transportation to the curious multitude, and many swam out the two miles which separated the vessels from the beach. All these visitors, the Admiral directed, were to be treated with attention, allowed to satisfy their curiosity, and be given something to eat, in return for the kindness they had shown the Spaniards. Among his guests was a chief who came from a town some distance to the west of Port St. Thomas, and he too pressed the Admiral to visit his place, promising him much gold if he would do so. The Admiral was unable to go himself, but he sent some of his men to get the proffered gold and learn what they could of its source. These emissaries were well received on reaching this chief's district; but could not get to the village, as they had to cross a wide river which the naked Indians swam without trouble, but the Spaniards dared not attempt with their arms and equipments. Altogether the arrival of the ships and their astonishing contents, both animate and otherwise, made a most gigantic commotion throughout all that thickly populated region, and the news was evidently spread far and wide with great rapidity, by whatever means, arousing the curiosity and interest of all who heard it.

The next day the Admiral would have left this bay and continued his voyage to the east; but the wind did not serve, and he had to remain where he was. He sent a party again to visit the village in the west whose chief had promised the gold, and this time placed Don Rodrigo Escovedo in command. By making a detour the party managed to cross the river and enter the town. The chief himself came out to meet them, and taking the notary by the hand, led the way to his own house, followed by all the population. Here the visitors were given all they could eat, and presented with some small pieces of gold, a quantity of cotton yarn, and, as a special mark of esteem, three or four live geese. In return they gave their host the presents sent him by the Admiral, and to the natives at large some trinket for whatever they had brought to the Spaniards. When they left, the chief sent with them a number of his men to carry their cotton and fowls, and to help his visitors across the streams and marshy spots on the road; both he and his people being greatly flattered by the visit made them by the white men.

Meantime, all day long the canoes were plying between the ships and the shore, coming from all sides of the great bay. The sailors counted more than one hundred and twenty of these craft, some large and others small, but all loaded with Indians bringing articles to barter with the Christians, — cassava bread, fish, jugs of water, cotton, fruits, — whatever they possessed, in short. A party of the sailors had taken their own boat and gone to cast their nets at a distance from the ships, when they saw a great canoe coming around a neighboring point and steering directly for them. On reaching the boat one of the savages in the canoe handed to the sailors a belt from which was suspended a mask carved from wood, and having its ears, nose, and tongue of beaten gold. Judging from the Indian's gestures that he had something of importance to communicate, the sailors made signs that the canoe should go on to the flagship, and the natives paddled off at once in the direction indicated. When they were brought before the Admiral he found it almost impossible to understand them, as the interpreters said that many of their words were unintelligible to them, and were unlike those of any of the other natives. At length he managed to gather that they had come on a mission from a great chief, or king, called Guacanagari, whose territory lay farther to the east, and who wished the Spaniards to visit him. If they would come, he had sent to say, they should have everything he possessed. From what the messengers told him, as well as from the decorations of the mask, the Admiral inferred that this king must have an abundance of gold, and accordingly he promised to visit him without delay. Leaving three of her crew behind to serve as guides for the white men, the canoe promptly set out on her homeward trip to carry the welcome news to the savage prince.

So impatient was the Admiral to verify the presumable wealth of this newly discovered monarch that he made ready to sail for his city on the next day, although it was Sunday; "and I do not usually leave a port on Sunday," he writes, "not from any superstition, but because I hope that all these people will become Christians;" on which account he desired to set a good example. But when the day came he found himself still wind-bound, and therefore decided to send a detachment of men in the small boats, under the command of the notary, to visit King Guacanagari, and make him such offerings as would likely be acceptable. Don Rodrigo was to assure the prince of the Admiral's early arrival, and inform himself as far as possible of the probable wealth and power of his Majesty. The boats set out under the guidance of the three savages who had remained for the purpose; while those of the Spaniards who stayed with the ships devoted themselves to the incessant stream of curious natives who thronged the vessels throughout the whole day, coming apparently from every quarter of the compass. The Admiral estimated that at least a thousand visited them in canoes, while half as many swam out from the nearest beaches. The one aim of these savages seemed to be to give something to the white men, whether they received anything in return or not. As soon as the canoes got anywhere near the ships, the Indians would rise to their feet, and holding up their offering, call out, "Take this! take this!" as if fearful lest the white men should refuse their gifts. To all of them some trifle was given, in obedience to the Admiral's orders; and those who seemed of chief importance he feasted on wheaten bread and honey, with such other celestial cates as they most appreciated.

Among his guests this day were no less than five chiefs, or *caciques*, as his interpreters called them, accompanied by their entire households, including men, women, and children, — all filled with wondering eagerness to see the marvellous creatures who had fallen from the skies. Some of these chiefs the Admiral had already seen on shore; and he now endeavored, through his interpreters, to get from them all the information he could regarding their own several parts of the country and the adjoining territories. All agreed that the island was of immense extent, and "full of gold." They told him that the people of the other islands came to Hispaniola to get this metal, by violence or by trade, according to their natures, and that the Spaniards could easily secure as much of it as they could possibly want. It is as well to remember, however, that these unlucky beings had not yet learned the boundless greed of the white men for this yellow stuff, or the lengths to which they would go to accumulate it; had they known, it is doubtful whether they would have been so unreserved in yielding their information. One of the caciques showed the Admiral how the gold was gathered in the interior; another pointed out the direction from which it came, and named the several districts in which it most abounded. The richest of all these, the Admiral understood, was situated far to the east, and called *Cibao;* and there, his informant averred, the king had banners of beaten gold. As if to give support to the welcome stories he was hearing, some of the natives had brought on board a few pieces of gold much larger and heavier than any he had theretofore seen; and he did his best to induce that one of his visitors who had been most frank and communicative to remain with him as a guide to the splendid region where this gold "grew." This the Indian willingly consented to do, provided he might bring with him another man who seemed to be a relation or intimate friend; and the two joined the other natives already attached to the fortunes of the white explorers.

This renewed talk of wealth and treasure had once more raised the anticipations of the Admiral to the highest pitch. He believed, on comparing all that he had heard, that Hispaniola was an island "larger than England itself;" and the latter was the greatest isolated body of land known to his experience. The rich territory of Cibao was clearly the Indian name for Cipango. The king with the golden standard was of course the sovereign of that mighty Asiatic island. If he could but reach this land of mines and riches, he felt that his utmost hopes would quickly be realized. "May Our Lord, who has all things in His gift, come to my help, and grant to me as shall be for His service!" is his pious exclamation in mentioning the tales of the caciques. And again he writes: "May God direct me in His mercy to find this gold, — I mean to say, this mine, — for many of these people tell me they know where it is." His thoughts were now no longer of cinnamon and mastic, of land-locked harbors and commanding sites for forts, of beautiful landscapes and peaceful natives; his one engrossing thought was gold.

It was after nightfall on this same busy Sunday when the boats returned with Rodrigo de Escovedo and the men who had accompanied him on his mission. He reported to the Admiral that King Guacanagari's town was situated on a river a long journey to the east of Port St. Thomas. On their way thither in the morning they had met a great flotilla of canoes crowded with Indians going to visit the ships, all of whom turned back when they met the boats and escorted the Spaniards, with much rejoicing, to their king. Some of them had paddled on ahead with extraordinary speed to apprise their ruler of the white men's coming, so that when they reached the mouth of the river on which the town was built they were received by a large concourse of natives, who led them in triumph to the settlement. This the notary described as being by far the most imposing he had yet visited; the houses being arranged in streets, with a broad and cleanly swept *plaza* in the midst of the town. To this place they were conducted, and were immediately surrounded by several thousand of the inhabitants, who made no effort to disguise their astonishment at the appearance of their singular visitors. In a short time the king himself arrived, and they presented themselves before him. He ordered food and drink to be set before them, and showed a keen desire to gratify them in all ways. The notary presented the Admiral's gifts, and announced his approaching visit, whereat the king expressed his delight; and after these formalities he took the Spaniards through the town. The people pressed upon them a multitude of presents, and for their own part seemed to consider as holy relics all the strangers gave them in exchange. The king himself bestowed upon each of the Spaniards a piece of cotton cloth, while to their commander he sent several pieces of gold and a number of parrots. In the afternoon, when they wished to return, he and all his chief subjects begged them to remain another day; but on finding their entreaties of no avail, the king took his leave with many declarations of friendship, a crowd of his people marching with the Christians to the boats, and carrying everything they were taking with them. On the whole the Admiral was well satisfied with Don Rodrigo's report concerning Guacanagari and his town. "If I can only celebrate the festival of Christmas in that port," he writes, "all the inhabitants of this island will flock to see it;" and from the effect produced on the inhabitants at the Port of Peace by the Feast of the Annunciation, he looked for a still deeper impression to follow from the ceremonies of Christmas Day.

At dawn on the 24th of December the ships weighed anchor, and stood out of the Sea of St. Thomas with a favorable land-breeze. Rounding the cape which forms its eastern limit, they coasted slowly along toward the port near Guacanagari's town. The wind gradually failed them as the day wore on, so that when night fell they were still ten miles from their destination, and barely making a steerage way.

As the night was clear and the sea calm, the Admiral, toward eleven o'clock, determined to turn in. He had been on the watch ever since early dawn, and had lost his sleep the previous night, so that he badly needed rest before undergoing the fatigues of the coming day. It was not his habit, he says, to lie down when the ship was sailing near the land; but on this one occasion he felt that he was peculiarly safe. Not only was the sea "as quiet as a porringer," as he puts it, but the sailors who had manned the boats with Don Rodrigo on the latter's mission two days before had carefully examined the whole course both going and coming, and reported that it was free and open, with no indications of reefs or rocks all the way to the king's port. Not satisfied to rely wholly on this apparently sufficient precaution, he called up the master of the vessel, a navigator of large experience, and handed over the tiller to him, charging him strictly to keep a sharp lookout, and rouse him at any indication of change in sea or sky.

Seeing the Admiral fast asleep in his cabin, the dead calm continuing, and the sea without a ripple, the master thought that he too might take his rest, and none be the wiser or the worse for his comfort. Summoning one of the younger sailors, — the Admiral calls him "a boy," perhaps in angry contempt; for his standing order was that the helm should never be intrusted to the ordinary seamen, — the master turned the watch over to him, and, wrapping himself in his cloak, went sound asleep in some sheltered nook. A little later on — not so much as an hour — the drowsy seaman who held the tiller felt a tremor in his hand, and noticed the rudder jar with a motion which was unmistakable. His loud cry of alarm awoke both master and Admiral; but the latter was the first to reach the steersman's side. He did not need the sound of the breakers close at hand to tell him what had occurred; the easy, steady rasp of the vessel's keel as she drove deeper into the sands thrilled through his whole frame with a message as plain as it was terrible. The ship had been carried imperceptibly on a sand-bank, upon which she was every moment drifting farther. The "Santa Maria," his flagship, was ashore in a savage country; the little "Niña" alone remained to carry a hundred souls back to Spain across that wide ocean!

Quickly observing that the ship was settling into the shoal broadside on, he ordered the master to take the barge and cast an anchor off as far as possible astern in the deep water, intending to work the ship off with the capstan if it could be done. But that worthy, either losing his head on seeing the consequences of his negligence or else from sheer terror, instead of obeying orders, set off with all hands in the barge for the "Niña," which was about half a league to windward. Here they found cold comfort; for Vicente Yañez, on hearing their story, railed at them for arrant cowards, and flatly refusing to let them put foot in his ship, bore down to render assistance to his commander as in duty bound. As for the Admiral, when he saw his barge disappear in the darkness in the direction of the "Niña's" light, he knew he was deserted, and promptly set about cutting away his mainmast and heaving overboard some of his cannon and other heavy truck with a view to lightening the ship. All his efforts were futile, however; for the one chance of salvation had been lost in the barge's flight. Little by little the "Santa Maria" worked on to the bank until she lay sunk deep in the sand with her broadside toward deep water. Seeing that he could not get her off in the darkness, and knowing nothing of the lay of the land, the Admiral took off all his crew and put them on board the "Niña" for safety.

As soon as it was dawn, he despatched Diego de Arana and Pedro Gutierrez in the "Niña's" boat to inform Guacanagari of his disaster, and ask him to send canoes and men to aid in unloading the wreck. Never did tale of distress fall on more sympathetic ears, if we may believe the report of the Admiral's envoys. The king shed tears of grief at hearing of the catastrophe which had overtaken the white men, and instantly ordered his people to go with their canoes, large and small, to the scene of the wreck, and do whatever the strangers should require of them. He himself came down to the beach soon after to watch the progress of the work; for the shoal on which the vessel lay was close to the site of his town. From time to time he despatched attendants to learn how the labors were advancing, and to repeat his offers of assistance. The Admiral was not to grieve over his misfortune, the king said, for he, Guacanagari, would give him all he owned to console him for the loss of his ship. As it proved at last to be impossible to get the "Santa Maria" off, the natives and their canoes were used in unloading the ship and transporting her cargo and stores to the shore. When he learned of this, the king caused a number of houses near the beach to be vacated, and directed that all the articles from the wreck should be stored in them. In a very short time the hulk was stripped of everything portable. So scrupulous were these savages in handling the goods intrusted to them that, notwithstanding the inestimable value they placed upon all they handled, the Admiral says "not a pin was missing, nor a crumb of bread." The king ordered two more houses to be vacated and swept clean as evening drew on, and these he gave to such of the Spaniards as were detailed to remain on shore over night; while he placed a guard of his own men to see that nothing was disturbed. The Admiral himself slept on the "Niña," anchoring her as near to the king's town as he could get with safety.

The prompt and generous help rendered by Guacanagari and his people made necessarily a profound impression upon the Admiral, and materially influenced his future course. Ever since landing on Guanahani, the Spaniards had had constant experience of the generosity of the natives; but between the indiscriminate liberality of the other savages and the thoughtful and painstaking hospitality of this prince, there was a broad difference. The one was dictated by a frank and magnanimous desire to be of service to friends in distress; the other by a childish anxiety to stand well with the superior beings such as the Indians supposed the white men to be. On the one Colon felt that he could rely; to the other he would not, perhaps, have been willing to trust after the first emotion of amazement had worn off. Moreover, in none of the other islands had he discovered any traces of discipline or government; but wherever he had landed in Hispaniola he had found some kind of a civil organization, although none of the caciques seemed to have so complete a command over their people as Guacanagari had shown that he possessed when this emergency arose. The king clearly had an individuality of his own which strongly impressed the Admiral, and the latter seems to have regarded him from the outset as a worthy comrade and ally. "These people are admirably faithful, and free from all covetousness," he writes in closing his account of the shipwreck; "and more than all others is this virtuous king." There were other reasons why he was drawn to the natives of Hispaniola to a greater degree than to any of the other islanders. The inhabitants of this region were industrious, so far as their needs demanded, as was shown by the care with which their fields were tilled and the pains bestowed upon their houses and canoes; they were numerous and, to all appearance, undisturbed by the neighboring tribes; and they were peaceable in disposition, as was evidenced by the total absence of weapons. Even the glaring colors with which they painted themselves, the Admiral had learned, were not worn to terrify their enemies, as he had at first supposed, but to protect their skins from the sun. Finally, the country was fertile, abounding in provisions and promising to prove rich in the products of mine and forest. For all these reasons it invited to settlement.

These considerations passed through Colon's mind, we may gather from his writings, even in the hurry and occupation of discharging the wreck of the "Santa Maria." He was ever a man of quick resolve and instant execution, and the problem now before him called for the exercise of both these qualities. The "Niña" was the only vessel remaining of the fleet, and therefore the one means left of communicating with that distant world beyond the broad Atlantic. Her company, originally of twenty-four, had been increased by the Indians taken on board from time to time; and now nearly eighty more souls, between the Spaniards and their native followers, were dependent on this single little bark for transportation. Vicente Yañez had thus far shown none of the spirit of insubordination which dominated his brother Martin Alonzo; but there was no assurance that a mutiny might not break out among the crews; and in such an extremity the captain might yield to the pressure and side with his townsmen of Palos. In such an event what would become of those who stood by the Admiral, and, above all, what would be the fate of the stupendous discovery which had at length crowned the toils and devotion of Colon himself? We do not believe for a moment that this man occupied his mind with concern about his own fate; we believe that, like other men of lofty aims, this was a matter of small concern to him in crises such as this was. But he knew that he carried in his own brain the secret of the route to this western world; and the thought that this might be lost, or if finally rediscovered by the labor of others after his own death or disappearance, might be used only for purposes of individual greed or sordid ambition, moved him to look upon himself impersonally as a guardian and trustee for these new lands which he believed the Almighty had intrusted to his keeping. In this persuasion he determined to go to any lengths rather than run the risk of his knowledge and purposes perishing with himself in that unknown corner of an unmapped sea.

Only the night before he had gone to rest planning fresh achievements and buoyed with new hopes, which had for their foundation the impression he would make upon Guacanagari by celebrating in all its pomp and circumstance the great festival of the Christian year in the capital of the heathen prince. Now he was a shipwrecked sailor, assailed by a flood of cares and dangers against which his only bulwark was the continued friendship of this naked savage. In so different a fashion from that which he had anticipated did the Admiral pass the first Christmas known to the New World.

XIX.

THE FIRST FRONTIERSMEN.

AS a measure of precaution and to curb any possible attempt at desertion on the part of the crew of his remaining vessel, the Admiral had transferred his flag at once to the "Niña" and remained on board that ship. On the morning after the loss of the "Santa Maria," shortly after sunrise, the king came to visit him and assured him of his earnest sympathy at the disaster which had befallen. Guacanagari repeated his former messages,—that he and his people, their houses, canoes, and all they owned, were at the disposal of the white men, and whatever the latter wanted should be done. While he and the Admiral were conversing, several large canoes came alongside, bringing numbers of Indians with pieces of gold to exchange for hawk-bells. On drawing near the ship, the savages rose in their boats and held up the shining bits of metal, crying out, "*Chuque, chuque!*" in imitation of the sound of the bells they were so wild to possess.[1] For a single tiny bell they willingly gave any piece of gold they had, regardless of its size, and after trading away all that they had brought, earnestly begged the Spaniards not to dispose of all their bells to the other Indians who should come, but to save some for the present

---

[1] *Chuqui* is "gold" in one of the languages of ancient Peru, and "dance" in another. It is possible, in view of the wide extent of the Inca Empire, and the extended traffic which we know existed even in those early times among the natives of the New World, that the word was used in one of these senses, and misunderstood by the Spaniards.

traders until the following day, for then they would bring lumps of gold as large as their hands. This the Admiral promised should be done; for he understood from the king, or those who were in his company, that these canoes came from a distance, and that wherever the tinkle of the little bells had been heard the natives were seized with a veritable passion for them. Soon afterward some of the sailors who had spent the night on shore came off to the "Niña," and reported that in the village, too, the Indians were offering gold in quantities, giving it to the Spaniards for anything at all, — a piece weighing an ounce or more in exchange for a brass lace-point, and other like extravagances. Nor was this only a momentary abundance, the seamen said; for the villagers had told them that what they then brought was nothing at all in comparison with what they should bring to the strangers in a few weeks' time. At this news the Admiral showed so much gratification that Guacanagari observed the change in his bearing and inquired the cause. On learning what it was, he bade his host be of good cheer, for he should have as much of this metal as he desired. Not far from there, he said, in Cibao, it was so plentiful that the people held it in such little esteem that it might be had for the asking, and he would send at once and have a great store of it gathered for the white men. These were welcome tidings to the Admiral, coming as they did just when the future was so doubtful, and he began to feel that good might, after all, come out of the evil he had suffered. The king remained to breakfast with him, and the Admiral took pleasure in watching the extreme propriety with which his guest acted. The meal finished, he presented the king with a silken shirt and a pair of gloves, with which elaborate raiment his Majesty was so delighted that he insisted on wearing at least the garments for his hands throughout the day.

Later on the Admiral took Guacanagari ashore in the barge and accompanied him to his town. The king showed his guest about the place, and then walked with him some distance through the adjacent forest, more than a thousand of the inhabitants following in their train wherever they went.

Their excursion ended, the king led the way to one of the principal cabins in the village, where a feast was spread for the Admiral and his party. In the preparation and service of this repast every effort was made to show the white commander in what particular esteem and honor he was held by the savage prince. The dishes consisted of everything known to the native palate,—yams, game, fish, shrimps, cassava bread, red peppers, fruits, and many eatables wholly unfamiliar to the Spaniards. Each dish on the table—or, properly speaking, on the ground—was pressed upon the surfeited guests, so that the entertainment lasted a long time. At its conclusion Guacanagari and the other natives present rubbed their hands with certain leaves which were brought them for the purpose; but to the Admiral and his suite water was offered, the king having remarked that the white men washed their hands after eating. When they rose from the collation, Guacanagari led the way to the beach, conversing as he went about the occasional inroads of the dreaded Canibals—or *Caribes*, as he called them—and the terrible weapons they used. The Admiral assured him that such arms had no terrors for the Spaniards, and, to give him a demonstration of the superiority of the white men in this respect, sent for one of his men-at-arms who was an excellent marksman with the Moorish bow. The skill and deadly power shown by this adept greatly impressed the king and all who were with him; but when, in obedience to the Admiral's orders, an arquebuse and cannon were discharged from the "Niña," and the balls went crashing through the forest, tearing off leaves and branches as they passed, the wonder of the savages knew no bounds. With these same thundering and irresistible weapons, the Admiral told his host, would the sovereigns of the white men send and destroy the Caribes, or bring them captive to Hispaniola, with their arms tied behind their backs just as they had done to the islanders. In such intercourse the day was spent, both the savage cacique and the white commander delighted with their experiences. At parting the king gave the Admiral another large mask, with eyes, ears, and nose of gold, together with a number of other golden ornaments, some of which he hung about his guest's neck, and one, a sort of coronet, he placed upon his head. To the other Spaniards he also made presents of pieces of gold, declaring, as they left, that before long they should receive still greater quantities of the precious metal.

The Admiral's purpose in spending the day with Guacanagari had not been one of mere pleasure. He had decided upon the course to be pursued, and wished to inform himself more fully upon certain vital points, and prepare the ground for the action contemplated. Now he was ready. To take all his people back to Spain in the "Niña" was clearly impracticable; to send her with despatches and await with part of his company the arrival of relief ships sent back to him by the Spanish Crown was to lean on a reed of the frailest; for the "Niña" might never reach Europe, or if she did, her crew might report Columbus and the others as dead, and so reap all the credit and reward for themselves. To build another vessel from the materials of the "Santa Maria" would take a long time; and the Admiral was constantly haunted by the thought that Martin Alonzo might return to Spain in the "Pinta," and not only claim the glory of the discovery, but propagate falsehoods destructive of the reputation and character of his leader. Relying, therefore, on the friendship and hospitality of Guacanagari, Colon had determined to erect at the mouth of the river, near the king's town, a small fortress, and garrison it with such of his men as could not be taken on the "Niña," choosing only those who were disposed to remain. The hulk of the flagship would furnish them with timber and iron; her cargo and supplies could be stored in the fort, and would be ample provision both for subsistence and traffic with the natives; and during his absence the colony could accumulate gold, cotton, mastic, cinnamon, and all the other products of the island, and have them ready to ship by the time he returned to seek them. He in person would make all haste to Spain, report his discoveries, and equip another and more adequate expedition with which to complete the exploration of these new lands and permanently establish the Spanish power. The more he reflected upon this plan, the more it commended itself to him. The loss of two of his vessels and the paucity of treasure in comparison with the fabulous quantities of gold and pearls, spices and silks, which he had confidently expected to bring back with him, would, he apprehended, be seized upon by his opponents at the Court, and used as arguments to belittle the merit of his achievement; they might even, he admitted to himself, succeed in deterring the Crown from sending out a second fleet, and then all his sacrifices and labors would go for naught. But with a colony planted in the New World the sovereigns would have to act, be the opposition what it might, and his garrison would thus be hostages to Fortune for the realization of his cherished aims. One more conception influenced him largely. These island regions were full of tantalizing mystery. Where was the country of the Great Khan? Where Babeque the golden? Whence came these already considerable quantities of gold which the simple natives treated as the dirt beneath their feet? What of those lands and monarchs of which the caciques and their people had told him? Partly for want of time, but chiefly from imperfect knowledge of the language, he had only learned enough about these several matters to keep his expectations keyed to the highest pitch. If his chosen followers were to settle among these friendly subjects of Guacanagari, however, it would be an easy thing for them to acquire the dialect, and thus, he argued, "discover the secrets of these lands." From every point of view he was satisfied with the project, and having formulated it definitely in his mind, announced his intentions to Vicente Yañez and the members of his own official household. Greatly to his content, it encountered little or no opposition. Many of the men, officers and sailors alike, had been charmed with the easy and indulgent life of the natives; others among them had had their avarice excited by the sight of so much gold and the promise of so much more; still others preferred the mere prospect of adventures in a delightful country and climate to the certainty of a long and tedious voyage across that endless ocean in a crowded caravel. Whatever their motives, it was evident that volunteers would not be lacking.

Thus it befell that what at first had seemed a desperate remedy, now that it took clearer shape, presented itself to the Admiral's sanguine mind as a direct ordinance of Divine Providence. Had the "Santa Maria" not been wrecked, he would only have passed Christmas Day in this port, and then sailed on in blissful ignorance of the stores of gold and valuable productions to be obtained here at so trifling an outlay. Had the master of the stranded ship obeyed orders and cast the anchor astern as he was told, the vessel would have been warped off the bank and the voyage continued. Had the people of Palos, even, done their whole duty as loyal citizens, and furnished a ship of lighter draught than the "Santa Maria," she might never have gone on the shoal, or even if she had, would have broken up in a few hours; whereas the timbers of the unwieldy flagship were yet sound and solid, and could be used to admirable advantage in the projected stronghold. Surely this was all foreordained by the Almighty, the Admiral thought. Now the garrison he should leave behind would be able to collect gold and spices in plenty, and discover the mines and forests where they grew; so that a vast treasure would be ready against his return. Beyond doubt they could gather at least "a ton of gold" and a vast quantity of precious spices in the time it would take him to go to Spain and get back; and at that rate within two or three years there would be sufficient treasure hoarded to warrant the sovereigns of Castile in undertaking his fond dream of freeing the Holy Sepulchre from the filthy grasp of the infidel Turk. He writes on the evening of December 26: —

"So many reasons at present occur to me, that this no longer appears to be a disaster, but rather a great good fortune; for it is certain that if we had not run aground I should not have ventured to come into this harbor, as it is difficult of entrance, and thus I should not have left a garrison here as I now intend doing; and even if I had wished then to leave them, I could not have furnished them with so large an equipment of ammunition and supplies, nor all that is wanted for their fort. Now it also appears that very many of my people who were shipwrecked wished to remain here, and they have asked me, or got others to ask me, to give them permission to stay. For this cause I have ordered that a fortress and keep should be erected at this place, all very carefully built, together with a large storage vault under ground. This is not because I have any fear concerning these people; for, as I have before said, with my present force I could take possession of their whole island, although it is, I am sure, greater than Portugal, and has twice as many people; but they are all naked, and have no weapons, and are cowards beyond all hope of recovery. The reason why I build this fort is because this place is so far away from Spain, and also in order that these people may learn something of the power of your Highnesses' subjects, and how much they can accomplish, and so obey them with fear and affection. From the wreck we can get timber and iron to construct the fort, and plenty of bread and wine for more than a year, and seeds for raising crops, and a barge for the use of our men. I shall leave here a calker, a carpenter, a gunner, and a cooper, and many of the other men who want to serve your Majesties and do me pleasure by finding out where the gold is gathered. And thus everything has turned out very conveniently for making this first settlement."

In such ready fashion was distress changed into rejoicing, and fearful foreboding into sanguine hope. Colon was not the only wise man whose mind has taken more kindly to the "ifs" than to the "buts" of futurity.

Work on the fortress was begun at once. The Admiral called the colony he proposed to establish the Villa de la Navidad (or Christmas Town), in honor of the day on which he had made his disastrous landing. The men set about their task with a will, — those who were to stay anxious to commence their independent life, and those who were to go as desirous to turn their faces toward Spain. It was no secret that the Admiral intended to return immediately across the Atlantic; and partly for this cause, and partly to impress the natives with the strength and skill of the white men, he pushed the construction of the little stronghold with all the energy he commanded. The king and his followers were pleased beyond measure when they learned that the strangers were going to settle among them, and lent themselves to the work with willing hearts; but when he understood that the Admiral himself was going away, Guacanagari was disconsolate. He begged his visitor to remain, saying that he had sent men in all directions to collect gold, and if the Admiral would only wait, he would cover him from head to foot with the metal he prized so much. On the 27th he came again on board the "Niña," with his brother and a chief who seemed to be a sort of privy councillor, and breakfasted. During the meal the king said that his two companions wished to accompany the Admiral to the country he was going to, and return with him when he came out again. To this Colon very gladly agreed, recognizing the importance of presenting to the Spanish sovereigns a native prince, the brother of a powerful and friendly monarch. As they were discussing this matter, a canoe arrived from shore bringing several Indians, who told Guacanagari that a great boat like the "Niña," filled with the same kind of white beings, was lying in a river at the eastern end of the island. The Admiral knew at once that this must be the "Pinta;" but, relieved as he was to learn that Martin Alonzo had not gone back to Spain to rob him of the credit of the discovery, he was much disturbed by the thought that his lieutenant was probably ransacking the coast for gold, and thus interfering seriously with his own intentions. Observing the anxiety with which the news affected his host, the king offered to despatch a canoe to the river mentioned to verify the truth of the report. This proposal was gratefully accepted by the Admiral, who also sent one of his reliable men to carry letters of a friendly tenor to Martin Alonzo, urging him to rejoin the "Niña" without delay. The knowledge that the "Pinta" was somewhere near and might make her appearance any day, placed Colon in a cruel embarrassment. On the one hand, could he but depend on her captain for loyal assistance, he would have been able to complete his examination of the shores of Hispaniola, and even continue his explorations in other directions, before resuming his homeward voyage; on the other hand, he might be placed in a most critical position were his headstrong subordinate to find him in this crippled and dependent condition. In this dilemma he resolved to hasten the construction of the fort and get under weigh at the earliest possible moment. It would be better, he argued, to meet the "Pinta" at sea, when he was bound ostensibly for Spain; even Martin Alonzo's men would probably side with the Admiral when the question was whether to remain longer in these distant waters or sail direct for Palos and home. Accordingly he spent most of his time now on shore, directing and animating the men in their work of digging ditches and setting up stockades; using meanwhile all his tact and diplomacy to confirm the favorable disposition of the king.

Guacanagari, indeed, seemed only to be anxious to win the favor of the white commander and convince him of his desire to enrich the strangers. He had evidently given orders that his people should not tell exactly where the gold came from, so that he might continue to be the only source from whom the Spaniards could obtain it; but his attempted monopoly was rather the fruit of a friendly jealousy than of greed, for he continued to shower presents upon the Admiral and the officers with all his original generosity. At one time it would be masks with golden decorations; at another plates of gold to hang about the neck; still again it was nuggets of the virgin metal. Nor did he prohibit his people from trading freely with the sailors; on the contrary, the latter continued to receive daily additions to their treasure, — or rather to that of the Crown; for they had to make a return of all they secured to the royal inspector, Rodrigo Sanchez. The king's one object in establishing this prohibition was, by being himself liberal and generous in supplying the coveted metal, to prevent the Spaniards from caring to seek beyond his dominions for the yellow stuff they thought so much of. In this and others of his dealings there was a transparent effort at mystery which reminds one of the elaborate devices of children at play. One evening, for example, he sent a handsome mask on board the "Niña" for the Admiral, with a request that the latter would let him have a water-basin and a jug; but Colon had no difficulty in discovering that the king intended to have others like them made of gold to present to his white friend and ally. On another occasion, when the Admiral went ashore in order to confer with him about the garrison which was to remain under his protection, Guacanagari, instead of meeting him on the beach as he usually did, hid himself in his house, and sent his brother to receive his visitor. The younger prince led the way ceremoniously to one of the houses set apart for the Spaniards' accommodation, and after seating the Admiral on a bench of honor which had been prepared, sent a messenger to advise the king of his distinguished guest's arrival. In a moment Guacanagari came running into the apartment, and, embracing the Admiral with every display of affection, hung a large plate of gold about his neck as an especial insignia of rank. All this performance, the Admiral remarks, was arranged for the sole purpose of doing him the greater honor. The king's artifices were not always successful, however, nor were his injunctions implicitly obeyed; and thus it happened that the Spaniards not only learned where the gold came from, but a member of the king's own family was their informant. The Admiral himself questioned every one he talked with upon this absorbing subject; but so far all his efforts had been in vain, for the Indians either evaded an answer altogether or feigned ignorance. A nephew of Guacanagari, a young man of quick intelligence and frank disposition, came one day on board the "Niña," and, as was his wont, the Admiral talked with him about the gold. Among other things, he asked him the situation of the mines whence it was drawn. Nothing loath, the young fellow told his interrogator that it all came from the eastern part of Hispaniola itself, — or Bohio, as he called the island, — and he named the countries of Cibao, Guarionex, Coroay, Macorix, Mayonic, and Fuma, where he said the metal was found in such quantities that it had no value at all. Happy in this discovery, the Admiral hastened to write down in his diary all the young man had told him, supposing these names to refer to islands in the vicinity of Hispaniola, although he later discovered that they all were provinces or districts of that same island.[1] As for the young man, he adds, when the king learned what had occurred, he read his nephew a serious lecture on his heedless conduct.

By the 30th of December the fortress was so far advanced that the Admiral began to make preparations for the long voyage before him. He wished to consult Guacanagari concerning certain of these matters, and went on shore to dine with him. He found the king surrounded by five of his subject caciques, all wearing coronets of gold and all, no doubt, deep in schemes to secure gold enough to satisfy the extraordinary fancy of the white men for such a useless material. On seeing Colon, the king ran forward and led him by the arm into the house prepared for his use, where he made him sit down on the bench of honor. Then he took off his own coronet and placed it on the Admiral's head with much ceremony and respect; apparently wishing to give this token of affection in the presence of his chiefs. Not to be outdone, Colon took off the necklace of beads he himself wore, and fastened it around Guacanagari's neck, and throwing off the short cape or mantle he had donned for greater ceremony, he placed it over the king's shoulders. He also sent to his chest for a pair of new red buskins which he had the king put on, and drawing a silver ring from his finger, placed it on that of his royal host. This completed the joy of Guacanagari; for silver was vastly more prized by the Indians than the more valuable metal, and the king had tried to get one of the sailors to part with a ring he wore, as the Admiral knew. It is evident that the latter felt that he had done all that could be expected of him, for in describing this scene he writes that the cape was a new one of

---

[1] Guacanagari's own district was called Marien, and was the territory near the cape now known as Haytien.

broadcloth which he was wearing for the first time, and the necklace was "of handsome colored stones and choice beads of beautiful tints, which was quite fit to be worn in any place." At all events, his audience was overcome by his generosity; for two of the caciques promptly came forward and gave him the large plates of gold hanging down from their necks in the palpable expectation of receiving in return, if not a mantle or a silver ring, at least a red shoe or a string of beads. In the midst of this second interchange of amenities, an Indian appeared and informed the king that only two days since he had left the other great boat of the white men in a port to the eastward of Navidad. On hearing this, the Admiral took it for granted that his messenger would surely reach the "Pinta," and she would speedily rejoin him; and he was mightily perplexed as to the best course to adopt toward Martin Alonzo should he arrive before the "Niña" had sailed from her present anchorage. Returning on board his ship to confer with Vicente Yañez, he was gratified to find that this one of the Pinzons at least was working for the success of the expedition; for he reported to his commander that he had that day discovered rhubarb on one of the adjacent islands, and believed a large quantity of it could be secured with little effort, as he had observed the same plant in the port of St. Thomas. This was a matter of no little moment in Colon's estimation, for the root had a high commercial value and was one of the precious commodities imported by the Venetian merchants from Asia. He accordingly directed Vicente Yañez to send a boat's crew to gather a supply of the rare drug as a sample to be shown the sovereigns on his arrival in Spain. It was one "spice" the more for the garrison to garner into their vault during his absence.

The last day of the year was passed by the "Niña's" company in laying in a stock of water and firewood for the impending voyage. The Admiral spent his time between the vessel and the fort, anxious to see that both were put in the best possible condition for the respective parts they had to play after the approaching separation. His impatience to set sail for home, to bear the tidings of his grand discovery, was tempered by a feeling of regret that he could not complete his exploration of the coasts of Hispaniola; but the loss of the "Santa Maria" warned him of the danger attending the navigation of these unknown harbors, and he shrank from exposing his last remaining ship to such constant risks. He seems to have left the "Pinta" entirely out of his calculations at this juncture. As was his nature, now that he was advised of her proximity, he was going to encounter the difficulty rather than let it overtake him; but even after finding the missing consort, he realized that she would be of no assistance. His desire had been to search out the ports and sites along the coast best adapted for settlement and colonization, so that on his return he might bring a contingent of colonists with their cattle and implements of agriculture;[1] but, as he was now situated, he would have to act upon such information as he had already acquired regarding the capacities of the country for permanent settlement by Europeans.

On the first day of the new year, 1493, the canoe despatched five days before by Guacanagari to search for the "Pinta," returned without any news of the missing ship, although the Spanish messenger reported that he had examined every harbor and inlet for many leagues to the eastward. The Admiral's disappointment at this failure was less than it would otherwise have been, for the "Niña" was now ready to set sail, and her course would lie in the direction where the "Pinta" was said to be cruising. His anxieties on this score diminished as the hour for departure drew near. What if Martin Alonzo had sailed for Spain eager to be the bearer of the great news and to secure the applause of his sovereigns for a success which he had done his utmost to thwart? The Admiral knew that soon thereafter he would himself arrive to confound the ill-gotten triumph of

[1] It has been objected by some historians that Columbus was to blame for not paying heed to anything but the superficial riches of the New World; but the censure is unjust. His language is explicit as to his rational and politic intentions in this respect.

his disloyal follower, and give the lie to the malignant falsehoods he felt sure the lieutenant would publish regarding his commander. A natural feeling of satisfaction filled his mind as he reflected that within a few weeks, if God so pleased, the whole truth would be in the possession of the Spanish monarchs, and the rewards and punishments be distributed as was of right. In a burst of indignation which brings him the nearer to our hearts from its perfect candor, the Admiral enters these sentiments without disguise in the diary intended for their Majesties' own perusal. He writes: —

"If I were certain that the 'Pinta' would reach Spain with that Martin Alonzo, I would not hesitate to make the exploration I so wish to make, trusting that in good time Our Lord would make all things right. But because I do not know what he may intend to do, and because if he reaches there he may fill the ears of your Majesties with lies, and thus escape the punishment he so richly deserves for having done so much harm by his desertion, and so greatly interfered with the benefits and advantages which would otherwise have resulted from this voyage, I have resolved to sail at once for home without completing my work of exploration."

As we have seen, it was his original intention to remain in the Indies until April, and it was now only the beginning of January; so the treachery of the "Pinta's" captain had cut short his leader's career of successful discovery by three whole months. Since he had accomplished so much in less than that time, after first sighting Guanahaní, what might he not expect to do in another equal term?

XX.

THE RETURN OF THE "PINTA."

BY the 2d of January all was ready for leaving the Villa de la Navidad and the hospitable capital of Guacanagari. The little fortress was well advanced toward completion; its magazines were filled with stores, ammunition, and goods for barter; its few small cannon mounted where they could best command the approaches by land and water. The garrison chosen to sustain the authority of Spain over the western hemisphere consisted of thirty-nine men under the command of three officers. In selecting the latter the Admiral had been largely guided by personal considerations. Not only were they to be representatives of the Spanish Crown, but they were to act for him as well, and he appointed those of whose loyalty to his person he had no doubt. To Diego de Arana, Rodrigo de Escovedo, and Pedro Gutierrez the joint government of the settlement was confided. The first was bound to Colon by ties of relationship, the second had proven himself worthy of the warranty given him by the father superior, and the third had shown his friendship for his commander both by services at the Court in earlier days and by his conduct since. The men who were to serve as the pioneers of civilization and exponents of its superior merits among the pagans of these hitherto fortunate regions were drawn from the crews of the "Niña" and the "Santa Maria." Only those who showed a cheerful willingness to remain were chosen; and it is significant to remark that not a single man of those selected hailed from Palos or its neighborhood. The mutterings of those trying days on the calm Atlantic were still ringing in the Admiral's ears, and he was leaving none of the Pinzon connection behind him to stir up strife and discontent in that lonely colony. In the list of those detailed to garrison Navidad it is interesting to see the names of "William Irish, native of Galway, in Ireland," and "Tallarte de Lajes, Englishman."[1] Thus early in its history did the rival races of the North and the South share the dominion of the western continent.

Diego de Arana was to be the nominal governor of the settlement, although in all things he was to act in consultation with his two associates; the fatal principle of divided authority, so dear to the Latin heart, handicapping the success of the colony from the outset. To them jointly Colon, as Viceroy of the islands, committed all the powers devolved upon him by the royal decrees. He left with them strict injunctions as to the maintenance of discipline in all things, and most particularly in their relations with Guacanagari and the natives surrounding them. As the major part of the garrison were seafaring men, he left his largest boat, the barge, with them to be used in coasting expeditions for the collection of gold and spices and the discovery of the mines. With the same provident care he included in the colony a ship-carpenter, a gunner who was also a handy workman in wood and metals, a cooper for their stores of wine, a physician, and a tailor. The store of provisions was, as we have seen, a plentiful one, and the stock of merchandise for the purposes of traffic was ample. Having made his dispositions regarding the essential welfare and safety of the people elected to uphold the authority of their Catholic Majesties under such difficult conditions, on the morning of the 2d he summoned the three governors and their thirty-nine men, and announced in terse and forceful sentences his orders for

---

[1] Various conjectures have been hazarded as to what English name this Romancized substitute represents. "Arthur Lake" is the latest; but the Spanish form of "Arthur" is *Artus* or *Artur*, and the *de* cannot be ignored.

their general guidance. For greater emphasis he divided his remarks into eight distinct injunctions. 1. They were to attend punctually to their religious duties, for without God's favor their endeavors must come to naught. 2. They were to obey their governors in all things. 3. They were to reverence King Guacanagari, and strive always to gain his good-will and that of his people. 4. They were to do no harm to the natives in property or person. 5. Under no circumstances were they to scatter through the neighborhood or go far from the fort in detail. 6. They were to keep up stout hearts, and not allow themselves to pine or become downcast in spirit on account of their isolation and strange surroundings. 7. They were to procure guides to the mines if possible, and obtain not only as great a store of treasure and spices as they could, but also inform themselves fully concerning the country and its products. 8. He pledged himself to ask the Spanish sovereigns to bestow special favors and distinction upon all who were remaining at Navidad, as a reward for their loyalty and devotion. His return to Hispaniola should be as prompt as was consistent with the distances to be traversed. At the conclusion of his address the men hastened to express, after their own fashion, their intention to abide by his instructions and their confidence in his protection of their interests. Only, they begged him, let his return be as soon as possible, and let their services never escape his memory when he found himself again on Spanish soil.

The Admiral now turned his attention to the ceremonies attendant upon his farewell interview with Guacanagari. So far as his colony was concerned, Colon felt that he had done all in his power to provide for its secure and prosperous administration. The site of the settlement was not, indeed, as favorable a one as he could have wished, for he would have much preferred establishing his people farther along the coast to the east, where they would be nearer the country where he believed the gold was found. In the absence of the "Pinta" this had been impracticable, and he had chosen the port of Navidad as being near the town of the friendly king and among peaceable neighbors. His final efforts were devoted to cementing the alliance already so promisingly established between the natives and their Christian visitors.

Guacanagari was to breakfast with the Admiral and his staff in the large house used by the Spaniards for their formal interviews. When the king entered the spacious apartment, accompanied by his brother and principal men, his whole deportment bore witness to the grief which possessed him at the prospect of losing his friend of a week. In the course of the banquet he repeatedly entreated the Admiral not to abandon him, promising him that he should have all the gold he wanted if he would only remain a little longer. One of the king's councillors took occasion to say to Colon that Guacanagari had sent out canoes and messengers in all directions to collect gold, with the intention of making a statue of the Admiral out of the precious metal, and that if the Spaniards would only remain for ten days the splendid gift would be ready. None of these inducements could shake the purpose of the white commander. His face was set toward Spain; if golden statues were to be had, the officers he was leaving behind would see that they were not lost. Declaring his intention to be unalterable, he commended instantly to Guacanagari the colonists he was leaving at Navidad, assuring the king of the gratitude and generous recompense of the Spanish sovereigns if he would aid and sustain the little party during their leader's absence. After the meal was finished, he gave the king fresh presents — a robe and other garments coveted by the savage taste — and also distributed liberal gifts among the other natives. The more to impress both king and people with the boundless power of the white men's weapons, a sham battle was fought between the men of the garrison and those of the ship, the Admiral assuring Guacanagari that so long as he had such redoubtable allies at hand he could laugh at the raids of the Caribes or any other foes who might assail him. Training the cannon of the fortress on the hulk of the stranded flagship, he fired several shots at this as a target. The stone balls crashed through the heavy timbers and plunged into the sea beyond, amazing and confounding the assembled savages with their prodigious force. With such mighty friends to fight his battles, the king felt that he would in very truth be safe from every enemy. That he would remain on good terms with the garrison was a foregone conclusion !

When the hour came for the Spaniards to embark, the king's lamentations could not be restrained. Colon soothed his distress by assuring him that in a few months at the most he would be back and would then make a long stay in his country; but nothing seemed to mitigate his woe. A great concourse was gathered on the beach when the " Niña's " boat was manned to make her final trip from the shore to the vessel. Colon was surrounded by his own officers and men as well as by Guacanagari's retinue. In the background was a dense throng of natives, gazing in wondering curiosity at the novel scene. Near by was the half-finished tower and palisade of the fortress, standing on the edge of the forest, in the clearing made for its greater safety. Behind all rose the dense wall of impenetrable woods, with the palm-thatched cabins occupied by the Spaniards showing among the nearest trees. Out in the offing rode the solitary " Niña " at anchor, and close by was the fatal bank with the dismantled and crumbling hull of the ill-fated " Santa Maria " outlined against the green plain of the shallow sea. Beginning with the weeping king, Colon embraced in Latin fashion all the group about him, bidding each of his thirty-nine devoted pioneers a separate and affectionate farewell, while his staff made their adieus in turn. Then, saluting the king with formal dignity, he entered the boat and was pulled from shore. The first colony of Europeans was established in the golden Indies.

It was the Admiral's intention to have set sail that same day; but the wind failed completely, and he was compelled to remain at anchor. The next day, the 3d, he was detained by the absence of several of the interpreters and their wives, who had gone on shore and were not able to return on account of the high sea which began to run. It was not until the morning of the 4th, that he was at length able to get under weigh, and even then it proved necessary to tow the "Niña" for some distance out of the harbor before her sails filled with the light land-breeze which prevailed. In a little while the rocky mass of Cape Caribata hid from the Admiral's sight the port of Navidad and its familiar scenes.

That he himself had no misgivings as to the welfare of the settlement is apparent from his writings, and, in fact, he had taken every precaution that knowledge and experience could suggest. Nor did those who remained entertain any apprehension of the future. There had been some natural display of emotion at the time of parting, but the members of the garrison had shown themselves willing and cheerful at the prospect before them. They were remaining of their own free will in the place of their choice; and whatever regret or sadness there was, existed rather on board the ship, among such of the crew as would have preferred the freedom of that pleasant life on shore to the arduous duty of manning the departing caravel. In the one case labor, privation, and no doubt danger were unavoidable; while in the other the fortunate colonists were assured of a long holiday of agreeable adventure and idle delight. Therefore the lighter hearts were those on shore. Confident that few though they were, they could withstand the attacks of every naked savage around them, even should their now hospitable friends be turned into open enemies by treachery or covetousness, the garrison anticipated no evil. What had they to fear? A few months would quickly pass in that favored region, and then their commander would be back, bringing them honors and rewards from their grateful sovereigns. The time did pass as rapidly as is its wont, and, true to his word, their leader landed at Navidad in less than ten months after leaving it. Some mutilated bodies, a burnt stockade, and a huddle of mouldy clothes and frippery were all that he found to mark the site of the colony from which he had hoped so much. From Diego de Arana, royal alguacil and vice-regal deputy, to the unnamed tailor, every man was slaughtered, and not a word remained to tell the tale of how or when. The "Niña's" crew had drawn the greater prize in the lottery of life, little as they thought it.

Doubling the neighboring headland, the Admiral steered his course along the coast. Throughout the day the land maintained its general character, — deep bays alongshore, wide plains near by, and lofty mountains in the distance, with native villages scattered here and there over the level districts. Owing to the line of shoals which fringed the shore, navigation was not wholly free from risk, and Colon made no attempt to land. He aimed to reach if possible a high and symmetrical peak which seemed to rise from the sea some ten leagues along the coast from Navidad ; but the wind fell as evening approached, and he had to anchor in a port not more than half-way to the landmark. On the morrow he reached it and named it Monte Christi, in honor of the Saviour whose protection he had invoked in starting on this homeward voyage, as he had in leaving Spain. The mountain served as guard to a deep and spacious harbor which offered so favorable a site for future settlement that the admiral landed to inspect it. He found traces of the presence of native fishermen, and was much pleased with the suitableness of the place, particularly as he found an abundance of colored stones, quarried as if by nature, and admirably adapted for the construction of churches and other public buildings, — "like those which we found in the island of San Salvador," he adds with a touch which shows his close observation. Here also he saw many mastic trees, and he returned to the "Niña" well satisfied with his examination. He enters with an appreciative pen in his diary the details of the noble panorama which was developing before his eyes as the ship pursued her course, apologetically saying that "far off to the south other very lofty mountains are visible, with very wide valleys fertile and sightly, and a very great number of rivers, — all this to such a degree delightful that I do not think I could enhance its beauty by the thousandth part." Well might he enjoy to the full the peaceful scenes on which his eyes were feasting, for a new season of trial and constant anxiety was close at hand.

On the following day, the 6th, soon after noon, the sailor who was posted aloft to keep a lookout for shoals ahead, sung out that he saw the "Pinta" in the distance; and shortly afterward that vessel appeared in plain view bearing down upon the "Niña" with a fair wind. The near prospect of meeting his insubordinate lieutenant, which was thrust thus suddenly upon Colon's mind, aroused at first a mighty impulse of angry resentment. The check given to his glorious career of success upon success by the desertion of Martin Alonzo; the knowledge that it would be imprudent, if not impracticable, to punish him for his rank disobedience; the apprehension lest other and greater troubles might yet be in store for him from the stubborn and independent nature of the "Pinta's" captain, — all these tended to break down his self-control and tempt him to indulge in reproaches and accusations. On the other hand, he reflected that although he had many men about him on whom he could rely, the Pinzons commanded both ships now, and had all their own friends and dependants in the crews, and it was by no means certain that should an open breach arise, he would gain the mastery. To have to yield to Martin Alonzo in such a trial of strength would be, he knew, to place all the fruits of this toilsome enterprise again in jeopardy. Under these circumstances he resolved to temporize and conceal as far as might be his resentment, accepting, at least in appearance, whatever excuses his derelict officer might have to offer. Therefore, when the "Pinta" came within hail, the Admiral answered her captain's salutations in kindly terms, and requested him to accompany the "Niña" back to the harbor near Monte Christi, since there was no safe anchorage closer at hand.

When the two ships were at anchor, Martin Alonzo came aboard the "Niña," and was received by the Admiral without any outward sign of indignation. Pinzon undertook to account for his defection by saying that on the night he separated from the flagship on the Cuban coast, the wind had driven him so far to the eastward that when day broke, neither fleet nor land was in sight.

"Your Excellency will well believe," the wily captain said with mock humility, "the terror and confusion which overcame me at this untoward discovery. All that it was in my power to do to regain the coast of Cuba, I did with my ship, — and men have said that I am no mean sailor; but despite my stoutest labors and all my indifferent skill, we were driven far away to the east until we reached some barren and rocky islands, I know not where. From there, with constant toil and peril, we have slowly made our way to this present coast, where, not many days ago, I learned from the natives that your Excellency was not far away with but a single ship. It needs not to be said that I lost no time in seeking for your Excellency, to offer my duty and place the 'Pinta' under your Excellency's orders; and grieved I am to find that one ship alone remains. I venture to hope that your Excellency received the letter I sent by the natives who brought me the joyful tidings of your Excellency's proximity?"

Of all this story the Admiral believed just one tenth. He was sure that in truth the "Pinta's" captain had heard of his presence in that vicinity and had come to meet him, as if voluntarily, in the conviction that at any moment the Admiral might fall upon him unawares. He was careful, however, to give no sign of anger or incredulity as he replied, —

"I thank you for your care and kindliness, Señor Martin, although by evil chance the missive you despatched has failed to reach my hands. Most heartily am I rejoiced to have you with me again, for the 'Niña' is but a doubtful dependence for the long and perilous journey that lies before us, and our course must now be hence direct to Spain. The 'Santa Maria,' good ship, lies on the shoals farther to the west, and a large part of her company remain near by for want of room to carry them; so the 'Pinta' is well come for more reasons than one. Were you fortunate in your search for gold, good Señor Martin?" the Admiral concluded, as blandly as a child.

"I found no great store, your Excellency," Pinzon answered, heedless of the trap into which he had fallen headlong; "and such as I sometimes got in traffic with the natives where we landed for wood or water, I caused to be preserved for the royal treasury, but now it shall be delivered to your Excellency."

"Not so, Señor Captain," the Admiral quickly replied, determined not to become responsible for any of his subordinate's possible misdemeanors. "'T were better to remain in your charge, since by you it was discovered; and when we are again in Spain a due accounting can be made of all to their Majesties. I doubt not," he added, changing the subject, "that your ship needs overhauling, Señor Martin, after her dangerous cruise. Please you, therefore, to order that she be put in condition to make the homeward voyage, while we are in so favorable a harbor. Again I thank you for your haste to join me."

With this the first interview between the two men closed. Neither was deceived by the attitude assumed by the other. But the advantage lay with the Admiral; for his forbearance robbed Martin Alonzo of any excuse for criticising his commander, while his own tale was known to be false by the commonest seamen. In the free intercourse which now set in between the crews of the ships which had been so long separated, the truth was bound to come to light; and the more the Admiral knew, the deeper grew his indignation. The very "Pinta" herself bore mute testimony to the falsity of her captain's tale; for her timbers were perforated up to the water-line with the tell-tale punctures of the dreaded *teredo*,— a fact eloquent of lengthy anchorages in land-locked ports.

From the reports of the Indian interpreters on the "Pinta" and others of her crew, the Admiral was soon aware of all that had befallen that ship from the night of the 21st of November, when she was lost sight of, until the day when she so unexpectedly hove into view. As he had suspected, Martin Alonzo's cupidity had been excited by the interpreter's tales of the fabulous wealth of Babeque; and on the night mentioned, finding the wind favorable and his vessel at some little distance from her companions, he had deliberately crowded all sail and left them to pursue their own way, confident that, as his desertion could not be discovered before morning, the "Pinta's" superior speed would frustrate any attempt at pursuit. Sailing to the east and northeast, in a few days he had reached a group of seven islands, which the Indians assured him were called Babeque;[1] but save for the few paltry ornaments worn by the inhabitants, no sign of gold was visible. Realizing that, either intentionally or ignorantly, he had been deceived by his guides as to the wealth of the island, he now changed his course southward toward a great island spoken of by the people of Babeque as *Hayti*, where, according to their statements, gold was as abundant as stones. In a few days he reached its shores, and found among the natives unmistakable proofs of the existence of the metal in great quantity. Following slowly along this coast, he gathered at every port new stores of gold, until, on reaching the mouth of a large river, he obtained it in such abundance that he spent sixteen days at this one place. While the "Pinta" lay at this anchorage, Martin Alonzo himself conducted a party of twelve of his men on a journey of several days into the interior, securing gold to the amount of a thousand ounces or more, and seizing four Indian men and a couple of women to serve as interpreters. This river he called the Rio del Martin Alonzo, after himself; and it was here that he first heard vague rumors of the presence of other white men in the territory of Guacanagari, not far off to the west. Either because he recognized the futility of trying to avoid the Admiral any longer, or because the "Pinta" had become so riddled by the worms during her protracted stay in bad waters that he dared not attempt the voyage back to Spain alone, or from a mixture of both reasons, Martin Alonzo decided at this juncture to go in search of his leader. Before leaving the river he shared with his men the whole

---

[1] It has been held, with some plausibility, that these were the island of Gran Caico and adjacent *cayos*, in the Bahamas group. Elsewhere the "shoals of Babeque" are frequently referred to.

treasure thus far accumulated, taking one half as his own portion and giving them the other half to divide among themselves. At the same time he urged his men to report to the Admiral's people, if they should meet, that the "Pinta" had been only six days in port, and had obtained very little gold. Sailing then westward, he had come within fifty miles of Navidad, reaching the point where he had been seen by the Indians who had reported the fact to Guacanagari. Failing to find his sister ships, he turned about to resume the collection of gold, and was coasting leisurely along shore, stopping wherever he thought advisable, when the "Niña" came in sight. Heading immediately for her, as though she had been the only object of his search, he had joined his Admiral in the manner we have seen. As for the letter he stated that he had sent Colon, and the anxiety with which he was seeking the latter after hearing of the loss of one of the ships, they were cut out of the whole cloth.

As little by little the Admiral fathomed the full extent of Martin Alonzo's treachery and baseness, he found it the more difficult to restrain his anger and contempt. It proved necessary to remain in the harbor of Monte Christi two whole days, in order to repair the "Pinta" and supply both ships with fresh water; and in his impatience to be once more under sail and bound for his sovereign's Court, Colon chafed under the delay. "I can no longer support detentions or tarry now for any cause whatever," he writes in his diary; "for I have found that which I was seeking, and do not want any further trouble with this Martin Alonzo before your Majesties know what I have accomplished and all the events of this present voyage. After that, I shall no longer brook the acts of evil persons and those devoid of honor, who presume to do their own will without regard for him who has brought them to such high fame." One single incident is sufficient to show how determined Colon now was to hasten his departure at all hazards. In filling their water-casks from a small stream which fell into the harbor not far from the anchorage, the sailors had found the sands on the bottom to be so full of gold-dust that on drawing the casks from the water the glittering particles were clearly visible, lodged in the crevices of the staves and hoops. At another time the Admiral would have become enthusiastic over such a discovery and taken the utmost pains to secure as much as possible of the wealth thus offered to his hand. But now, after verifying in person the correctness of his sailors' report, he contented himself with naming the stream the River of Gold, and noting in his diary that the fine grains must have been brought down by the stream from mines near by. He explains : —

"I did not think it necessary to take any of the sand which contains so much gold, for in any case your Highnesses have it all at the very doors of your town of Navidad; and it seems wiser for me to make the more haste to bear the news of these riches to your Highnesses and get rid of the evil company in which I now am. They are people without shame, as I have often said before."

He was, in fact, living in hourly expectation that Martin Alonzo would attempt some new "work of Satan," as he calls it; nor, as we shall see, was his apprehension unfounded. It is amusing to find the great navigator, notwithstanding his anxieties and cares, solemnly entering in his journal that on the day when he went to examine these golden sands he "saw three mermaids, who raised themselves high out of the sea; but they were not as beautiful as they are painted, although they bear a certain resemblance to human creatures in their faces. I had seen them before when voyaging to the Guinea Coast and Manegueta," he adds. It was in keeping both with the times and with the other marvels of the region he was exploring that he should have seen in a group of seals, or perhaps the seacows of these waters, veritable sirens such as would have lured Ulysses to his doom.

During the sojourn of the ships in this harbor word must have been borne to Guacanagari that the white men were still lingering on his coasts; for a messenger arrived from the king, who sent to beg the Admiral to return and receive the *diaho* which had been promised him. The purport of the message was not intelligible to the Admiral; and he asked Vicente Yañez, who was standing by, what he understood to be its meaning.

"By your Excellency's leave," the "Niña's" captain replied, "*diaho* in the speech of these people would seem to mean figure or effigy; and I conceive the messenger to say that the king craves that your Excellency go back to Navidad, that he may present your Excellency with the statue of gold which he pledged himself to give at the banquet on our taking leave of him. It were truly a royal gift, Señor Admiral."

"Could we believe that such were indeed the king's intent, Señor Vicente, I might be tempted to sail once more to Navidad; but in the doubt I care not to turn our backs on the homeward course," the Admiral answered, his distrust of Martin Alonzo rising as a barrier loftier than Monte Christi itself to warn him from returning to the colony.

"As your Excellency wills, Señor," Vicente Yañez said, with no little disappointment. "Yet again, by your favor, could your Excellency of a truth obtain the effigy, it would yield not less than two hundred *cuentos*,[1] and be a worthy example of the wealth of these realms for our gracious sovereigns, whom may God preserve!"

"The thought is loyal, Señor Captain," Colon responded, after a moment's reflection; "but it behoves us not to linger on these shores. In our hold we bear abundant measure of all that is needful to instruct their Majesties as to the surpassing value of these new domains, and the rest can well await our next coming. See that the messenger of our good friend the King Guacanagari is rightly entertained, Señor

---

[1] A *cuento* is a million maravedies. Two hundred million maravedies would amount to about two million and eighty thousand dollars of our money. The story rests on the authority of one of the bystanders, Francisco Garcia Vallejo, who gave it in evidence in the great lawsuit. Much of the material in this chapter is drawn from the records of the same suit.

Vicente; but when our sails are spread again, it must be for Castile."

The Admiral's decision, when it became known, gave rise to much wondering comment among his people,—perhaps as was his intention. In any case, it was an unmistakable declaration as to his purpose to loiter no longer on his way to Spain. He himself had already concluded that he had sufficient gold to convince even the most incredulous of the plentiful existence of the coveted metal in the Indies he had found, and had even counted upon deriving some advantage from the disobedience of Martin Alonzo. "For I recognize, Señores Sovereigns," he writes, addressing his royal patrons with the extraordinary frankness habitual to him, "that Our Lord miraculously ordained that this ship [the 'Pinta'] should remain in that place; for it is the best situation in all the island for making a settlement, and the nearest to the mines of gold."

At midnight on the 8th of January the two vessels weighed anchor and left the shelter of Monte Christi. After sailing for forty miles to the eastward along the coast, they anchored on the afternoon of the 9th under a cape, which the Admiral named Punta Roja, or Red Point. The following morning they continued their voyage, and reached the river which Martin Alonzo called after himself, and where he had remained so long and so profitably with the "Pinta." Although the Admiral remained here all the afternoon and night of the 10th, he did not set his foot on shore. Refusing to recognize the name given to the locality by his faithless officer, he rechristened it himself the Rio de Gracia, or River of Thanks,—as if from a feeling of gratitude that at last he was bound for home, and drawing daily nearer the end of all his trials. Here, too, he insisted upon the "Pinta's" captain restoring to their tribe the six captives he had taken when he landed here before. His lieutenant protested vigorously against this order; but the Admiral was inflexible. In his view it had been an unwarrantable assumption of authority for his subordinate to molest the natives, and he compelled their release as an assurance to the population that no harm was to be feared by the Spaniards. That Martin Alonzo was willing at length to yield to his commander's insistence and surrender his prisoners, is the first indication we find of his intention to submit again to his commander's supremacy.

In the great lawsuit brought by Colon's son, Diego, against the Spanish Crown, the relatives of Martin Alonzo and especially his eldest son, Arias Perez Pinzon, tried to turn to the advantage of the senior Pinzon all the incidents attending the defection and return of the "Pinta." What was the one dark blot on their friend's fame they heartily endeavored to establish as a grand achievement entitling him to the glory which they claimed Colon had appropriated to himself. To accomplish this, they indulged in what modern lawyers would consider some very adventurous swearing, and among other things sought to make capital out of the change made by the Admiral in the name of this river. The alteration, they claimed, was an act of pure spitefulness and malice, meant to deprive their kinsman of the credit to which he was entitled. As they swore, however, at the same time that Martin Alonzo had been the first to discover Hispaniola; that he had immediately sent a letter and chart to the Admiral *in Cuba* advising his leader of the discovery, as a loyal officer should; and that he urged his commander from whom he had parted *by agreement*, to hasten and rejoin the "Pinta" in a country so abounding in treasure, — we need not pay much heed to the Pinzon side of the case. So long as he faithfully followed his Admiral and gave him frankly his counsel and assistance, Martin Alonzo was entitled to a generous share of the glory of the whole stupendous success, for both his knowledge and influence had been invaluable to Colon. But when he abandoned his companions and started off to acquire riches and reputation at his leader's expense, the captain of the "Pinta" became that most contemptible of men, — an envy-eaten and treacherous subordinate, ready to betray his principal and sacrifice his own honor so long as his greed was satiated and his vanity gratified. His folly cost him his life, and he is entitled to his part of that charity which is the one virtue practised by the writers of obituaries. In those stirring days in Palos, enlisting men and equipping ships for the great voyage, and on the trackless western ocean encouraging his crew and upholding the authority of his commander, Martin Alonzo made a name which must ever be remembered with honor, so long as the New World has a history. Pity that his end could not be like that of his younger brother, Vicente Yañez, whose less overweening ambition yet sufficed to place him in the front rank of the world's boldest and most fortunate seamen, the discoverer of the mighty Amazon and the vast territory we call Brazil!

XXI.

NORTHEAST BY EAST, FOR SPAIN AND IMMORTALITY.

LEAVING the Rio de Gracia at midnight on the 10th of January, the Admiral pursued his easterly course for two days without coming to anchor, on account of the dangerous nature of the ground alongshore. With a lively breeze and a strong current both in its favor, the little squadron rapidly ran down the coast, and by the afternoon of the 12th was abreast of a tall headland which was apparently the limit of land in that direction. On doubling this, a great bay appeared, setting far back into the island; and beyond it the coast trended to the south and southwest, as in the case of Cuba. Judging by this analogy, the Admiral argued that he had reached the confines of Hispaniola, and was, he confesses, "frightened" as he reflected upon its probable extent. He anchored within this great bay, which we know as Samaná, and sent a boat on shore in charge of Pedro Alonzo Niño to hold communication with the natives, if possible, and secure a stock of peppers for the long sea-voyage before them. The Indians hid themselves at the approach of the Spaniards, and Pilot Pedro Niño had to return empty-handed. On the next day the Admiral would have weighed anchor and gone in search of a better anchorage, for his present one was too much exposed to be to his liking; but a strong sea-breeze detained the vessels, as an off-shore wind was needed to let them escape from port. He sent a boat again on shore, and this time the natives received the strangers at the water's edge. Unlike any of the tribes heretofore encountered, these savages were armed with bows and arrows, and carried long two-edged war-clubs of heavy wood. They were totally naked, had their faces blackened with charcoal, and wore their hair, which was decorated with feathers, in long locks down their backs. Altogether they were ugly and repulsive-looking, and wholly dissimilar from the more western races. The boat's crew offered them beads and trinkets in exchange for some of their weapons, and induced one of the men to go back with them on board the "Niña," so that the Admiral might converse with him. From the appearance of this individual and the description of the rest, Colon supposed them to be the much talked of Canibals of the Cubans, or the Caribes, as the natives of Hispaniola called them; but on inquiring of the Indian before him, the latter shook his head and pointed still to the east, in the direction of a shadowy looming of land which the Spaniards had remarked as they rounded the cape on the previous afternoon. The interpreters had hard work to understand the language spoken by this savage, as it differed materially both from their own dialect and that of Guacanagari's people, — a difference which Colon attributes to the distance separating the various tribes and islands. After repeated efforts, they informed the Admiral that the Indian said that the Caribes lived on an island not far to the east of Hispaniola, where there was so much gold that it was found in pieces as large as the ship. This fortunate country was called *Guanin*. In the same quarter was another island called *Mantinino*, which was inhabited wholly by women.[2] The Caribes ranged among all the neighboring islands, carrying off captives to fatten and devour, and the savages of Samaná had to fight them constantly. From the contrast between the natives at this end of Hispaniola and the handsome and pacific tribes to the west, Colon concluded that the fierce appearance and war-

---

[1] *Guanin* was the native name for a base alloy of gold, containing much copper.
[2] Mantinino is supposed to have been Martinique.

like instincts of the former were probably due to some intermixture with the ferocious Caribes themselves. As he could extract no further information from his visitor, he gave him his fill of biscuit and honey, and sent him back with a number of presents to his companions, telling him to ask them to bring whatever gold they had to the ships for barter. When the sailors took this Indian to the beach, he called out to his fellow-tribesmen that the strangers were friends; so that, laying down their weapons, they fearlessly approached the Spaniards. The latter again tendered beads and pieces of scarlet cloth in exchange for bows and arrows, as the Admiral desired to obtain a number of these savage arms; but for some cause the Indians became alarmed, and rushing for their discarded weapons, presented a startling front to the astonished sailors. Fitting their arrows to the bows, and flourishing cords as a token that they intended to bind the white men and carry them away, they shouted their uncouth cries and appeared to be on the point of making a general attack. This was too much for the Spaniards to bear. Although but seven in number, they leaped out of the boat and cheerily rushed into the midst of the savage mob. One of the sailors who bore a cross-bow, drove a bolt full into an Indian's breast; another, with his sword, hamstrung a native as he turned to fly; in a moment more the terrified heathen would have been massacred in the approved Castilian fashion, had not Pilot Pedro, who had the command, ordered his men to desist and return to the boat. When the skirmish was reported to the Admiral, he was inclined to feel keenly regretful. It was the first blood shed in anger in the new world he had discovered, and it was an unhappy close to the long series of kindnesses and generous hospitality which he had elsewhere encountered. On second thought, he reflected that since no greater harm had resulted, it might be for the best. These savages, who were plainly of a more fearless and quarrelsome disposition than any he had as yet met, had learned something of the power of the white men; and if the colonists of Navidad should reach this shore on the coasting journeys which he had ordered them to make, the natives of Samaná would hold them in wholesome dread, and not lightly attempt to do them violence. The argument, no doubt, was good. What the two mutilated Indians on shore would have said to it we should like to know. Probably they were disposed of in the thrifty Caribe manner by their relatives, and their views were not considered of moment. It is with almost a sensation of relief that we find some aborigines who did not hold any theory as to the celestial origin of the Europeans. It spoke well for their courage and saved them a bitter disillusion.

These people acted as though fighting Spaniards were an ordinary pastime. The next morning they flocked in numbers to the beach, making gestures that the strangers should come again on land. When the Admiral despatched a boat toward them, the Indian who had already visited the "Niña" came forward accompanied by another, who, he explained to the interpreters, was the cacique of that country. This chief offered to the men in the boat, through the Indian who had done the talking, some strings of rude beads in token that he came in peace; and on understanding this the Spaniards took him and three of his followers into the boat and rowed off to the "Niña," as this was what he seemed to want. Here he was hospitably entertained by the Admiral, and received a quantity of presents; so that on leaving the ship, he promised to return on the following day and bring his host a golden mask as a pledge of friendship. When the next day came it brought no cacique, although he sent to the Admiral a coronet made of beaten gold as a substitute for the mask, with a message excusing his non-appearance, on the ground of the distance he had to travel from his town to the ships. The Indians flocked down in numbers to the beach on seeing the boat arrive which had been despatched for the expected cacique, and showed no further opposition to exchanging their weapons and other scanty possessions for the trinkets of the Spaniards. Four young natives asked to be taken aboard the caravel; and they showed themselves to be so intelligent and communicative that the Admiral induced them to remain with him as guides to the islands of the Caribes, which he had resolved to visit, since they seemed to lie directly in his homeward course. From these men he learned that there was not much gold in this eastern end of Hispaniola. His informants pointed to the west as its source; and hence he inferred that the mountainous region which he had passed, lying between the territory of Guacanagari and that of this warrior tribe, must be the country of the mines. What seems to have interested him most at this landing was the superior character of the arms borne by the savages. "These people have no fear," he says, "and are not like the other tribes, who are cowards and have no weapons, in a senseless fashion." The bows of this tribe, he remarks, were as long as those of the English and French archers, and were, he thought, made of a species of yew. The arrows were often two yards in length, made of light reeds with heads of a hard wood, a foot or eighteen inches long, tipped with a fish-tooth. "The most of them are touched with some kind of herb," he adds. The method of drawing these bows was different from any he had seen in his military experience, and altogether he speaks of them as formidable weapons. From the description, they would seem to be identical with the arms still used by tribes of the southern continent, and the "herbs" were doubtless the poisonous composition in which the arrows are often dipped. As for the prospects of future commerce with this part of Hispaniola, he records that although there were indications of copper and gold, the main product of value would be the *aji*, or red pepper, which the natives employed largely in all their dishes. "This is much better than pepper," he writes; "nobody eats anything without it, and it is very wholesome. It would be easy to load fifty ships a year with it in this island."

Navigation in Colon's time was the art of carrying on trade by sea with the grace of the keenest blade and surest aim; but he was one of the few who knew it to be capable of higher uses. One of the reasons he gives for accepting his detention in the bay of Samaná so patiently, allows us an insight into that scholarly side of his character which is too generally overlooked in forming a conception of the man. He was expecting, he says, on the 17th of January, "the conjunction of the moon with the sun, and wished to observe how this would result." Besides, there should occur at this season, according to his tables, "the opposition of the moon to Jupiter, and her conjunction with Mercury, and the sun's opposition to Jupiter;" and all this led him to be prudent, "for it is the cause of great gales." How much of this astrological forecast may be correct, we do not pretend to say. Las Casas, in editing Colon's diary, observes that "these planets do not appear to be correctly collocated, through the fault of the scribe who copied the diary." Whatever may be the proper expression of the phenomena, it is characteristic of the great sailor that he should be anticipating their advent with so lively an interest, and should be anxious to observe them in as favorable a spot as possible. Unfortunately, his editor has not preserved Colon's subsequent entries concerning this first astronomical observation in our waters.

Before the eclipse and its attendant conjunctions were due, the Admiral was compelled to leave the bay. Both of the ships had been taking in water freely for a long time through their opening seams; but now they began to admit it in such quantity along the run of their keels that he realized that it would be dangerous to loiter any longer on the voyage. On the night of the 15th a fresh breeze sprang up which would carry him out of the bay; and, fearful of becoming wind-bound for an indefinite time, he directed the vessels to get under weigh and stand out to sea. He steered his course a little north of east; for in that quarter lay the islands of the Caribes, according to his savage guides, and since it would not take him far out of his homeward track, he was disposed to visit the famous people whose canoes roved at will through these peaceful seas and imparted such terror that their very names choked his earlier interpreters. After sailing some sixteen leagues in this direction his Indian pilots suddenly changed their minds and pointed to the southeast as the course to be followed. The Admiral, although reluctantly, gave orders to steer as they indicated; for if the distance was not too great, he would rather make the deviation than not explore the islands of which he had heard so much, and where he hoped to find at last the subjects of the Great Khan. The ships held on their way for a few miles, in a direction which would soon have brought them within sight of the blue mountains of Porto Rico, when the wind shifted and came out fresh from the quarter that was fairest for their homeward voyage.

So long as they had hugged the northern coast of Hayti they had known and cared nothing about the winds which were blowing out on the open ocean. Now that they had left land behind them and were sailing once more at large, the sailors were quick to recognize that the first steady wind they encountered would give them a free run home. How many weeks was it that the breeze blew them ever westward on the outward voyage? It all seemed so long ago that it was well-nigh forgotten, with the stupid fears of which the merest boy was now so heartily ashamed. But whether three or four, it was an east wind for one week after another, and as it had blown before so it might blow again, and when, then, should they see Spain? At first these remarks were confined to themselves, — merely Jack Tar's "wondering" why his commander did not act in a manner to suit his crew's ideas. Soon the pilots caught the burden of the seamen's lament and bore it, couched in duly respectful representations, to the Admiral. The ships were leaking fast; the stock of provisions scanty; the men's hearts sinking with longing to be on the other side of the mighty ocean which stretched so far ahead; the winds had proved uncertain among the islands, and the one prevailing was fresh and steady for the shores of Spain. "By the favor of your Excellency," this, and "Under the Señor Admiral's honored pleasure," that; but it was plain that reasons were plentiful and good for postponing to another time the visit to the Caribes. Colon needed no urging to convince him of the wisdom of these arguments. Had he been able, he would have liked to see the ferocious creatures who devoured their fellow-men, and carry a few with him to exhibit to his royal patrons; but it was not a matter of much import. More than any other he was impatient to set foot again on Spanish soil, and he would run no risk of losing so fair an opportunity of making a rapid voyage. To the joy of pilots and men, after scant reflection, he ordered the ship about and laid her head northeast by east, — the quarter where lay the distant coast of Andalusia.

The Admiral fully shared the apprehensions of his crews regarding the perilous condition of the two caravels; probably from his more intimate knowledge of the vessels' weakness, his anxiety was greater than theirs. Those leaks along the keel particularly disturbed him, for they were well-nigh inaccessible, and in his diary he reverts with bitterness to the malice of the Palos calkers who had so recklessly imperilled the safety of his people. He adds with quiet confidence : —

"But notwithstanding the quantity of water which the ships are making, I have faith that our Lord who brought me here will, in His mercy and loving-kindness, watch over my return; for His High Majesty well knows the toil I suffered before I could get away from Castile, and that no one was on my side except Him only, because He alone could read my heart; and, next to Him, none but your Majesties, for all others were opposed to me without any cause whatever. To these latter is the blame due that the royal crown of your Highnesses has not had a hundred millions of revenue more than all it has enjoyed since I came to serve your Majesties, — which will be seven years on the 20th day of this very month of January, — besides all that shall be received in the future. But the same Almighty God will not fail to set all straight."

With such lofty courage and sublime faith did this great man face the long and dangerous voyage which had now begun, as he had the still more daring one which had confronted him on leaving Palos. The day wore' on; the wind held good; by sunset the last dim trace of Hispaniola had sunk below the horizon. Behind him lay the " golden Indies;" before him was Spain and a deathless fame. The next land he sighted was within the confines of the older world.

Colon had spent three months and five days in cruising among the new lands he had discovered; barely one half the time that he had intended, as we have seen. Following the coast of Cuba for nearly four hundred miles east and west, he had in turn believed that it was the island of Japan, then the eastern provinces of Asia, and finally a great unknown island off the Asiatic shores. The immense extent of Hispaniola tended to restore his conviction that Cuba was part of the mainland; but as the natives of the former always referred to Cuba as likewise an island, he continued to refer to it as such until his second voyage. At that time he skirted its southern shores, as now he had its northern, for several hundred miles in one direction; and this restored him to his original belief that no mere island could have such gigantic proportions, and that it was the continent itself. In this faith he continued until his death, and his contemporaries still longer; for it was not until later years that men questioned his having discovered the veritable Indies *extra* Ganges.[1] His three subsequent voyages — the second to the Caribbee Islands, Cuba and Jamaica; the third to the coast of Guiana and Venezuela; and the fourth to Honduras and Central America — only strengthened this belief. The character of the natives, the products of the whole zone, the conditions of climate, and the strange coincidence by which the mistaken distances of the ancient maps made the Asiatic continent and its adjacent archipelagoes fall in the longitude of the Gulf of Mexico, all supported his theory. It is true that Colon did not find, either on this voyage or later, the vast cities and countless population celebrated by Marco Polo and Mandeville; but he heard (or fancied he did) the names of the Great Khan and Cipango, of Quimsay and Cathay, repeated on all sides, and hence was led, naturally enough, to expect to reach at any moment the civilized portion of the Indies. In the tales of cannibals with dogs' heads, of islands inhabited by Amazons, of others formed of

---

[1] And then it was *not* Americo Vespucci who opened their eyes.

solid gold, and the like, he was but unconsciously fitting to the vague descriptions of the Indians the ideas already gathered from the veracious tales of the Venetian merchant and the English knight. He followed no lead blindly; for when he failed to find Cipango and Babeque in the places assigned to them by the natives, he frankly attributed it to his own want of comprehension, and tried in another direction. But nothing ever shook his belief that these were the very Indies which he had found; and when, after ten years of unsuccessful effort to reach the borders of the true Cathay, he undertook that last terrible voyage whose hardships led directly to his death, it was to search for a strait connecting the western ocean with the middle seas of India.

Now, as he was hourly carried farther and farther away from the glorious region he had visited, his mind was at rest concerning the fruits of his undertaking. He had noticed that the Indians navigated fearlessly from island to island, even when these lay out of sight of one another, and that they knew the situation of other lands ten and even twenty days' journey away. This sustained him in arguing in his own mind that if the wealthy cities and provinces which he had come to seek had not been actually reached on this first attempt, it was merely a question of ampler time and more adequate equipment when they should also be discovered. The road was opened; it would not be long before the world knew whither it led. It is not singular that his opinions as to his whereabouts and the exact relations of his surroundings to Asia and to one another should fluctuate. The two islands he had skirted so vastly exceeded in extent any known to the navigators of those days, that, until they had been circled, it was impossible to avoid a doubt as to their insular character. Colon's instruments of observation, at best defective, became in time deranged and well-nigh wholly useless. When he applied to his pilots, skilful seamen as they were in the opinion of their times, he received as many different solutions as there were voices. Moreover, an intuitive distrust, which his subsequent experience amply justified, withheld him from taking his associates unreservedly into his confidence. The Indies had been found by *him*, at the direct instigation and under the individual protection of the Almighty. He was under a sacred and ever present vow as to the disposition to be made of the fruits of this discovery and the methods by which its future was to be regulated. "I protested to your Highnesses," he wrote in his diary on the day after the wreck of the flagship, "that all the revenues from this my enterprise should be spent upon the conquest of Jerusalem; and your Majesties laughed and said that you were willing and had the desire to do that even without my aid." The people of the new countries, as we know from his own words, were to be evangelized and converted to the true faith. Such as refused the Gospel and continued in their darkness were to be sent to Europe and sold as slaves. None but "true Christians" were to be allowed in these fortunate regions, even for the ordinary pursuits of commerce, and all intruders were to be repelled at the cannon's mouth. The natives of the new-found Indies were to be, in this world, subjects of the Spanish Crown; and hence they were to go direct to the Christians' heaven, there to partake of the joys of the faithful. With such beliefs and projects stirring in his mind, Colon never revealed to his companions the full result of his observation and reflections. He guarded these for the knowledge of his sovereigns alone.

One strange instance of the perplexity which often assailed the Admiral as to where he really was on the broad face of the earth, occurred just as he was sailing out of Samaná Bay. At this eastern end of Hispaniola he had found quantities of the same kind of seaweed which had attracted his notice on the outward passage and been heralded by his pilots and himself as a sure sign of neighboring land. Observing now closely this marine herbage he saw that it grew on the rocks and reefs at little depth below the water's surface, and thence concluded that what he had seen before must have been equally near some coast. As his log-book showed that he had first passed through this weed when only four hundred leagues west of the Canaries, the inference to his mind was obvious that some of the islands of the Indies must extend to within that distance of the Canary group. The first one he had encountered, Guanahaní, was, indeed, nearly three times that far from Ferro; but this he explained by supposing that he had passed too much to the north or the south of the most easterly of the Indies. On his subsequent voyages, he hoped, he would meet with them when journeying west. Needless to say that he never found them, and that the sea-weed he had first sighted was only one of the detached fields of floating Sargaco which encumber the Atlantic along the parallels he sailed. But the little incident, unimportant in itself, gives us a vivid idea of the groping and uncertain way in which even the great explorer, with all his keen sagacity and undaunted courage, was feeling about in the vast expanse which lay beyond the limits of the then known world.

For an entire week the two ships kept on their northeastern course, favored by a smooth sea and fair winds. As they proceeded, the air grew cooler and the nights longer; and this the Admiral conceived was due to the fact that the earth grew narrower in that direction. On the 23d the breeze became variable and often baffling; so that the "Niña" was called upon to shorten sail on account of her consort's inability to sail close to the wind. The "Pinta" was originally the better sailer; but in her six weeks' solitary cruising she had sprung her mizzen-mast, and was now unable to use those sails. This renewal of anxiety on Martin Alonzo's account was evidently hard to bear. To the Admiral every day's delay meant fresh danger and increased risk of never seeing Spain again. "Had her commander," he writes, in commenting upon the detention to which he was again exposed by the "Pinta," "taken as much pains to provide himself with a new mast in the Indies, where there are so many and such excellent ones, as he did to separate from me in the hope of filling his ship with gold, he would have had everything in good condition." Happily the sea continued calm; and the Admiral does not fail to return thanks for this renewed mark of Divine protection. On the 25th the sailors succeeded in catching some large fish and a shark of enormous proportions; and this also was a cause of rejoicing with their leader, — "for we had brought with us from the Indies only wine and bread and peppers for food," he states. That the squadron should have been so ill supplied with provisions for the long voyage back to Spain can only be accounted for on the supposition that the Admiral had left with the garrison at Navidad whatever stores of dried flesh he had, finding that the island of Hispaniola produced no animals from which meat could be obtained in sufficient quantities.

The winds were now more often adverse to the progress of the vessels than favorable; and their course varied from one day to another all the way from due north to southeast. They saw constantly the same sorts of birds, both large and small, which had been greeted as harbingers of land four months before; but now the sailors drew no hopeful auguries from their presence. Whatever land was nearest must lie far in the west; and their faces were set this time toward the rising, not the setting, sun. On the 3d of February they had come so far to the north that the Admiral records that the polar star seemed to be at the same elevation as at Cape St. Vincent in Portugal; but owing to the unsteadiness of his little ship he was unable to take a correct observation with his rude astrolabe and quadrant. If his estimate was exact, he must have been about in the latitude of Cape Hatteras, and a matter of one third across the Atlantic. The wind here changed for the better, and the vessels were able to hold steadily on their easterly course for the space of ten days, making eight or nine miles an hour day and night. The variations in their direction and the want of reliable observations had by this time destroyed the value of any computations as to their precise whereabouts; the squadron was driving whither the wind compelled, all hands contented in that their advance was mainly toward the east. The sea was covered with a kind of weed which the Admiral had seen in the Azores, differing widely from that which grew near the Indies; but he judged by the coolness of the air that he was not yet near the Portuguese islands. On the 6th and 7th the pilots compared notes, with as wide a variance in results as that of the traditional physicians. Vicente Yañez claimed that they were to the south of Flores, the westernmost of the Azores, with the island of Madeira due east of their bows. Roldan thought they were almost past the easternmost of the Azores, and were heading straight for Porto Santo. Pedro Alonzo Niño was for insisting that they were passing between the islands of the Portuguese group, although no land was visible. By the 10th they had made four hundred miles farther easting, with a considerable reach to the southward; and as no signs of land appeared, the pilots began to be anxious. The ships were leaking like sieves, the provisions were growing scarce, firewood and water alike were at a low point, and it was plain to the crews that the pilots did not know where they were. Another consultation was held in the Admiral's cabin. He and all the hard-headed and stout-hearted navigators who were with him had each drawn, according to their respective lights, their own charts of this extraordinary voyage. Whether one man could understand another's map is more than doubtful; but in those days what men did not understand they undertook on the strength of an unflinching courage and a muttered Paternoster. Vicente Yañez and the three pilots Roldan, Sancho Ruiz, and Pedro Alonzo were now unanimous in placing the ships well to the east of the Azores and in the near vicinity of Madeira. There was much hot disputation and jotting down of crabbed figures to sustain their several contentions; but the Admiral differed from them all.

"Against so many and such able navigators, 't is ill contending with a single voice, good masters," he said, after hearing their opinions; "but for my part 't is clear that you place us a full one hundred and fifty leagues too near Castile. Under your correction, I hold that we are only now in the longitude of Flores, and that Madeira lies not far to the southeast. Were we to keep still eastward, if my judgment does not greatly err, we should reach land not far from Nafé, on the coast of Africa. But all this is as yet conjecture; and we shall only know with certainty when, by the grace of God, we get a glimpse of some shore."

' In his own mind the Admiral was sorely perplexed as to where he was, although he believed that his calculation was much more nearly correct than that of his companions. Not only had he kept a careful and painstaking reckoning of each day's run, with allowances for drift and currents, and checked this whenever possible by stars and sun, but he had maintained a scrupulous watch over the surface of the sea as well. Each trifling indication which might serve as a hint to fix his knowledge as to what portion of the sea they were sailing was noted; and he compared his observations with his previous studies of these same waters on earlier cruises. His journal told him that on the outward voyage he had first seen the western sea-weed at about three hundred leagues from Ferro; he now argued that as they had but recently lost the last of that weed, they must be approximately in that same latitude, which would be that of Flores. As this coincided closely with his computations, he had the greater confidence in their exactness, and so maintained them against the united opinions of his pilots. These latter, however they might differ from him, adopted his reckoning without remonstrance, keeping the while a sharp look-out for land. In a few hours they were to have abundant cause both to praise their leader's sagacity as a navigator and be grateful for his skill as a cool and fearless seaman.

XXII.

"THERE WERE NO TEMPESTS IN THE INDIES."

FOR six months Colon's tiny ships had been at sea, the greater part of the time in untravelled waters, and thus far he had been spared the one danger which was most reasonably to have been expected. The proverbial terrors of the deep had been but words to conjure by; and even the perils of shipwreck had been passed without a timber parting or a green wave being shipped. For such an unhoped blessing he had not failed on frequent occasion to render thanks where they were due, and to enter in his diary his sense of the vast importance to his work of so providential an ordering. Now, however, both his faith and his fortitude were called upon to bear a strain which was all the more bitter because, like Cæsar's bark, the little caravels were freighted with the fortunes of a world. Unknown and unlocated, save by those on board, the new hemisphere must disappear if disaster should befall the frail squadron which bore the mighty tidings.

On Tuesday, the 12th of February, the sky was overcast, and the wind changed to a roaring gale, lashing the sea into frothy rage, and from the very outset putting the undecked vessels to imminent danger of destruction. As the night wore on, the tempest increased until both ships were running before it under bare sticks, their seams yawning, and the only doubt as to their otherwise assured fate being whether they should founder from the weight of water entering them from underneath or overhead. As the Admiral stood at his lofty post on the "Niña's" castle, scanning as far as might be in the gloom the yeasty confusion through which his craft was driving, he saw with still increasing anxiety three vivid tongues of forked lightning flash out in quick succession from the pitchy blackness toward the northeast. To his companions this was only an incident in the furious gale; but to him it was a boding of greater trouble yet in store.

"Three times it lightened from the selfsame quarter. Saw you that, Señor Vicente?" he asked of the captain, who stood at his elbow. "My heart misgives me that from there, or its antipodes, we shall have still wilder blasts before the morning light."

"'T were then a case for *Miserere Domine*, Señor," shouted Vicente Yañez, in reply; "for little more can this poor ship endure. I have not seen the 'Pinta's' light since early evening, and I fear her plight is worse than ours, — so riddled are her timbers by those voracious worms."

"God's will be done, good captain!" the Admiral responded. "He holds us all in the hollow of His hand. But I think not that evil has befallen our companion, for I saw her lantern astern within the hour."

When the morning came both of Colon's anticipations proved to be well founded. For a brief spell the wind lost some of its violence; and the "Pinta," which had weathered the night in safety, rejoined her sister ship. But later in the day, with a shriek of warning, a fresh gale fell upon the caravels and drove them staggering and helpless through the thundering seas, now dashing and crossing in blind fury as far as the eye could reach. So long as the tormented vessels were forced in one direction with the rolling billows they had some chance of riding out the storm; but now that the wind had shifted and heaped great walls of angry water against the course of the earlier surge, the short, round-bottomed tubs were tossed at large in this direction and in that, threatened with annihilation by every swelling crest that rose skyward alongside their weak hulls. All the night of the 13th this merciless plunging continued. To lift his ship a little out of the crazy dance of the cross-seas, the Admiral ordered a corner of the mainsail to be raised,

— a measure which steadied her somewhat, though at imminent risk of carrying the mast overboard at each fresh blast. A little additional relief was had by filling all the empty wine and water casks with salt water, to serve as ballast. The Admiral had not ballasted the ships in Hispaniola, intending to do this at the Caribes' island, where he had expected to touch on leaving Samaná. As their stock of liquids was exhausted, the vessels grew lighter until, had it not been for the preservation of the empty casks, they might have been swamped a dozen times in the course of these terrible days.

Daylight broke on the 14th over so wild and frenzied a whirl of angry sea and hopeless sky, that the bravest seamen gave themselves up for lost, and crouched sullenly in the lee of the bulwarks, waiting the end in stolid impotence. With anxious hearts the Admiral and Vicente Yañez had tried to pierce the driving mist of spray and rain, to catch some sign of the "Pinta;" but nothing met their eyes but flying scud and combing crests. During the night the "Niña" had been driven several miles away from her consort; but for many hours an answering flash had come from Martin Alonzo's vessel as the Admiral burned his flares to signal his own safety and inquire for that of his companion ship. Even when the latter ceased to respond, he had not thought the worst, for the night was thick and both craft were plunging wildly, so that distance and the mountainous waves might account for his failure to see the answering gleams of the feeble torches. But when the full light of day showed no sign of the "Pinta," he gave her up for lost, mindful of her leaky condition and the weakness of her masts. As the word passed among the sailors that the other ship was gone, they merely shook their heads and muttered a short prayer for their comrades' souls. To them it was only a question of a few hours, more or less, when they too should meet a like evil fate. The Admiral himself abandoned all hope of seeing another night unless by a miracle of the Almighty; but in his deep extremity he called upon Him with constant prayer and unshaken trust.

As became a good son of the Church of Rome, he also invoked, after the manner of his times, the intervention of those saints whose aid was likely to prove most efficacious. Sending for a handful of flat beans, he counted out as many as there were souls on board, and marking a single one with a cross, shook them thoroughly in a seaman's cap, and called upon the crew in the order of their rank to draw one. He upon whom the lot fell was to vow that if the ship were only spared, he would make a pilgrimage to the famous shrine of the Virgin of Guadaloupe, bearing as an offering a weighty candle of pure white wax. His being the first turn, the Admiral solemnly thrust his hand into the cap and drew out a bean from the sixty or more therein contained. It bore the cross. Reverently making the same sign, he confirmed his vow and called upon his companions to invoke each the aid of his own patron saint in this hour of desperate need. It was suggested that a pilgrimage should also be vowed to the shrine of Our Lady of Loreto, whose miracle-working powers were famous throughout the South of Europe. The lots were again drawn, and this time the marked bean fell to one of the sailors, — Pedro de Villa, from the town of Santa Maria, near Palos. As the journey to Loreto would involve considerable expense, the Admiral promised to defray the costs if they reached land in safety. Some of the seamen whose piety was of a more local type, now asked that a pilgrimage be vowed to Santa Clara of Moguer, a church much sought by the mariners of Andalusia when setting out on voyages. Whoever should draw this lot, it was established, was to watch a whole night at the altar of that church, and have a Mass of thanksgiving celebrated as well. Once more the cap was shaken, and a second time the cross lay in the Admiral's hand. This repetition of his former fortune served greatly to animate and console Colon. He pointed out to his awestruck men that since he had been chosen by Providence to make two pilgrimages, it must be because he was to be saved; and if he, their leader, was to escape, it was clear that they must also. As a final token of devotion and humility, he now registered a vow, in which he was joined by the whole ship's company, that wherever they all or any of them should first set foot on shore, there would they march in pious procession, dressed only in their shirts and bearing lighted tapers, to the nearest church, and solemnly render up thanks for their miraculous preservation.

Somewhat soothed by these devout exercises, Colon set about a measure of a more worldly nature, but one not the less near to his heart on that account. If his vows and petitions should not prove acceptable to the Almighty, he was distressed to think that the glorious outcome of his long life of struggle and contention would be lost to the world at large, and his royal patrons in particular. Withdrawing, therefore, to his cabin, he wrote down on a sheet of parchment, as best he could in the desperate circumstances of the moment, a plain and succinct relation of his voyage from the Canaries to San Salvador, his discoveries in the Indies, the incidents of the return voyage, and the perils by which his ship was at that hour surrounded. Rolling this up, he endorsed on it a request that whoever should find it should forward it to their Majesties of Spain, for which service he promised a reward of one thousand ducats. The parchment was wrapped securely in a piece of waxed cloth, and the parcel enclosed in a tightly bound cask which he caused to be heaved overboard. To no one did he communicate his action, lest they should lose heart still more at his apparent want of hope; and those men who saw the cask thrown over the vessel's side, supposed that it contained the effigy of some saint or other pious token consigned to the waves, as was not infrequently done on occasions of dire distress at sea. In the entry calmly made in his diary after completing this act, we can read the soul of the man as though it were mapped and charted before our eyes in copperplate. Without, the gale raged with unabated fury, and at almost every word Colon must have had to suspend his writing, as the ship lurched here or plunged there in the whirling caldron of waters. As he wrote down the record of his stupendous achievement, and reflected on the countless obstacles and dangers he had already been permitted to surmount, his hopes ran high that the present extremity also would pass away, and his work be spared for the benefit of mankind. He wrote:—

"Mayhap the fervent desire which I have to bear this marvellous news, and to show that what I maintained and offered to discover has proved to be exact, has led me to feel this great fear lest I should not be spared; so that at present every mosquito has it in its power to disturb and vex me. Surely this is due only to my own weak faith and want of confidence in Divine Providence! The thought of the many mercies which God has shown me in permitting me to achieve so great a victory, notwithstanding the many adversities and embarrassments which I suffered before leaving Spain, should sustain me in this hour. To His hands I committed my undertaking, and to His guidance I left it all; and He has heard my prayers and granted all I asked. Why should I doubt, then, that He will complete what has been commenced, and bring us all to safety? On the outward voyage I had far greater cause for fear in the trials which I had to endure with the seamen and others with me, all of whom determined with one voice to turn back, and arrayed themselves against me with many threats. Yet the Eternal God not only gave me courage and strength to overcome at that time, but afterward showed to me and through me many other marvels, besides saving me from the evil designs of certain of my own household. With these instances of His mercy, I can have no cause for dread in this present tempest. It is my own weakness and lack of faith which will not allow my mind to be calm. My heart also fails me when I think of my two boys, who will be left without father or mother in a strange land if aught befalls me; and I grieve to think that my sovereigns should not know of the services I have rendered them by this voyage, and that God has given their Majesties the victory in all they desired from this enterprise. I would also that their Highnesses should know that there were no tempests in the Indies, as may be clearly seen from the grasses and trees which grow down to the water's edge."

It was for all these reasons, he concludes, that he had prepared the story of his expedition, and committed it to the waves.

But what a touch of character lies in that last clause! Come what might, he wanted justice to be done to that new world beyond the Ocean Sea, — his world. Despite all the baleful prophecies of ignorance and fear with which for twenty years he had been surfeited, it was not in the western seas that he had been in jeopardy. It was here, near home, in the waters claimed by Portugal and Castile. In the Indies were no tempests!

As that trying day drew to its close, the wind fell somewhat, though the sea was as boisterous as ever and the "Niña" shipped great quantities of water. After dark the sky began to clear, and by midnight the Admiral was able to set a small sail and run before the wind. By morning on the 15th, the sea too had abated, and shortly after sunrise the welcome cry of "Land!" came from the lookout in the bows. So confused had the pilots become by the erratic course taken by their ship as the gale drove them hither and thither over the face of the ocean, that they did not agree within a thousand miles as to what the land, now showing plainly in the southeast, should be. Some held that it was the island of Madeira, while others were as confident that it was the Rock of Cintra, at the mouth of the Tagus; and a third group insisted that they were in sight of the coast of Spain itself. The Admiral, however, had followed the wanderings of his vessel with a narrow attention, and was of the opinion that they had before them one of the Azores. The pilots, he contended, allowed too easterly a position in their surmises. It was evidently an island they discovered on drawing nearer; but the strong head wind and sea prevented them from approaching it. In the afternoon they descried another island, just before darkness fell upon them and hid both from their sight.

As the "Niña" was beating about in her effort to fetch the coast first seen, Colon again sat quietly in his cabin, completing the letter which he had been writing on the homeward passage to his friend Don Luiz de Santangel, the Treasurer of their Majesties for the Kingdom of Aragon. To this courtier's courageous intervention, as we have seen, he owed the change of Queen Isabella's purpose after she had declined to accede to his demands in the camp before

Granada; and to him the Admiral felt was due a personal account of the results of the enterprise to whose success he had so largely contributed.[1] With the prospect before him of so soon being once more in port, Colon closed his letter in a strain of gladness which forms a striking contrast to the phrases of the previous day. He wrote: —

"All Christendom should rejoice and make great festival because Our Redeemer has given this victory to our illustrious King and Queen, and to their mighty Realm; and to the Holy Trinity should solemn thanks be offered, with many prayers, for the mighty glory they shall have in the addition of so many peoples to our Holy Faith. Thanks also are due for the temporal blessing in that not only Spain, but all Christian men shall receive from this enterprise, and that very soon, so great comfort and advantage."[2]

The night of the 15th was passed in cautiously tacking to and fro in the vicinity of the two islands; but when day dawned, the "Niña's" company could discern neither on account of a fog which had suddenly shut down. All day long they cruised about, on the 16th, searching for the lost landfall; but the only indication they had was that one of the sailors saw a light to leeward, as the night was closing in. Again they beat about under shortened sail until the morning, and for the first time in four days the Admiral threw himself on his bed and tried to take some rest. The ship was barely making a wake, the sea had subsided into the rolling swell which follows a storm, the sky was clear, and the breeze light; so he felt no apprehension. The long exposure to cold and wet on these fearful days and nights, coupled with the impossibility of obtaining food for most of the time, had caused his legs to swell to such an extent that

---

[1] It has been often held that Santangel furnished individually the funds for the voyage; but that this is an error is shown by the documents from which extracts are given in Note F.

[2] This letter is dated "On board the caravel, off the *Canary* Islands, the 15th of February, 1493." Either this was a slip of the pen, or the Admiral at the moment was leaning to the opinion that the Canaries were, in truth, at hand. A postscript was added at Lisbon, as will appear later on.

they could no longer bear his weight. For the greater part of his life he was a sufferer from gout, and in many of the later crises in his career we find him assailed by this, the most vindictive of his adversaries. Fortunately for him, this night passed without incident, and he was allowed to rest in peace. When the sun rose on the following morning, — Sunday, the 17th, — the land they had lost sight of was distinctly visible again to the southeast. Baffling winds obliged them to waste the day in fruitless attempts to make the coast, and it was evening before they reached it. Even then the haze was so thick that no one could assert with confidence what land it was, and they crept slowly alongshore looking for a harbor. At last they came to anchor in what seemed to be a favorable spot, only to have the cable part and be obliged to put to sea for another night. By sunrise the caravel had made nearly the entire circuit of the island, and reached a place which promised better anchorage. Seeing a few houses on the beach, the Admiral sent a boat on shore to inquire just where they were. The men soon returned with the news that it was, in fact, Santa Maria, one of the Azores, and that at San Lorenzo, a short distance farther along the shore, a good harbor would be found. The inhabitants with whom the sailors had spoken, had looked upon it as a miracle when they heard that the little vessel had weathered the fearful gales of the previous week, and said that among the islands the tempest had lasted for a fortnight without intermission. If they were amazed at seeing the "Niña" emerge in safety from such an ordeal, their wonder knew no bounds when they heard that the same tiny vessel had twice traversed the mysterious Western Ocean and visited the Golden Indies on the other side of the world. When the boat left them, the islanders set off at full speed to carry the astonishing tidings to the little government town.

The Admiral weighed anchor without delay, and made for the port of San Lorenzo. The sun had set when he reached it and brought his ship again to anchor as near the beach as was safe; but three men were already standing on the shore in evident expectation of his arrival. Hailing the ship, they said they wished to know the object of her visit; so Colon sent the boat to shore with one of his pilots to make the necessary report. The three men invited the Spaniards to accompany them to the town, which was some distance away, in order to converse with the governor or captain of the island, Señor Juan de Castañeda, who represented in Santa Maria the Crown of Portugal. This official received the pilot and his companions with marked civility, and was profuse in his admiration of the extraordinary exploit which he heard they had accomplished. In earlier days, he declared, he had known their commander, the honored Señor Cristoval Colon, very well, and had the highest admiration for him as an intrepid and sagacious navigator. After offering them such refreshment as he had on hand, the governor urged the pilot and two of his companions to spend the night with him on shore, proposing to send back his own messengers with the rest of the boat's crew to the "Niña." The invitation was promptly accepted. The party returning to the ship were laden with a generous supply of chickens, fresh bread, fruits, and other eatables likely to be acceptable to men who had been so long at sea; and these were presented to the Admiral by the Portuguese messengers with the governor's respectful compliments. His Excellency would have called in person upon his distinguished visitor, they assured the Admiral, had it not been for the late hour of the latter's arrival. In the early morning, however, he would present his respects and bring with him the three Spaniards whom he had detained on shore. The governor had only taken the liberty to invite these men, the messengers explained, on account of the passing delight he anticipated in listening to the recital of their astonishing adventures. Meantime his Excellency begged the Señor Colon to accept these poor refreshments as an addition to his evening meal, and on the morrow whatever the island afforded should be placed at his disposition. The Admiral expressed his appreciation of the governor's courtesy, and showed the Portuguese every attention in his power, answering freely their inquiries, and exhibiting to their admiring vision his Indian interpreters and some of the curious articles he had brought from the lands beyond the sea. The hours passed so rapidly in this agreeable intercourse, that when the messengers talked of returning on shore it was so late that the Admiral would not permit their attempting it, but gave orders that they should be lodged as comfortably as possible on board the ship.

In all this exchange of civilities and compliment there was something which caused the Admiral an undefinable uneasiness. Delighted as he was to find himself once more among the subjects of a friendly Christian power, there was a certain hollowness, a want of hearty cordiality, in this welcome, which made an unfavorable impression on his mind. He had no such vivid recollection of Señor Juan de Castañeda as that worthy professed to have of him, and he was none too well pleased with the detention of three of his crew, on never mind how plausible a pretext. He had lived too long among the Portuguese not to know exactly what value to attach to their ceremonious protestations, and there was a false ring about all this which put him on his guard. It was not the greeting to which he had looked forward when he had thought of once more landing on Christian shores. Still, he reflected, Spain and Portugal were certainly at peace, and therefore he had no legitimate ground for apprehension. The governor might have really fancied it was too late to call upon a strange ship, as he had alleged, notwithstanding the unusual nature of her mission. As for the three sailors, — well, the messengers were a fair equivalent, and if it came to a trial of wits his pilot would be able to give no information as to the whereabouts of the wonderful lands which would be of any use to the Portuguese in case they should want to go there. All that knowledge the Admiral had locked up in his sea-chest or in his breast; and he felt confident they would gain no advantage should they attempt any new trick this present time.

With these considerations he sought his rest, worn out with the cares and vigils of the past week, and devoutly grateful that at last he was within a measurable distance of his sovereign's Court.

XXIII.

THE GRACES OF CIVILIZATION.

AS the "Niña," on the previous afternoon, had rounded the point of land which formed one side of the harbor, the Admiral had noticed a small chapel, which stood a little distance inland on the side toward the sea. No sooner had the sun risen on the morning of the 19th than he reminded his men of their vow to go in their shirts in solemn procession to the first church they should find, and there return thanks for the miraculous escape vouchsafed them. Telling off the whole ship's company into two equal parties, he directed that the first should visit the chapel at once to perform their pious duty. He himself would head the second detachment of thanksgivers; but for the present he would remain on board the vessel in attendance upon the governor's anticipated visit. In answer to his inquiries the Portuguese messengers informed him that there was no priest attached in permanency to the oratory; but on hearing of the vow, they volunteered to go to the neighboring town and request the parish curate to meet the Spanish pilgrims and say the Mass. This offer the Admiral concluded to accept, his suspicions as to their good faith having been allayed by their friendly conduct while on the ship. The first party of the crew accordingly entered the boat, and were soon lost to view around the point. A motley sight they must have presented as, barefooted and barelegged, clad only in their scanty garments, they leaped ashore before the little building and marched in line to fulfil their singular vow! Their commander meanwhile remained with the other half of his men, quietly awaiting the promised appearance of Señor Juan de Castañeda. Hour after hour passed without any sign either of his Excellency or the absent sailors. Toward noon, becoming anxious, and a little suspicious as well, Colon determined to weigh anchor and sail around the point to see what was detaining his people. He could not imagine that any harm had befallen them on land, not only because Castile and Portugal were friends and allies, but because of the elaborate and unsolicited tenders of assistance which he had received on the previous evening from the governor of the island. The worst he feared was that the ship's boat might have come to grief on some of the rocks which lined the rugged coast; and the possibility of such a disaster sorely troubled him. It did not take long to double the point, and on coming within sight of the chapel a scene presented itself which roused the Admiral's anger to the highest pitch. Around the little edifice was gathered a great crowd of the Portuguese residents of the island, — some on horseback, but most on foot, and a large proportion of them bearing arms. Not a sign of a Spaniard was to be seen, although their boat was safely drawn up on the sands in a little cove near by. To the Admiral's mind it was clear that some treachery had been practised; but in the absence of any means of reaching the shore he could only strain his eyes in the vain hope of discovering what was passing in the distance. The "Niña" was run in as close to the beach as was prudent, the better to observe what was going on. As she drew nearer, a squadron of horsemen galloped down to the deserted boat, and dismounting, shoved her off and rowed out to the "Niña." As they approached, the Admiral noticed that they were all well armed, and were plainly people in authority. Coming within easy hail, they lay on their oars while their leader, rising from his seat, hailed Colon, who was standing on the castle consumed with an overpowering wrath.

"Señor Colon," said the Portuguese, "I am your Worship's very humble servant, Juan de Castañeda, the unworthy governor of this island of Santa Maria for his Most Serene Majesty King John of Portugal. Have I your Worship's warranty that I may come and go in safety upon your ship?"

"Of a surety, worthy Señor Governor," the Admiral answered, as the hope dawned that the governor might indeed come on board and put himself in his power. "The Crowns of Portugal and Castile are living in friendly peace, and ill would it become an officer of their Catholic Majesties to show affront to the captain of one of their ally's possessions."

Upon this some conversation ensued in the boat, which the Spaniards could not hear; and then the governor said, —

"I should esteem it a high honor, noble Señor Colon, if your Worship would accept my poor hospitality, and accompany me to my modest cabin with such of your people as you may designate. For that purpose have I come out to pay my compliments to your Worship with these few gentlemen of my household, and we shall grieve if we have made a bootless journey. It was our expectation to have met your Worship at the chapel, or otherwise we should have visited your vessel, as was our first intent."

"Nay, Señor Governor," Colon replied, as he grasped the situation; "it were not Castilian courtesy to allow your Excellency to return to shore without tasting the quality of our wine. I pray you consider that my poor ship and all that it contains is at the bidding of your Excellency and your gentlemen."

Again there was a brief consultation in the boat; but it was apparent that neither the governor nor his attendants cared to come to closer quarters with the Spaniards. At length he called out, —

"If it be not unseemly interference, Señor Colon, may I ask your Worship's purpose in putting into my port of San Lorenzo with an armed vessel, and sending a large body of men on shore without so much as asking for the permission of his Majesty's chief officer?"

At this the Admiral's temper nearly got the better of his discretion; but with a violent effort he controlled it yet a little longer, and responded, with an assumption of deference fully equal to that exhibited by the governor, —

"I put into your port of San Lorenzo, worshipful Señor de Castañeda, to escape the fate of my other vessel, which was lost in the tempests of the last few days. For many a long year have I sailed on many a sea; but it has been reserved until this day for me to find the shelter of the nearest port refused me by the officers of a friendly king. I bear with me the commission of their Catholic Majesties of Castile, Señor Governor; and if you will but come on board my unsightly craft and examine it, you shall find that I am strictly enjoined to show all aid and assistance to the subjects of his Majesty of Portugal, wherever found, and treat them with the honor I should myself expect, as a servant of my sovereigns, to receive at their hands. Your Excellency must be well aware that in Castile the subjects of Portugal are as safe as in their own Court of Lisbon. It would seem, nevertheless, from to-day's strange happenings, that the subjects of Castile enjoy no such welcome at the hands of Portugal."

Some hesitation was evidently felt by Castañeda as to the course he was pursuing, for he betrayed no little embarrassment when next he spoke.

"And may I, then, worthy Señor, make so bold as to demand upon what commission it is that your Worship thus freely invades the dominions of a friendly prince?"

"That may you, Señor Governor, and right glad I shall be to answer your demand, though its phrasing is none of the kindliest," replied the Admiral, speaking a few words to the pilot at his side, who quickly disappeared. "And may I ask, in turn, what news your Excellency can give me of my men who landed this morning under your Excellency's protection, and have been restrained by your people from returning to their ship?"

To this the governor answered nothing; for at that moment the pilot despatched by the Admiral returned with a case, from which the latter drew several parchments. Unfolding these so as to display their seals, he held them up toward the boat, and said in measured tones, —

"Your Excellency has here, Señor Governor, the royal decrees of their Catholic Majesties constituting their unworthy servant Admiral of Castile and Viceroy of the Indies, which, by God's blessing, I have but now annexed to the Spanish Crown. In their Majesties' names I demand of your Excellency the release of those of their subjects whom you are holding prisoners this day. As their Highnesses have ordered me to show such special favor to the ships and subjects of Portugal, so your Excellency's own sovereign shall not fail to be grievously angered that any officer of his should show so foul an affront to the envoy and servants of his Majesty's allies of Castile as your Excellency has seen fit to offer to me and my people."

The exhibition of the documents bestowing so high a rank upon Colon evidently made a profound impression on both the governor and those who were with him; but he answered defiantly, —

"In this island of Santa Maria we know nothing of the King and Queen of Spain, worshipful Señor Admiral; neither have we any fear of them nor concern for their commissions. What we do is for the Crown of Portugal; and if needs be we shall show that the power of our sovereign is no whit less than that of their Majesties of Castile."

This open threat filled up the measure, and away to sea blew the Admiral's long-tried patience. Dropping all further effort at pretended urbanity, he exclaimed in desperation, —

"Now may the consequences of your acts lie on the head that hatched them, Señor de Castañeda! Because your Excellency has foully trapped the half of my ship's company, think not we shall all fall into your treacherous hands. There are stout men enough remaining to take this caravel to Spain; and with God's blessing we shall be in Seville before many days are past. 'T will best behoove you, therefore, Señor Governor, to put your house in order; for his Majesty of Portugal will not deny the demand of my sovereigns of Castile that he who has done this traitor's act in time of peace shall meet his due reward."

There was more probability of truth in this declaration than was pleasant for the governor to hear. He well knew that the Portuguese king was not bent upon having a breach at any cost with the Spanish monarchs. If formal complaint was made, he was quite aware that King John would readily disclaim the act of his governor; and in that event he, Juan de Castañeda, would have an awkward account to settle. So he answered somewhat more pacifically this time, —

"Rest your Excellency assured, Señor Admiral, that I have done naught without the express orders of my gracious king. But if you will put back to our port of San Lorenzo, I will gladly consider with your Excellency what may best be done in this most difficult conjunction."

Colon saw at once the advantage he was gaining. Calling upon those around him to bear witness that the governor claimed to have acted and spoken under direct orders from the Crown of Portugal, he sent this parting shot at the boat, which was now turning about prior to putting back to shore : —

"So be it, then, Señor Governor, although the responsibility is none of mine, nor the difficulty of my making. I would but have your Excellency bear in mind that unless my men are incontinently released I pledge myself by my word and faith, as an Admiral of Castile, that I shall neither leave this ship nor set my foot on land until I have come back to this port with force sufficient to strip this island of its people and carry them all to Spain. I speak not hastily, Señor de Castañeda : mark well my words!"

The "Niña" was thereupon put about and steered back to the harbor. The Admiral was vastly disturbed over the day's occurrences. Neither the governor nor any of the islanders had intimated that there was any breach of the peace between Spain and Portugal, and yet the former's action was neither more nor less than one of open hostility.

His declaration that what he had done had been by his sovereign's orders, pointed to an intentional and premeditated provocation against Spain; while his contemptuous reference to the sovereigns of that country showed that, in the first flush of his success, he had counted upon the support of his own government in the high-handed outrage he had practised. As Colon reflected over what had passed, he was satisfied with his own course. If war really existed between the two powers, he had done what was spirited and right. If the governor's proceedings were only the excess of a mistaken zeal, the consequences would fall on him and not on the Admiral. "I could not suffer his insolence to pass without replying as regard for propriety demanded," the latter writes in summing up the incident. As for his attempt to capture the governor himself under promise of safe-conduct, he found a sufficient salve for conscience by arguing that the Portuguese had broken faith with him, and no pledge was binding as toward a traitor. The recollection of his narrow escape from the Portuguese fleet on leaving the Canaries a year before was present in his mind, and he only regretted that he had allowed himself, even for a single night, to put faith in the protestations of any subject of that jealous nation. He was tempted to carry out his threat in good earnest, and set sail without delay for Spain, to lay the matter before his king and queen and ask for the redress which he knew would instantly be granted; but the weather was unsettled and the winds unfavorable to the course he had to sail, so that he scarcely ventured to run the risk in the crippled condition of his crew. The party which had made the first pilgrimage and fallen into the islanders' hands contained nearly all his pilots and seamen. Of really able mariners he had not more than four left on board; so there seemed to be no remedy but to remain in the harbor for a few days and see what diplomacy could do to secure the release of his people.

San Lorenzo was a poor port to lie in, especially in such a stormy season as then prevailed. On the following day, while Colon was awaiting with ill-disguised impatience the promised conference with Juan de Castañeda, the "Niña's" cables parted under the constant strain to which they were subjected, and she had to seek a safer anchorage. The island of Santa Maria offered no other harbor; so there was nothing for the Admiral to do but to stand for San Miguel, another of the Azores, which is distant some seventy miles to the north of the first named. The little ship was doomed to suffer many a buffet, however, before she reached a haven of peace. No sooner had she left the shelter of Santa Maria than a storm arose which drove her so far out of her course that two days and a night passed without a sight of land. The danger to which she was constantly exposed throughout this gale was in no degree less than that which had confronted her before; and short-handed as he was, the Admiral looked for disaster to overwhelm them at any hour. "God showed us mercy," he writes, "in making the seas come from one direction only; for if they had crossed one another as they did in the other tempests, much greater evil must surely have befallen us." At the end of the second day, as the heavy weather still continued and no sign of San Miguel was visible, Colon resolved to return to the refuge of San Lorenzo, which, bad as it was, was better than beating about in a stormy sea with a crew of four available men to handle the ship. In these hours of trial his thoughts reverted persistently to the smooth seas and balmy breezes of those fair regions beyond the Ocean Sea. He enters in his diary: —

"Not for one single hour did I find the sea in the Indies so stormy that it was not easy to navigate; but here we have been constantly exposed to furious tempests, and the same fate befell us on our outward voyage when we were sailing to the Canary Islands. Well did the sacred writers and the wise philosophers of old say that the earthly Paradise lies in the extreme limits of the Orient; for the countries which I have discovered are temperate beyond description, and they must verily constitute the eastern end of Asia."

On the afternoon of Thursday, the 21st of February, the "Niña" came to anchor again in the port of San Lorenzo.

Her unexpected departure the day before had clearly alarmed the bellicose Señor de Castañeda, for as soon as she approached the shore a man appeared signalling her from the water's edge, and calling out that she should remain where she was, as the governor desired to communicate with the Admiral. Shortly thereafter the captured boat hove in sight, rowed by five of the Spanish sailors and containing two Portuguese priests and a notary, — evidently a pacific embassy. A pledge of security being asked and given, they came on board the caravel and delivered their message. His Excellency the governor, they assured their hearer, had no desire to embarrass in any way the noble Admiral; he had but acted in accordance with his instructions, which were to call to account any vessel putting into a port of his jurisdiction without the special permission of the Portuguese king. If the noble Admiral would satisfy his Excellency that he had come with no hostile intent, and had not invaded any of the territories of Portugal in the voyage from which he was returning, his Excellency would release the men and render the noble Admiral any service in his power. It was very difficult for Colon to listen to this rigmarole with patience. He saw that it was a mere pretext on the governor's part to escape from his dilemma; that having failed to secure the commander himself, he was now anxious to retire as gracefully as possible from an untenable position, and restore the men who were of no use to him; and that he hoped thereby, since the game was lost, to escape any serious consequences from his act of treachery. Colon had no idea of yielding too readily to the proposition of the governor. He declared that he must reflect upon the matter; and as it was now dark and the weather blustering, he induced the emissaries to remain on the ship overnight.

In the morning he inquired of them what was the nature of the assurances they demanded as to his intentions and authority. They replied that if he would show them that in reality he was sailing under the orders of the Spanish Crown they would be content. The impudence of this proposal nearly upset again the Admiral's self-control. That he, an officer of the highest rank in the navy of Castile, a Viceroy of the proudest monarchs in Christendom, the discoverer of a new path to the Antipodes, should be stopped by a petty official of a rival nation as he was bearing to his own sovereigns the tidings of his prodigious success, and called upon to give an account of his actions to an unknown scrivener and two nameless priests, — the very thought was gall and wormwood to the Admiral's proud mind! Conscious of his own mighty deeds, and eager to communicate them to his royal patrons, the interference of this petty Portuguese tyrant was as humiliating as it was insolent. His instant impulse was to send the three messengers back to Castañeda with a biting answer of scorn and defiance; but a moment's reflection restored his self-command. If he secured his men, be the cost to his pride what it might, he could sail at once for Spain, and, once before his haughty masters, could obtain all the redress and satisfaction he so righteously desired for the affronts now offered to their standard and representative. Curbing his wrath with a mighty effort, he accordingly consented to produce his commissions. When the priests and the notary read the ample powers vested in the man who stood now so quietly before them, and saw the signatures of Ferdinand and Isabella attached to the summons addressed to the princes at peace with Castile to grant all friendly aid and succor to their Admiral and Viceroy, they realized the mistake the worthy governor had made. Profuse in their expressions of respect and recognition, they were now all anxiety to return with their report; but their entertainer would not allow them to go empty-handed. Choosing from his stores a number of curiosities and strange productions from the distant Indies, he pressed them upon his embarrassed visitors, who, when they finally took their leave, were overwhelmed with the graciousness and magnanimity of him whom they had so lately scorned and outraged. Within the hour the boat returned to the "Niña," bringing all the Spaniards who had been detained. Without further delay the Admiral hoisted sail and left San Lorenzo, to seek some other place along the coast where he could take on board a supply of wood and water before laying his course for Spain.

The restored members of the crew, in giving him an account of their experiences while in the hands of the Portuguese, declared that the whole affair, from the moment the "Niña" was first hailed on the evening of the 18th, was a plot to secure the person of the Admiral. When the landing party of pilgrims had settled down to their devotions inside the chapel, the sacred edifice was surrounded by the whole male population of the island, under the governor's immediate command, and every one of the praying Spaniards was taken prisoner. As soon as Castañeda found that the Admiral was not in the party captured, he rode off in a towering rage to the boat on the beach, determined to go off to the caravel and seize Colon, either by stratagem or force. Foiled in this second attempt, the governor seems to have devoted his energies to extricating himself from the predicament into which his hot head had led him, and the men had no other ill-treatment to complain of. They had learned while in durance that orders had been sent out some months before by the King of Portugal to the authorities of all his islands and colonies in the Atlantic Ocean and along the Guinea coast, directing them to seize the Spanish vessels wherever they should appear, and take the Admiral prisoner. That the governor of Santa Maria had failed in his amiable design was due only to the fact that Colon had decided to accompany the second party of pilgrims to the chapel. The messengers who had taken the news of the intended pilgrimage to Castañeda when they had offered to get the priest, had not been aware of this arrangement, and so a very prettily laid scheme had ended only in chagrin. What wonder that the Admiral, as he contrasted the reception of the savage king of Marien with that extended by the civilized governor of Santa Maria, should have thought that not the elements alone were better regulated in the Indies! As one reads Colon's account of this first welcome offered by the people of the Old World to the finder of the New, one is tempted to regret that he did not leave his band of pilgrims in Santa Maria and adjust the score in the manner he threatened.

It was not until early evening on the 23d that the Admiral found a place where he could come to anchor and procure the supplies he wanted, and even then the surf was running so high that he would not send the boat ashore. Sunday, the 24th, broke with a strong southwest breeze which threatened to drag the vessel and cast her on the rocks if she were kept any longer where she was. This wind, too, was fair for the Spanish coast, and the prompt completion of his voyage suited better the Admiral's present humor than losing another day in waiting to take in water. An inspection of the stock on hand showed that with proper husbanding it would last the remainder of the journey, and he therefore ordered the anchor weighed and the ship's head laid for Home. Great was the rejoicing among officers and men when they thought that the next port they should make would be within the borders of Castile. Had they known what still lay before them, they would have preferred remaining in Santa Maria, even in their shirts.

XXIV.

KING AND COMMONS.

FOR three days the weather held good, and the "Niña" made fair progress to the east and northeast; but on Tuesday night the wind changed to a gale, and she was driven off her course and wandered at the mercy of the storm for forty-eight hours. This constant succession of tempests "at the very door of home," as Colon puts it, seemed to him to be meant as a judgment upon the pride and satisfaction with which he was looking forward to the reception with which his great news would be greeted when he reached Spain. After all, what was he but an instrument of the Almighty in this stupendous event? To God was due the glory, and to Him alone; and the Admiral piously reproaches himself for having appropriated too large a share of the credit of the enterprise.

On Friday the weather changed for the better, and on this and the next day the ship was able to make good headway. On Sunday, the 3d of March, another storm set in which came nearer to bringing the voyage to a fatal termination than any of its predecessors, pitiless as they had been. The Admiral believed himself to be not far from Cape St. Vincent, and was steering east when the storm fell upon him. Without a moment's warning a cyclone struck the little ship; and before an order could be shouted or a hand stretched out to seize a rope, the sails were split into a thousand shreds, and the "Niña" was plunging blindly along under bare poles. The sea, already heavy from the previous gales, now mounted in heaping masses about the terrified crew, crashing down upon the devoted vessel from every direction and threatening her with instant annihilation. Again the despairing company appealed to Heaven for the aid they could no longer render themselves, and, casting lots, vowed that whoever should draw out the cross-marked bean should make a humble pilgrimage to the Virgin of the Belt in Huelva, near their native port of Palos, and in his shirt give thanks for the infinite mercy shown in saving them from this imminent destruction. Strange to say, for the third time the Admiral was indicated by chance to do this act of penance; and in this fact he discerned the Divine intention of rebuking him publicly for his vainglory. Not content with this vicarious deed of penance and contrition, the whole crew now joined in vowing that the first Sunday they should spend on land they would touch no other food than bread and water, — not a small matter for men to promise who had been living on little else for six weeks and enduring the while so many other hardships.

The storm continued without a break all that day and night, accompanied by frequent violent rains and a ceaseless play of lightning. The fury of the seas — not regimented billows, but a frantic confusion of gigantic waves, — cast the tiny caravel from the ragged summit of one watery mountain into the seething hollow of the next; and not for a single moment did the worn-out mariners draw a breath in peace. "It pleased Our Lord to sustain us," Colon records, "although through infinite peril and distress; and when daylight came He showed us land." Two sailors caught sight of a lofty rock in the dismal light of the early morning; but it was only an additional source of danger. The coast proved to be iron-bound, and as it lay on their lee they were lost beyond the hope of salvation unless they could wear their ship farther out to sea. To make any sail at all was to expose them to scarcely less danger of foundering; but there was at least a fighting chance for their lives, and they took it. As the light grew stronger, the Admiral recognized that he was off the mouth of the Tagus, and that the headland in sight was the far-famed Rock of Cintra. The knowledge brought him little consolation; for to enter the Tagus was to put himself irrevocably in the power of Portugal. What choice had he, however? Better deliver himself up as a prisoner and trust to the Almighty and their Majesties of Castile to rescue him, than to expose his whole ship's company to almost certain death! Putting the "Niña's" head about, he slowly and laboriously beat toward the mouth of the river, and after hours of torturing suspense made the entrance and came to anchor off the little village of Cascaes, where the water was fairly quiet. Many a time in previous years had he sailed gladly into the Tagus, homeward bound from distant climes; but on this one occasion, when he most needed her shelter and yet was loath to avail of it, did she play the churl and strive to bar the way against him. The residents of the fishing hamlet put out at once to the caravel to see what the new arrival was, and were loud in their expressions of wonder that the ship had been able to live in such a gale. All morning long, they said, they had watched the "Niña" as she fought her desperate battle, and over and over again had given her up for lost, although they never ceased their prayers that she might reach their harbor in safety. When they heard of the voyage she had made, they could not credit their ears. So fearful a winter had never been known along the Atlantic coast within the memory of the oldest sailor. They reported that on the Flemish shores alone five-and-twenty vessels had been lost, and there were others in the Tagus, bound for Flanders, which had been waiting for four months for a chance to put to sea with reasonable safety.

Later in the day, when the tide served, the Admiral left his anchorage at Cascaes, and continued up the river to Rastelo, just below Lisbon, where incoming ships had to lie until permitted to go on to the city. He was determined to put a bold face on his arrival, since he was completely at the mercy of the Portuguese. Not only might they seize him on the pretext that he had been filibustering in their newly acquired African dependencies, as Castañeda had attempted; but there were old scores against him, dating ten years back to the days when he plead his cause at King

John's Court, and kept the wolf from the door by making maps and sailing ships. He would act as became a man of courage and an officer of the Spanish Crown, at all events; and so he at once addressed a missive to the king, announcing his presence in the Tagus, and asking permission to take his vessel up to Lisbon. He based his request upon the fact that there was no sufficient protection at the station where he was, and as the report had gone abroad that his ship contained great treasures, he was exposed to attack from the lawless inhabitants of the river-bank. In order to remove all idea from the king's mind that the Spanish vessels had been trespassing in the countries claimed by Portugal, Colon added that he had not been near the Guinea coast, but had come direct from the Indies, which he had reached by crossing the Western Ocean. He put himself under the protection of his Majesty in obedience to the orders of his own sovereigns, who had directed him to ask whatever aid he might require from their ally of Portugal, and to pay for it at its full value. This letter he despatched to the king, who was at the Valle do Paraiso, some nine leagues from Lisbon. It shows the shrewdness of the writer's mind, notwithstanding the open frankness which was one of his chief characteristics. He had every reason to suppose that King John was disposed to make him prisoner, either from envy of Spain or from a grudge against the Admiral himself for having left his Majesty's service and gone to seek his fortunes in Castile. By boldly appealing to the king for assistance and protection in the name of the Spanish Crown, he threw the Portuguese monarch into the unpleasant dilemma of affronting his allies by an act of undisguised hostility, or of smothering his resentment and allowing the Spanish Admiral to refit his vessel at leisure and depart in peace. The event proved the wisdom of Colon's move. King John was anything but prepared to seize the Viceroy of his neighboring allies by an act of open violence, and had no remedy but to put as good a face as possible upon his envious disappointment, and welcome the Admiral as the representative of the Spanish monarchs.

One more trial, and that a bitter one, was in store for Colon before he tasted that rare wine of triumph of which he was to drink so deep. When he had anchored at Rastelo he had noticed with admiration a huge man-of-war lying not far off, which he knew, from her size and appointments, was the flagship of the Portuguese navy. "A better ship, or one more nobly provided with artillery and all manner of arms, I never have seen," he writes, in a genuine seaman's delight at so splendid a craft. The morning after his arrival, while waiting for an answer to his letter to the king, he saw an armed boat put off from the great ship and make direct for the caravel. On coming alongside the "Niña," the officer in charge of the boat gave a hail and asked for her commander. The Admiral at once presented himself and inquired what was wanted of him. Rising in his boat, the Portuguese officer replied, with little attempt to choose his words, —

"His Excellency Dom Alvaro Dama, captain of his Majesty's flagship yonder, desires to know your business in the Tagus, good Señor, and has sent me to bring your Worship aboard his vessel. For myself, I am your Worship's humble servitor, Bartolomé Diaz, a poor lieutenant of his Majesty King John, whom may God preserve!"

"Amen, Dom Bartolomé!" said the Admiral, cut to the quick by the cool impertinence of the summons, and reflecting bitterly on the vast disparity between his weather-beaten cockleshell and the magnificent war-ship before his eyes. "Your vessel is a noble one and worthily commanded. But I am Admiral of the Ocean Sea, a humble servant of their Catholic Majesties of Spain, and I have never heard that it was the usance of a Spanish Admiral to give account of his actions to every Portuguese captain he chanced to meet. If your worthy commander wants me he can take me without a doubt, for he has ten times my power; but save by force of stronger arms, I stir not from this ship. Take that for my reply to Dom Alvaro Dama, good Señor Lieutenant, and God speed you as you go!"

The easy-going lieutenant saw that he had a harder task

on his hands than he had thought, or his captain either, and changed his tone at hearing the high rank claimed by the tall stranger who had answered him so harshly,

"I crave your Excellency's pardon, Señor Admiral, for an offence that was not intended. No doubt the requirements of my noble captain will be fulfilled if your Excellency but sends with me the master of your vessel, or any one to answer for your Excellency."

But the Admiral's wrath was at a white heat. All the treachery and insults he had received from the Portuguese, from the time when, years before, they had tried to steal the glory of his enterprise, up to this present moment when a supercilious subordinate was bandying words with the bearer of a new world, came flooding into his mind and broke down the last barriers of his self-control.

"I doubt not that such a token of submission would be welcome to your chief, Señor," he responded, with a ring of irony in his voice; "but neither master of the ship nor sailor of the crew shall go on board your vessel except by stress of better fighting. As willingly should I go myself as let any one go for me, and 't is easier for me to die fighting, as is the custom of the Admirals of Castile, than live at the behest of every underling of Portugal."

Lieutenant Bartolomé began to see that prudence would be golden, and strove to allay the storm his careless insolence had raised.

"I protest, most noble Admiral," he said with great deference, "that neither my captain nor myself, your Excellency's servant, has any wish to attack the dignity of Spain or assail your Excellency's authority. If your Excellency will but deign to let me see your powers, I shall be able to certify to Dom Alvaro that I have performed my duty, and report your Excellency's exalted rank to my commander."

The Admiral was tempted to look upon this as a fresh piece of impertinence; but the thought of the imminent necessity of avoiding any overt quarrel with the Portuguese authorities led him to yield a little of his dignity, and he sent for his commission.

"So be it then, Señor Lieutenant," he answered; "a drop more in the ocean will not cause it to overflow."

When the parchments were brought, he exhibited them to the officer, who saluted the signatures of Ferdinand and Isabella and returned at once on board the flagship. Colon remained in an anxious frame of mind, determined to resist to the uttermost any attempt at violence, but distressed at the prospect of meeting with disaster just as he had escaped such mighty dangers and was so near the end of his weary journey. But the report made by Dom Bartolomé Diaz on reaching the flagship had opened many eyes. In a short time the Admiral saw the great barge of that vessel put off from her side and head for the "Niña" with a company who were plainly bent on no deeds of arms. Seated in the stern was a gayly dressed party of officers, and over the water, in advance of the approaching barge, floated the martial music of cymbals, drum, and pipe. Seemingly a visit of high ceremony was intended, and all on board the Spanish caravel awaited with eager interest the explanation of so stately a proceeding. When the boat drew near the "Niña," it proved to contain Dom Alvaro Dama and his staff, who saluted the Spaniards and asked leave to present their compliments to the Admiral. Like a brave and generous sailor, the Portuguese captain had resolved frankly to make amends for the error of the morning as quickly as he heard who the new arrival was, and had come with the pomp befitting the rank of the caravel's commander. Colon received his visitors at the ship's side with all the honors, and conducted them to his own cabin. There Dom Alvaro tendered his apologies for the recent occurrence, excusing himself on the ground that he was unaware of the distinguished rank of his host, and begged to be allowed to supply whatever the Admiral might require. The latter accepted willingly the captain's explanations, and promised to avail himself of his tenders of service should occasion arise. He then entertained his guests with an account of the voyage to the Indies, exhibiting his savages and other curiosities for their inspection. After an agreeable conversation, the Portuguese took their leave, charmed with their reception, and having equally delighted the Admiral by their courteous and hearty bearing. He had no longer any fear of petty treacheries at least, for he knew that the visit just ended was a sincere tribute of respect and amity.

The extraordinary nature of the "Niña's" voyage and cargo was soon noised through Lisbon, and for the next two days the ship was overrun with visitors, and her commander burdened with well-meant civilities from the most distinguished residents of the capital. To all their compliments and flattery he answered simply that it was God's doing; that he had merely been an instrument of the Divine Providence in what had been accomplished. To such questions as seemed to be designed to draw from him a more particular knowledge than he cared to give concerning his late discoveries, he returned politic and guarded replies. He was not going to be led into betraying his secrets by the smooth tongues of the Portuguese courtiers. As for his visitors, their amazement knew no limits, and on all sides was to be heard the remark that this dazzling acquisition was palpably the direct gift of God to the Spanish monarchs in return for their zealous piety in conquering the Moors and driving from their dominions the infidel children of Abraham. In the scanty leisure permitted him by these constant demands upon his hospitality, Colon prepared a letter to Ferdinand and Isabella in which he announced the chief results of his expedition. This he sent overland to Barcelona, at the extreme border of the Spanish territories, from Lisbon, as he had learned that the Castilian Court was established in that city. By the same bearer he forwarded the letter he had written on shipboard to Don Luiz de Santangel, having only added to it a postscript on the day he had come up the river, in which he told his friend of his safe arrival at Lisbon, and contrasted the inclemency of the weather with the benignity of the "Indian" climate. "It was always like the month of May," he wrote, as if drawing a comparison with the harsh months of February and March in the North Atlantic.

On Friday, the 8th of March, being the fifth day of the "Niña's" detention in the Tagus, Dom Martin de Noronha, one of the royal chamberlains, came aboard the caravel, bringing the answer of King John to the Admiral's appeal. His Majesty therein expressed his very great satisfaction in hearing of the safe arrival of the Spanish vessel and the desire he had to learn from the distinguished navigator's own lips the details of his astonishing exploit. He therefore begged Colon that, since the weather was yet so tempestuous that he could not put to sea, he would visit the royal palace of Valle do Paraiso as the honored guest of his Majesty. The letter added that Dom Martin de Noronha, its bearer, was instructed to wait upon the Admiral and furnish him with all he might require. In presenting this reply, the chamberlain also stated that the king had directed the authorities of Lisbon to supply without charge both the ship and her crew with whatever they might need, and that he himself was to remain exclusively at the orders of the Admiral. All this was very flattering and gracious; but Colon was loath to leave his ship and go so far into the country to visit King John. He had lived too long among the Portuguese to have forgotten their sententious proverb, that "Feathers and words both float on the wind," and he had hard experience that the royal breath was no weightier than that of commoner mortals. "The word of the king cannot turn back," the same people were fond of saying; but he had seen it not only turn back, but roll in the mire as well, and he hesitated to trust it now. However, he had no excuse for declining the royal invitation; the more especially as any display of reluctance would probably give rise to suspicions as to the real nature of his voyage, and thus afford a plausible pretext for his detention. He accordingly signified to Dom Martin his intention to comply with his Majesty's commands, and ordered his trusty pilot, Pedro Alonzo, to be prepared to accompany him on the journey. The party set out in the afternoon, under the guidance of the royal chamberlain and escorted by a proper guard, and went as far on their road as the town of Sacambem. The following morning they continued their journey, despite a drenching rain, and reached the Valley of Paradise late in the afternoon.

The Admiral was met at the entrance to the palace by all the dignitaries and officers of the Court, and treated with the utmost distinction. After changing his travelling-dress for a garb more befitting the occasion, he was conducted to the audience-chamber, where he found King John, surrounded by his whole court as on a state occasion. Advancing toward the dais, the Admiral bent his knee and kissed the royal hand; then rising, waited for the king to speak, as etiquette demanded. The king, however, directed that a chair be brought, and affably insisted that the Admiral should be seated while in his presence. This honor was the more marked by reason of its excessive rarity in that punctilious Court; and at this moment Colon must have felt a triumph in some degree commensurate with the trials and hardships of the bitter past. It was only ten years since he had left Lisbon overwhelmed with debt and almost despairing under the weight of grievous disappointment. It was only five years this same month of March since King John himself had offered to him, as an inducement to return to Portugal and renew the negotiations for his western enterprise, that he "should not be seized, detained, accused, cited, or tried on any charge, whether civil or criminal." To-day he was sitting in the presence of this very prince, the one member of all that glittering company for whom such a condescension was admissible!

The Portuguese sovereign engaged in an earnest and even cordial conversation with his guest, as if bent on removing all possible doubt or distrust from his mind. He congratulated the Admiral upon the happy termination of his adventurous expedition, and asked him many questions about the new lands he had visited, and their people and productions. Colon answered all the royal inquiries with frankness and simplicity, but was ever on his guard against surprise. He knew the man he had to deal with, sovereign though he was; and that his caution was not superfluous soon became apparent. The Admiral having said that beyond all question the countries he had discovered were the eastern confines of Asia and the isles of the Indies, King John raised his hand as if in dissent, and remarked in his suavest tones, —

"There we cannot accompany you, Señor Don Admiral, without far greater study than we have as yet been able to give to so grave a matter. As we read the charts, by sailing so far to the west you have come within the eastern world which was conceded to us by our allies of Spain in the capitulations of seventy-nine. But there is no cause for disputing now this matter; after we have taken the judgment of our most skilled astronomers and map-men regarding it, we will discuss the question amicably with their Majesties of Castile. Both the Crown of Spain and ourselves wish for nothing that may not be of right our due."

The Admiral suspected a trap he could not see. Even the assumed indifference of the king seemed to him suspicious. So, bowing toward his royal host, he answered with great deference, —

"Your Majesty most surely knows far more of such weighty affairs than a poor sea-captain, for neither of the treaty nor of other concerns of State do I know aught. But I crave your Majesty's gracious license to say that my sovereign's strictest orders were that I should touch neither at the Gold Coast nor other part of Guinea, nor explore in the direction of any of the territories claimed by Portugal. The warning that my ships were forbidden from all such interference with the labors of your Majesty's own hardy navigators was proclaimed formally in every port of Andalusia before I sailed last year. If, therefore, despite my anxious precautions, I have approached too near the eastern world allotted to your royal Crown, I most humbly entreat your Majesty to believe that it was due to my poor skill in navigation, and not to any desire to invade the limits of your Majesty's possessions."

Whether King John knew anything about the "eastern world" which he had claimed in the partition of the Ocean made in 1479 with Castile is more than doubtful; he certainly had no ambition to dispute the point with the foremost geographer of the age. So he blandly dismissed the subject with a smile.

"Without doubt, without doubt, Señor Admiral. The matter calls for no immediate adjustment, and I question not shall be settled between our Crown and their Catholic Majesties without the need of an arbitrator."

With this the king brought the audience to a close by a renewal of his former offer of assistance in anything the Admiral might need. He assigned his guest to the care of the Prior of the Convent of Crato, as being the principal personage of the Court, and announced his desire of continuing the conversation at an early opportunity. The eminent ecclesiastic proved to be a nobleman in more than the conventional sense; and from him Colon received a sincere and generous attention. What would the worthy Governor of Santa Maria have thought had he but known that the commander of the dingy little caravel whom he had held in the harbor of San Lorenzo was the honored guest of his most serene monarch? That it was hard to fathom the purposes of kings, perhaps.

Early on the following day the Admiral was summoned to the king's presence, and spent a long time in detailing to his Majesty the information he was eager to acquire concerning the regions his visitor had explored and the ocean he had twice traversed. The king informed Colon that the queen was residing for the time being at the Monastery of San Antonio at Villafranca, near Lisbon, and greatly desired to converse with the Admiral; whereupon the latter asked the king's permission to leave the Court on the next day, in order that he might do his homage to her Majesty as he returned to his vessel. To this King John perforce assented, having no pretence for further detaining his guest; and the Admiral made his preparations for departure. From all the royal household, from monarch to man-at-arms, he had received unequivocal marks of respect and admiration; but he bore himself with a studious moderation and simplicity. Those who applauded his deeds were not his friends; and this he knew without the need of any monitory incident. Both national and personal jealousy were actively fermenting, and he acted in all respects with the circumspection of a trained courtier. If the Crown of Portugal could not hope to rob the Spanish sovereigns of their new-gained world, there was many an intriguer attached to it who would do his best endeavor to destroy the fame of its discoverer. What was he to them, at best, but a map-drawing merchant sailor, dressed in red velvet? If he gave no indication of the thought that was in his mind, the Admiral kept it none the less ever present; and it was well for him that he did. Some faithful ally of his numberless detractors hastened to advise the Spanish Court that their Admiral was negotiating in secret the delivery of the Indies to the King of Portugal, and that his arrival in the Tagus was due to this intended treachery! To the credit of Ferdinand and Isabella be it said, the venomous tale was wasted in the telling; but it rankled long in Colon's heart, and years afterward he referred to it as one of the crowning indignities to which he had been exposed. There is no evidence that he was aware of the malicious deed at the time; but his path in the Vale of Paradise was so beset with pitfalls that it is no marvel he was anxious to exchange the glory that beats about a throne for the safer quiet of his narrow quarters on the caravel.

After breakfast on the morning of the 11th he had his final audience with the king, and kissed the royal hands on taking leave. King John was graciousness itself, and confided to the Admiral various messages he desired to send to the Spanish monarchs. He also directed Dom Martin de Noronha to act as escort for the Admiral back to Lisbon, and, in fine, bade him farewell with as many demonstrations of friendliness as he had shown in receiving him. For the first league out of the Valle do Paraiso Colon was accompanied by a large party of the courtiers, who testified in this manner their esteem, whether real or feigned, for their departing guest; and when they at length parted from him, it was with every outward show of distinguished honor.

Late in the afternoon of the same day the Admiral and his escort arrived at the Monastery of San Antonio. He was received with much cordiality by the queen and royal princes. Her Majesty in particular showed a lively interest in all his exploits, and dismissed him with many assurances of her highest consideration. That night he slept at Llandra, on the road to Lisbon, intending to reach his ship the next day and set sail without delay, as the weather was now propitious. In the morning, however, a royal page arrived from the Valle do Paraiso with a message from King John. His Majesty sent word that after the Admiral's departure he had bethought him that perhaps his visitor would find it more convenient to make the journey overland to Spain, rather than continue on by sea, and had therefore sent one of his pages to accompany the Admiral to the Spanish frontier should he so elect. The king had also sent a couple of excellent mules from the royal stables for the use of the Admiral and his pilot on the proposed journey; and the page had authority to provide all else that might be requisite for Colon's comfort. This hospitable offer the Admiral declined, with many expressions of gratitude and recognition. The page therefore took his departure, leaving the two mules for the Admiral's use on the remainder of his road to Lisbon, and bestowing upon the pilot a purse of golden sequins.[1]

This proposal of the Portuguese king, coming as it did at the eleventh hour, is not easy of explanation with the light we now possess. Some have held, looking through Spanish glasses, that if the Admiral had accepted the offer he would never have reached any frontier this side the Stygian shores. Certain of King John's counsellors, this school affirm, had poisoned the royal ear with dastardly suggestions of the vast increase likely to accrue to the Castilian power from the Admiral's discoveries, and pointed out a ready way of preventing their being utilized, at least under his leadership. Others again, dipping their pens in Portuguese ink, deny this

[1] This incident is related with some variations by Las Casas; but the diary gives it, in greater detail, as above recorded.

imputation as a malicious slander, and attribute King John's offer to an hospitable afterthought intended to spare his illustrious visitor the tedium and uncertainty of completing his journey by water. We see no cause to question the substantial accuracy of the latter view, although there seems to be no doubt that the king was in fact urged to seize the tempting opportunity to dispose effectually of the man who promised to raise Castile beyond the wildest dreams of Portuguese rivalry. Colon himself, who certainly evinces elsewhere no tenderness for the sensibilities of Lusitania, makes no remark upon the possible motives of King John. In relating the various incidents of his visit to that sovereign he simply adds, "I have recorded all that the king did to me, so that your Majesties should know." The Delphic oracle itself could not be more sibylline.

At nightfall on Wednesday, the 12th of March, Colon reached Lisbon, and went directly on board the "Niña."

XXV.

HIGH NOON AND THE TIDE AT FLOOD.

AT eight o'clock on the morning of the 13th of March the "Niña" weighed anchor and stood down the Tagus on her way to Spain. The weather was fair and the wind favorable for her southerly run, so that by daylight of the 14th she was off Cape St. Vincent. It was the Admiral's intention, on leaving Lisbon, to make direct for the mouth of the Guadalquivir and ascend that river to Seville, where he would be within comparatively easy reach of his sovereigns; but as he changed his course for the eastward run he also altered his plans, and decided to put into Palos, and there determine upon his future movements. All that day and evening he coasted along the shores of Portugal, making but slow progress, for as night shut in he was only off the harbor of Furon. By the time the sun rose on the 15th, however, the coast presented a familiar appearance to the joyful crew; for as far as the eye could follow stretched the "fat sands" and flat beaches which form the seacoast of Andalusia. The wind was light; but the tide was in their favor, and before long they sighted the entrance to the estuary of the Tinto and the Odiel. Slowly the "Niña" crept toward the well-known harbor, until the excited sailors could see the little town of Saltes, then the hills behind Palos itself, and at last the white walls of La Rabida on the height. Onward swept the little caravel, borne rather by tide than wind. Willing hands executed the Admiral's orders to hoist the royal standard on the "castle" and the banner of the green cross at the mainmast head; and with such sorry pomp as she could muster the battered vessel moved steadily to her goal. She had not many miles to go; but she seemed almost reluctant to traverse them, as if loath to close her glorious career. The sun was nearly overhead when she reached the Saltes bar; a few rolls and plunges and she was past it. As the dial marked high noon and the tide was touching flood, the "Niña" entered the Tinto and sought the anchorage she had left seven months and fifteen days before. She had seen strange sights and done brave deeds, had this "Little Girl," in the interval.

There had been ample time for the report to spread from the riverside to Palos and Moguer that "one of the Señor Colon's ships" was coming into harbor; and as soon as the "Niña" had swung around, she was surrounded by boatloads of eager townspeople. Heartily responding to their greetings, the Admiral gave them such tidings as he could at the time; but he himself was anxious to reach the shore. Entering his boat at the earliest possible moment, he was rowed to the landing-place. The welcome which he received was a foretaste of what the ensuing months had in store for him. The whole population of Palos and its vicinity for miles around had crowded to the beach; and as Colon stepped from the boat, loud shouts of gladness and unstinted praise arose from every side. The good Fray Antonio was waiting with ready arms for the man he loved and had served so well; and as the two friends were locked in a warm embrace, there were more tears seen than words spoken for a few minutes. After him there was the young physician to be greeted in a manner scarcely less earnest. Then Juan of the hard head pressed forward, eager to report right then and there his fulfilment of "the Master's" orders. Burly Sebastian, the privateersman, claimed recognition too; and Diego Prieto and his fellow-functionaries were impatient to give his Excellency the Señor Don Admiral a practical demonstration of the flexibility of the official knee. Besides these, there were a hundred questioners to answer as to where the voyage had led the fleet and what had befallen the "Pinta" and the "Santa Maria." The Admiral was, of course, the centre of attention, though every sailor was encompassed by his own small circle of joyful friends or curious listeners. If in the midst of the general rejoicing and enthusiasm there was heard now and again a broken sob or a choking prayer to Our Lady of Sorrows, it was only some stricken woman bewailing the loss of husband or son who was not a member of the "Niña's" crew. Such things must happen, of course, even in the victories of Peace; and it was too much to expect an Andalusian peasant to care more for the aggrandizement of the Spanish Crown than for her own happiness. As for the copper-colored savages who stood together in a wondering group apart, they divided with the Admiral himself the honors of the day. Unhappily, they left no record of their impressions of the white man's "heaven" which they had now reached. It would be worth while to know what their ideas had been while they were being pitched around in the storm-tossed ship and stared at by the Lisbon crowds. By the time they had reached Palos they must have had grave doubts as to the celestial origin of their bearded shipmates.

Colon was the first to remind his men that their earliest duty lay within the walls of St. George's Church. Forming in ceremonious procession, they all marched into the sanctuary, and devoutly offered up their thanks for the manifold tokens of Divine favor which they had received. *Te Deum Laudamus* was solemnly intoned; and voyagers and townsfolk alike joined in the praise for the triumph which had been vouchsafed to what all were now overjoyed to claim as "the ships of Palos." The service of thanksgiving completed, the men were pulled hither and thither by those who claimed them, and appealed to their commander for his instructions as to their future movements. The Admiral would not let his men disperse beyond his reach, for he was half inclined to complete the journey to Barcelona by sea; but he gave them liberty to go at pleasure within the reach of his summons. Little by little the throng broke up and drifted off in sections, with one of the pilots or some seaman as the axis of its independent motion. The news the travellers had to tell was too marvellous even in its naked truth to be easily grasped by their hearers, and we may be sure it lost none of its strangeness in the telling; so the loss of their relatives and gossips on the "Pinta" was of more ready comprehension by the townspeople, and came nearer to them by far than wild stories of countries where one-eyed men ate those with two eyes, and all alike went naked from one year's end to the next. The Admiral himself went with the superior and Garcia Fernandez to the convent, and was soon deeply immersed in informing himself as to the condition of affairs in Spain, and in relating to his sympathetic auditors the chief events of the voyage so happily concluded. It was late at night when the three friends separated; and Colon for the first time in many months lay down to rest undisturbed by care and unharrassed by suspicion. That night, if we mistake not, it would not have been in the power of "any mosquito" to have interfered with his slumbers.

For the next few days the Admiral's energies were taxed to the utmost. He had abandoned his idea of passing through the Straits of Gibraltar with his caravel and going to Barcelona by sea, and had despatched a courier to announce to their Majesties his arrival at Palos, and his intention to go overland by way of Seville at the first practicable moment. He now had to make all the arrangements both for this journey and for closing up the most pressing matters connected with the voyage. There was the "Niña" to be unloaded and disposed of; the crew to be discharged, or dismissed on liberty; his reports and charts to be completed and prepared for their Majesties' inspection; and many letters written to the Court and his friends elsewhere announcing the result of his expedition and future plans. Nor were the obligations of religion less exacting. The very day after his arrival was a Saturday; and in compliance with their pledge he and his men again all walked in procession to St. George's Church in airy attire, and there heard Mass, both as a complement to their fast on that day and to complete the pilgrimage so rudely interrupted at the Portuguese chapel in Santa Maria. Another day he had to spend in going to Santa Maria of the Belt, in Huelva; while a night was passed at the altar of Santa Clara of Moguer. Pedro de Villa must also be despatched on his long trip to Loreto in the territories of the Pope, to perform the penance thrust upon him by his lot. As for Our Lady of Guadaloupe, she had to wait for her five-pound candle of pure white wax until the Admiral came within more convenient distance. The debt was as good as gold; for those who went down into the sea in ships in those days settled with the saints as punctually as they fleeced their fellow-sinners.

While the Admiral was thus busied with his manifold duties, secular and religious, what might well have passed for a miracle happened, throwing the little town into an excitement even greater than that attending Colon's own arrival. One day a vessel stood up the broad estuary, and crossing the bar, dropped anchor by the "Niña." Those who saw her rubbed their eyes and crossed themselves in terror; for either the new-comer was a phantom ship or she was the "Pinta," which was supposed to be lying at the bottom of the deep Atlantic. Strange to say, from the ship herself no word was brought at first. A boat put off from her side; but instead of boarding the "Niña" or making for the landing-place, it headed for a little cove, and there discharged its passengers. It was only when the people of the port had rowed out to her that they learned her tale. The "Pinta," for such she was in veritable hemp and timber, had weathered the terrible storm of the 14th of February; but on seeing no trace of the "Niña," Martin Alonzo had concluded that his sister ship was lost. After excessive toil and peril, he had made the port of Bayonne in France, and having there refitted, had sailed direct for Palos. The "Pinta's" crew were as much amazed to find the "Niña" floating quietly at anchor in the Tinto as were their friends on shore to see the missing ship; for no one on the "Pinta" had doubted that their companions on the other vessel were long since beneath the waves. So much of their story the crew told now. Their captain, Martin Alonzo, was sorely ill, they said; and it was he who had been landed in the cove, the better to go direct to his home, and thus avoid the agitation and confusion of passing through the town.

Such tidings were not long in reaching the Admiral. When he heard of the "Pinta's" arrival, he sent for her officers and inquired the exact particulars of their separate cruise. They repeated what they had told the first inquirers, but added sundry important details. On the very day that they had anchored at Bayonne a ship entered the harbor coming from Flanders, on which by a strange coincidence was Arias Perez Pinzon, the oldest son of their captain, who joined his father as soon as he learned that the "Pinta" was so near.[1] After this, the men continued, Martin Alonzo had despatched a courier across the Pyrenees to bear to the Spanish sovereigns the tidings of *his* safe arrival and *his* wonderful discovery of the Golden Indies, and to announce to their Majesties that he would sail thence directly for Palos and hasten to lay before them a report of *his* voyage, and of the lamentable fate which had befallen the Admiral and his companions. From Bayonne they had made their way to Palos; and when Martin Alonzo had found the "Niña" safe in port before him, he had ordered out his boat, been rowed ashore with his son, and gone to his home in the manner already related. As Colon heard this story, his face grew sterner than was his wont; but he gave no other sign of the wrath which was consuming him. He treated the "Pinta's" men and their vessel precisely as he had the "Niña" and her crew, and set them to work putting their affairs in order. As for Martin Alonzo, the Admiral would bide his time. Palos was the home of the Pinzons, and their voices would be heard before his by most ears. Ere-

---

[1] This singular fact is reported by the younger Pinzon and other witnesses in the great lawsuit, and seems to be beyond dispute. We surmise that it furnishes the basis on which the story has been built as to the "Pinta" coming into Palos *on the very day* of Colon's arrival. Herrera first gave currency to the attractive fable, and has been followed by many later historians; but we find no trace of any such occurrence other than the coincidence mentioned above.

long he should be able to tell his story where it would be hearkened to to some purpose. With this resolution, the Admiral continued his preparations for setting out to Barcelona. Martin Alonzo himself avoided all contact with his chief; and by degrees the report gathered strength that the Spanish captain had been unjustly treated, and that to the Palos seamen, and not to the Italian navigator, was due the greater credit for what had been accomplished. Colon held his peace; and few even of the townspeople paid any heed to the whispers. It was enough for them just now that the sea had given up its dead, and that of all who had sailed on that wild and desperate adventure, neither man nor boy from Palos or its neighborhood was missing.

It was nearly a fortnight before the Admiral could start upon his journey overland to Barcelona. From the moment he left the little seaport until that of his triumphant reception by his grateful sovereigns and their obsequious Court his progress was one continued series of enthusiastic acclamations. In order to enhance the popular estimate of the importance of his discovery and establish at the outset a realizing conception of its truly Oriental splendor, he took with him an extensive retinue, consisting of his pilots and principal seamen, the Indian interpreters as a matter of course, and a long train of pack-mules laden with the varied spoils of his pacific campaign. As he passed, in easy stages, along the highway leading through the plains of Andalusia and the mountains of Granada, the shepherds left their flocks, the vinedressers their vineyards, the peasants their fields, and one and all — men, women, and children — thronged to see the wonderful beings from another world and the brown-faced mariners who had crossed the Western Ocean under the guidance of that blue-eyed leader riding in stately dignity at their head. The Admiral was ever somewhat given to proper pomp and circumstance, as we have seen; and when his route lay through any town of sufficient importance, he caused his Indians to don their ornaments of gold and feathered plumes, and bear their fragile weapons in their hands; while his own more sturdy people displayed some of the impressive trophies of his victory over the ignorance and superstition of his age. Wherever they halted there were compliments and flattery to be received from supple dignitaries, and the wondering curiosity of lord and hind alike to be satisfied by the recital of the incidents of the voyage and an exhibition of the golden masks and strange animals from the distant regions beyond the sea. The rumor of their advent preceded the slowly moving train, and the villages off the line of march were emptied, says an eyewitness; such was the eagerness of the people to behold this astonishing display.

On the 31st of March the notable procession entered the famous city of Seville. The day was Palm Sunday, — one dedicated by the populace of all Catholic countries to festivity and gladness, — and the town was already in holiday attire; but the arrival of Colon and his companions increased by a thousand fold the interest of the festival, and made it memorable in the annals of even that historic capital. He was met by the principal cavaliers and officials without the gates, and accompanied by them as an escort of honor to the lodgings "next to the arch which is called 'of the Images' at San Nieblas," which had been secured for him and his cortège. The streets were thronged to impassability with sightseers, while every window framed a group of eager faces. From balcony and window-sill hung gayly colored tapestries; and at short intervals, stretched from house to house, festoons of banners fluttered in the breeze. As the Admiral paced slowly up the leaf-strewn street, accompanied by his honorable retinue and followed by the groups of bronzed sailors and dusky savages, every neck was craned to catch a glimpse of the man who had been — where? and done — what? Few in the great concourse gazing at him as something more than human could have told. Perhaps it was better so; for as their ignorance of the world they lived in was complete, so much the greater was their amazement and credulity at the sight of so much they had never heard or dreamed of. We, who live in the continent which Colon discovered, — and know so much more about it than he, —

have sometimes been invited to consider him a person of very ordinary attainments.

Loud as were the plaudits of the good people of Seville, and welcome as was the tribute of their undisguised wonderment, a far more momentous triumph awaited the Admiral here. A few days after his arrival and while he was yet receiving the attentions of the learned and the powerful, of priest and layman, a courier arrived from Barcelona and delivered to him a packet sealed with the royal cipher. On its face was the superscription: "From the King and the Queen. To Don Cristóval Colon, Their Admiral of the Ocean Sea and Viceroy and Governor of the Islands discovered in the Indies." At last his success was indeed complete! Their Majesties had made good their pledges, and now greeted him by the titles he had won at the cost of such years and years of patient faith and hard endurance.

The royal missive ran: —

"We have read your letters, and had great delight in learning what in them you have written to Us, and that God has vouchsafed you so happy an ending to your labors and directed favorably what you began, in which both He shall be so greatly glorified and Ourselves and Our Kingdoms shall receive so much advantage. If God pleases, besides what you have done in this matter for His service you shall receive from Us many favors which, you may be assured, shall be such as your trials and labors deserve. And because We desire that what you have begun, with God's help, may be continued and carried further, We wish that your coming hither should not be delayed. Therefore, for Our better service, We desire that you make the utmost haste you can in your journey, and in good time all shall be arranged as may be necessary. As you know, the Summer is already commenced, and in order that the season for returning to those regions shall not elapse, see whether you can do anything in Seville, or the other places you may visit, to advance your return to the countries you have discovered, and write to Us immediately by this same messenger, who has orders to return at once. Thus whatever is to be done can be provided for while you are on your way hither and stopping here, in such manner that when you leave here everything may be ready.

"Done at Barcelona, the 30th day of March, ninety three.

"I, THE KING. I, THE QUEEN."

It had taken the Spanish sovereigns nearly seven years to give their consent to the first voyage; but on learning of its result it took them less than as many days to determine on a second one. The Admiral saw no inconsistency in this frantic haste. His own most earnest wish was to return as quickly as possible to the beautiful regions in the Western Ocean and complete his work by finding the mainland of Cathay, and opening up the dominions of the Great Khan to Spanish commerce and the Christian religion. The letter of their Majesties was, therefore, a source of keenest gratification to him, assuring as it did their hearty co-operation in the preparation and despatch of his second expedition. Hence he exerted himself diligently to set out from Seville as soon as possible, and continued his journey to Barcelona in the early days of April.

Owing to the distance between the two cities and the slow rate at which he was obliged to travel, it was not until towards the end of the month that the Admiral reached the royal Court. Here he was welcomed by a great gathering of the attendants upon their Majesties, bent upon conveniently forgetting their former treatment of the "Genoese adventurer." To all alike he showed himself as oblivious as themselves of the awkward past; but it was only in the society of his tried and proven friends, Fray Diego de Deza, Luiz de Santangel, Alonzo de Quintanilla, and the few others who, like these, had been steadfast in their support when friendship cost an effort and was of corresponding value, that he threw off his reserve and spoke freely of his work already done and that which remained for him to do.

He had barely entered the city when he received a summons to repair at once to the royal presence. Entering the audience-chamber, which was filled with the glittering array of grandees and courtiers, soldiers and prelates, which formed the brilliant Court of Spain, the Admiral advanced, we are told, "with the air of a Senator of Rome," through this resplendent company intending to beg permission to kiss the royal hands. Then occurred a miracle as startling and notable as any he had so devoutly noted in all the history of that eventful undertaking. As he bowed low before the dais whereon were set the equal thrones of Ferdinand and Isabella, the king and queen rose from their thrones and *stood* to receive their Admiral! The proudest and most ceremonious of Christian monarchs offered princely honors to the man to whom for seven years they had doled out a few ducats at a time, and who had served as a laughing-stock for many a one of the bewildered courtiers who were now watching in open-eyed amazement this unheard-of mark of condescension. Extending their hands for his dutiful salute, the king raised the Admiral from his kneeling posture and, directing a stool of ceremony to be brought, bade him be seated, — a mark of honor seldom shown even to the most eminent nobles. Both king and queen then plied him with mingled thanks, congratulations, and inquiries, with a frank absence of all formality which plainly showed their extreme interest both in the man himself and in the mighty work he had performed.

After that the sequel was foreordained. The *Te Deums* in the chapel royal; the honors heaped upon the ex-adventurer and present hero; the vast excitement and enthusiasm which spread through the circles of the Court at the sight of the raw gold, rare drugs, strange fruits, and other evidences of the abounding wealth and fertility of the new lands, — all these were matters of course in comparison with that first act of crowning condescension. Ferdinand of Aragon and Isabella of Castile had risen to receive Cristóval Colon! The cranium of the average Spanish courtier in the year of Grace fourteen hundred and ninety-three could not hold any other impression while that phenomenon filled his mind. Acting on the unmistakable example set them by their kings, with one accord the ready placemen vied with one another in heaping honors upon the great discoverer whom they themselves had just discovered; but the greater nobles — the grandees proper — still held haughtily aloof from other than formal intercourse with the parvenu thus suddenly thrust upon them. Yet it was from that one of their Order, so pre-eminently high in rank and powerful in authority that he was called "the third king," that the nobility of Castile learned that Genius, as well as Death and Misery, ignores all factitious distinctions. One day, soon after Colon's arrival at the Court, as Pedro de Mendoza, Grand Cardinal of Spain, was leaving the palace, he encountered the Admiral and asked him to dine. At his kindly solicitation Colon went with the Cardinal to the archiepiscopal palace, where scarcely less state was maintained than in the royal saloons proper. The Cardinal placed his guest in the seat of honor next himself, ordered that the dishes should be served to him covered, and saluted him with the *salva*, or greeting of ceremony, as the person of greatest distinction present. "Thereafter," we are dryly informed, "the Admiral was always served with covered dishes, and treated with the consideration and formality befitting his high rank." To him it was all one, now that his work had been passed upon by those he had served so faithfully. In the past he had been neglected because he was not great; now he was great because he was not neglected. That was all.

He made no mistake as to the value of this sudden homage. Both his faith in Providence and his distrust of the Court remained unchanged until his dying day, and the one was as abundantly justified by subsequent events as the other had been by those precedent. He wrote, in closing his diary : —

"This voyage has marvellously shown to me that without God's will it is vain to plan or attempt anything, and this can be plainly seen both in this record from the many singular miracles which He has done and from my own life, who so long a time was at your Highnesses' Court combating the opposition and disfavor of so many of the principal persons of your household; all of whom set themselves against me, saying that this deed, which now is done, was but a piece of folly. And yet I believe that, with the blessing of our Lord, it shall nevertheless prove the greatest glory that has thus far ever been vouchsafed."

"These are the final words," certifies Las Casas of the quotation just made, "of the Admiral Don Cristóval Colon concerning his first voyage to the Indies and to the discovery thereof."

XXVI.

AFTERWARD.

THE Admiral remained at Barcelona until the 30th of May. What with the settlement of his accounts, the completion of his records and charts, and the preparations for the return to Hispaniola, both days and nights were consumed in constant labor. Scarcely a day passed that he was not at the palace in close consultation with the sovereigns. Ferdinand and Isabella had thrown themselves with extraordinary ardor into all his plans; it was enough for him to propose a measure, and instantly a decree was issued for its accomplishment. The second expedition was to consist of a score of vessels. Twelve hundred men were to be under the Admiral's orders, including all the best seamen of the kingdom. In this number were also men-at-arms, both foot and horse, a large party of civil officers and adjutants, a detachment of miners, another of artisans and agricultural laborers, and a dozen priests. Nothing was to be left undone to provide for the colonization and proper government of the lands already discovered, and hasten the exploration of the remaining coasts and islands of the Indies. Horses, cattle, and seeds were to be taken in ample quantities to secure their establishment on the fertile soil of the western world, and immense stores of provisions and ammunition for the supply of the colonies to be planted and the expeditions to be conducted throughout the newly opened regions. Who spoke now of excessive cost or doubtful returns? The treasurers of the Crown were directed to pay the expenses of the armament without stint; for were not one half of the ships to unload on reaching Hispaniola and be freighted with the gold and spices, the rhubarb, cinnamon, aloes, dyewoods, cotton, and pungent peppers accumulated, in their leader's absence, by the industrious garrison left behind at Navidad? There was no cause in this case for reading of harsh orders in parish churches, and holding village authorities responsible for the enlistment of unwilling men. Rather the difficulty was to choose from the multitude of applicants who — men of birth and rank and those with neither — jostled one another in their efforts to gain the Admiral's favor and be elected by him to join the new crusade. Where he had made one enemy before by having to seize on ships and impress men, he made ten now by having to refuse the offers of those who volunteered. Don Cristóval Colon, Admiral of the Ocean Sea and Viceroy of the Indies, was a power in those days.

Nor was a merely local fame his only reward. Both from Lisbon and from Seville the news had spread through Europe that the Spanish navigator had broken the bonds of Ocean, as Seneca had prophesied in Nero's time, and found that the western sea was no longer the Sea of Darkness, but the highway to an unknown world (presumably Asia) teeming with wealth and riches. Bartholomé Colon, the Admiral's brother, had long been in England, soliciting the same aid from Henry VII. which the Admiral himself had for so many years sought in vain from Ferdinand and Isabella. He had not learned of his brother's final success or of his departure on his voyage of discovery; but now, himself successful in his application, as he hastened to Spain to communicate to Cristóval the welcome news that the English Crown would furnish the means for their projected enterprise, he heard with astonishment on reaching Paris that his brother had sailed, had found the world he looked for, and was again at the Spanish Court,— a famous and renowned man. The pens of the men of learning in Spain and Portugal published the great achievement far and wide. " Columbus has returned from the western antipodes," wrote one. " He brings gold and cotton, dyewoods, and pepper keener than that of Asia. He followed the sun's course for more than a thousand leagues, and discovered six islands, of which the largest exceeds all Spain in size." "Christopher Columbus has reached Lisbon," wrote another, "frόm the voyage he made for the sovereigns of Castile to the islands of Cipango and Antilia. He brings with him some of the people of those countries and specimens of the gold and other productions, and has been made Admiral of those seas." It was not long after his arrival at Barcelona when a garbled version of one of his letters relating his discovery was printed at Rome in Latin, and circulated widely through the civilized world; and it is worth remarking that a copy of this famous product of the early press will now bring in the hemisphere discovered by its author a sum equal to one third of the total cost of finding the western world.

But what must have been the praise of sweetest savor to the pious mind of the Admiral was that the Holy Father himself—that Alexander the Sixth, who to us is best known as a Borgia worthy of the name, but who to Colon was Head of the Church and Vicar of Christ on earth—proclaimed throughout Christendom his apostolic approbation of Colon's work. "Our beloved son Christopher Columbus," so ran the words of the successor of Saint Peter, "a man fit and well chosen for so great an undertaking, and worthy to be held in high honor, has with ships and people suitable for the purpose, but not without enormous labors, cost, and dangers, sought by the Ocean those continents and islands which have hitherto been remote and unknown, and, where no man had before navigated, has, by Divine favor, found them after much sacrifice. In the which lands, according to the reports, live many nations who dwell together in peace and go naked and know not how to eat meat." The Bull in which the Pope thus dilated upon the merits and deeds of the Admiral was dated at Rome on May the second, only six weeks after the "Niña's" arrival at Palos, and is an interesting evidence of the quickness with which the Spanish Crown grasped the vast importance of the outcome of the enterprise to which they had so tardily given an insufficient support. No sooner had Ferdinand received the first announcement from the Admiral than he despatched an envoy post haste to the Vatican to secure from his Holiness — as presumable guardian for the Almighty of all the earth's surface not already appropriated by alleged followers of the Cross — a pontifical decree awarding to Spain whatever territories might lie on the other side of the Atlantic. For value received (for the waters were rough around the Fisherman's craft just then), the Servant of the Servants of God agreed to do this; and this singular Bull, in which he handed over to the sovereigns of Castile a third of the habitable globe, was the result. What is still more strange is that although neither Pope nor monarch had any more title to these countries — of whose very existence they knew nothing — than the author has to the reader's watch, this award of a mighty continent was acquiesced in and respected for centuries by the obsequious potentates most interested in foiling one another's plans. The same princes were wont to gird at one another over the flimsiest trifles, and would cheerfully ruin every subject in their kingdoms in a war about the ownership of half-a-dozen hovels anywhere in Europe; but they did not dispute the Vatican's power to do as it pleased with what had no owners whom anybody feared.[1]

Besides the renown to which he was so pre-eminently entitled, the Admiral received from Ferdinand and Isabella many substantial proofs of their consideration and gratitude. Letters-patent were issued confirming to him and to his heirs the dignities and emoluments which had been granted the previous year on condition of his finding the lands beyond the sea. Another royal decree gave him a new and honorable coat of arms symbolical of the great enterprise he

[1] If there is a limbo where departed heathen foregather, there must have been some interesting exchanges of experience in late years between the shades of the aboriginal Americans and those who arrived more recently from equatorial Africa. The ghostly representatives of each savage race must have been puzzled to hear the others explain how they got there in the cause of Christianity!

had so successfully concluded.[1] Others still allowed him to appoint the officials and authorities for the government of the Indies; permitted him the use of the royal seal and the right to employ the royal names in his proclamations and laws; and prohibited any voyage to or traffic with the newly opened regions except by his special permission or that of the Crown. In addition to decreeing that whenever he should travel he and his retinue should be served at the cost of the royal treasury, the sovereigns also settled upon the Admiral the pension of ten thousand maravedies for first seeing land, which has already been mentioned, and ordered their treasurer to pay him in one sum a merced, or bounty, of three hundred and seventy-five thousand maravedies. This latter amount was equal to one fourth of the whole outlay on the first voyage, and, though we have been able to find no record of its disposition by Colon, it is probable that it was solicited and used for the repayment of the funds advanced by the Pinzons when the million of maravedies furnished by the Crown proved insufficient for the equipment of the expedition.

So urgent was the haste and so energetic the measures adopted for the despatch of the second fleet, that within six months after the solitary "Niña" crossed the bar of Saltes the imposing array of crowded vessels was ready to sail. Throughout this period there had been a constant fencing with the Portuguese king, who endeavored to impede by all available means the departure of the Spanish armament. The Court itself was so filled with unfaithful servants retained as spies by Portuguese bribes, that Queen Isabella was obliged to excuse herself to the Admiral for retaining so long the diary he had left with her Majesty to be copied, "because it had to be written in secret, so that

[1] These were granted on May 20, 1493. They were: in the upper right-hand field a golden castle on a green ground; beneath it a group of golden islands in a blue sea; in the upper left-hand field a purple lion on a white ground; beneath it Colon's own arms, five golden anchors on a blue ground. "There are not many handsomer escutcheons in all Spain," remarks Las Casas, with a complacency which does honor to his friendship for the great sailor.

those of Portugal who are here, or any one else, should not know its contents. For this reason," she added, "and to finish it the more quickly, it has been copied by two persons, as you will perceive." Notwithstanding all these intrigues and the peculiarly dilatory methods of Castilian administration, the preparations were completed and the ships all ready within the comparatively short time named. On the 25th of September the Admiral went on board his flagship, the "Maria Galante," in the port of Cadiz, and at the head of the seventeen vessels which composed his fleet stood out to sea bound for Hispaniola. He had been just six months and ten days in Spain, and in that time attained the very summit of such power and glory as the world had to offer to one not to the purple born. Ere next he saw the shores of Andalusia he was to know how hard it is to maintain oneself at so giddy an elevation above the dead level of envy and detraction which the mass of weak humanity maintains.

With the events of this second cruise we have not here to deal. It is grateful to leave the high-souled, hopeful, and intrepid sailor pursuing an even course in the van of so worthy an armada toward the new world he had found, while the older lands he was hourly leaving more distant still resounded with the fame of his great deeds.

Of the companions of his first adventurous journey, there is both good and evil to be told. The letter sent to the Spanish sovereigns by Martin Alonzo from Bayonne, unfortunately for him, reached their Majesties after they had received the Admiral's announcement of his own arrival. They thereupon sent a brief reply to the "Pinta's" captain, saying that as the Admiral was in command of the expedition, they could only receive Martin Alonzo when presented by his leader, — a blow which so aggravated the mortification of the unhappy man that he died at his home in Palos while Colon was making his triumphal progress to Barcelona. Vicente Yañez, as we have seen, became a mighty man of the sea, and lived to a green old age, distinguished by many marks of his sovereign's favor, and contributing some of the most brilliant pages to the glorious history of Spanish navigation.

Arias Perez, Martin Alonzo's son, lived for thirty years after his father's death, ever keen to belittle the Admiral's fame and to claim for his own house the chief glory of discovering the Indies. We find some light thrown on his character by a petition he made to the king and queen in 1500, complaining that since his father's death his four brothers had left their weak-minded sister on his hands to take care of; "the which," he pathetically remarks, "causes me great annoyance and trouble." The good father superior, Fray Juan Antonio Perez, of Marchena, was called upon to mourn the loss of the nephew he had sent with the Admiral on the latter's first voyage, but lived to the close of a long life of honor and usefulness. We would gladly know more of this attractive personality, but the records are silent regarding him. Scanty as is our knowledge, his name should be printed in larger letters than hitherto in the history of the hemisphere he helped so effectively to find. Garcia Fernandez was also a man of many years when he died; for, twenty-five years after the memorable conference in the convent of La Rabida, he did yeoman's service in breaking down the attempt of the Pinzons to cloud the dead Admiral's fame. He also had yielded meantime to the impulse of his heart, and gone to visit the marvellous countries his friend had found; and it is in his report, as royal notary on the spot, that we read of the first discovery of Brazil and the Amazon in 1499. Juan Rodriguez Cabezudo was a pretty old man in 1513; but he came down to the royal commission when they were taking testimony as to whom belonged the credit of finding the lands beyond the sea, and gave his evidence in behalf of his dead "Master." Stiff-necked as ever, he swore to all that occurred at the time of Colon's first coming to La Rabida, and laid no little stress on his having loaned his mule to the great navigator when he wanted her for his Reverence the Father Superior. "And I know," he insisted on saying in his own stubborn way, "that the Admiral set out from this town of Palos in ninety two to discover the Indies, and returned to this same port, safe and sound, after finding them; because the Señor Admiral himself told me he had found many islands in the Indies, and showed me six or seven Indians he had brought from there, and pieces of gold and golden masks; for he said that there was a plenty of gold there. And many others heard him besides myself," he concluded, with a hit at some of the hard swearers of the Pinzon connection. The old seaman's quondam charge, Diego Colon, accompanied his father on his second voyage, and assisted him ably until the Admiral's death. He then engaged in the long struggle with the Spanish Crown for the dignities and profits to which he was entitled as his father's heir, and after a contest worthy of the elder Colon's persevering courage, won the recognition of his claim, and became Viceroy over all the lands discovered by the Admiral. Diego Prieto, of obstructive memory, appears to have continued in his efforts to carry water on both shoulders, for we find him in after years condemned for stealing one of the Indian captives brought back to Spain by his kinsman, Vicente Yañez, from one of his western voyages.

Of the pilots and seamen who had shared in the finding of Guanahani, many attained to their full share of the glory attendant upon the exploit. Several of the former accompanied the Admiral on his subsequent expeditions; while others undertook voyages of their own in search of *terra firma*, or of a shorter route to the famed Cathay that still remained so far. Many of the sailors became pilots in turn, and guided other ships through the waters of the Caribbean Sea and the Sinus Mexicanus up to the times of Cortes and Pizarro. Others we find, plain seamen yet, sailing with Ferdinand de Magellanes on his immortal cruise around the world. Before the days of newspapers it was no such mighty thing, apparently, for a man to take part in the discovery of the western world and afterward join the ships which circled the whole globe for the first time. At least we find no special mention made of these doughty Juans and Antonios in the history of their times, and only know of their adventures from the incidental mention of their names in ship-list or the roll of dead. The Indians who arrived in Spain on the "Niña" and the "Pinta" were all baptized, with Ferdinand and Isabella as their sponsors. After that they died off rapidly, and went to the Christians' heaven, no doubt. One only reached his native shores again, to delude his unsophisticated countrymen into trusting their bearded visitors. We have alluded already to the fate of the devoted men left to garrison the fort at Navidad. Neither governor nor tailor, Irishman nor Basque, lived to tell the tale of how the rest had met their death in that ill-fated outpost of an unworthy civilization. If what Guacanagari and his people related to the Admiral when he landed to visit the ruined settlement was true, even Charity herself cannot deny that they deserved their doom.

As for the Admiral himself, we can best read his character from his own words, penned from day to day amid the trials of his outward voyage and the triumphs of his first hours of success; on the summer seas of the long-sought Indies and the boisterous waters of the Atlantic at its wildest; among the exquisite delights of those noble scenes he opened to the enjoyment of his fellow-men, and in the hurried confusion of sudden shipwreck. Whether dealing with a nameless savage or measuring phrases with Portugal's King, whether writing his report to his distant sovereigns or chatting with his men over their strange surroundings, we find him ever the same, — direct, simple-minded, trustful, fearless. If he, a man of the people, had what we (who have none such!) call the vices of his times, he also possessed virtues which seem to have grown rarer as time has passed. He was loyal to his friends, over-generous to his foes, and what he promised he performed. Among other things, he pledged himself to prove that there was another side to the world, and he did it. His minor inconsistencies might be set aside in view of that performance. In after years he met with bitter disappointment, rank ingratitude, and unmerited indignities; but in this he was not wholly a martyr. A matchless seaman and intrepid explorer, he gave at no time any evidence of superior executive talent. In undertaking to colonize and govern the territories he discovered, while continuing at the same time his more remote investigations, he was attempting a task far beyond his powers, — perhaps beyond those of any one man, considering the instruments then available. The misconstructions and disputes which arose naturally enough with a jealous Crown, when we consider the vast and undefined nature of the authority intrusted to him, were fanned and distorted by the active efforts of envious and malicious courtiers. That he suffered gross injustice is beyond dispute; that it was intentional and foreplanned by either Isabella or Ferdinand, we do not believe. The absent were ever wrong, and the great Admiral was no exception to the ancient rule. A Governor and Viceroy for the Spanish Crown, with one breath he held out hopes of obtaining untold riches, and with the next talked of seeking the earthly Paradise with three or four teredo-eaten ships. In one letter he proposed to find tons upon tons of virgin gold, and soon after had to report that his own followers would not allow him access to the mines. It is not strange that his sovereigns should have found it necessary to establish a stronger and more systematic government than his in the immense dominions the Admiral had brought under their control. That they pursued a considerate or magnanimous course in providing this, no one will affirm; but they hastened to make him ample amends for the severity of their servants as soon as they knew the outrages inflicted on the man they seemed sincerely delighted to honor. The Admiral's claims were somewhat of the broadest, and that they were not immediately liquidated is not to be wholly wondered at. That he died in poverty and distress is not to be credited, unless we mean by "poverty" that he did not die possessed of the fabulous wealth he looked for from the Indies, — not for his own aggrandizement, be it ever borne in mind. The altercations between himself and the fiscal officers of the Crown regarding his portion in the products of his discoveries are by no means all one-sided; and while it cannot be denied that influential enemies threw every obstacle in his way, his impetuous temperament and quick sensibilities often interpreted as intentional indifference what may well have been only the needful caution of sluggard officials in dealing with unauthenticated demands. The Admiral himself was not remarkable for financial method. We find repeated instances in the formal records of those years of gifts and bounties to the great explorer; of the constant payment of considerable pensions to his sons and brothers, and of large sums due by him as his contribution to the " eighth " excused and released by the Crown. We think it wholly probable that had an exact balance been struck between the expenses paid by Spain for all her ventures concerning the Indies and the actual money value of the gold and other products received during Colon's lifetime, there would have been but little for him to collect his share upon. In his own will, written on his death-bed, he admits that the Indies had thus far furnished no revenue commensurate with the outlays made; and he disposes, in advance, of the great sums he expected the future to produce. True, he ascribes the absence of such returns to the mismanagement of others, and there was much force in his contention; but we must remember that the Indies were "golden" to him until his latest breath, and he failed to recognize the amount of time and systematic toil required to derive a fixed and adequate income from a region thinly populated by savages, however fertile and abundant it was in valuable products. In saying, in the last year of his life, that he " had not a roof he could call his own," and that he " lived on borrowed money," we do not assume that he was in absolute penury. His expenses were necessarily large to sustain the dignity he thought was becoming; but he found no difficulty in securing whatever funds he required, pending remittances from Hispaniola. His grievances, indeed, — real though they undoubtedly were, — seem rather the wounds done to a proud and sensitive spirit, than any actual hardships suffered in the flesh. He had his full share of the latter in the course of his adventurous life; but of these he makes little moan. We do not intimate that the services of their Admiral were open to commercial valuation by the sovereigns of Spain, or that they themselves so believed; but this aspect of his relations to the Crown was unavoidable, and much of his correspondence turns upon the fulfilment of the contracts made with him. So long as Queen Isabella was alive, we find both her and the king dealing generously with the claims advanced by Colon. Unfortunately for the latter, his royal benefactress died just as he arrived in Spain from his last and most disastrous voyage, and the surviving monarch cared not to be worried with the importunities of one of his officers, even if that officer was of all the most distinguished. Ferdinand had other irons in the forge much nearer to his hand than the farther side of the Ocean Sea. Like a prudent king, he had abundant control of the sentimental side of his nature, and so he deferred the consideration of Colon's petitions to a more convenient season. "Ferdinand enters into an enterprise with enthusiasm, and concludes as chance or necessity dictates; nor has he hitherto had reason to complain either of Fortune or his resolutions." Such was the opinion of a man who knew him well, — one Niccolo Machiavelli, of undeservedly mal-odorous renown. In Colon's case the king simply followed the dictates of his nature. By the time he was prepared to give heed to his Admiral's representations, Cristóval Colon had said his *In manus tuas*, and been gathered to his obscure fathers.

Whatever were his mistakes and short-comings, Colon was neither a visionary nor an imbecile. Had he been perfect in all things and wise to the point of infallibility, we could not have claimed him as the glorious credit he was to the common humanity to which we all belong. His greatness was sufficient to cover with its mantle far more of the weaknesses of frail mortality than he had to draw under its protection; and it becomes us who attempt to analyze his life in these later days, to bear in mind that, had his lot befallen ourselves, the natives of the western world would still, beyond a peradventure, be wandering in undraped peace through their tangled woods, and remain forever ignorant of the art of eating meat. In his trials and distresses the Admiral encountered only the portion of the sons of Adam;

but to him was also given, as to few before or since, to say, with the nameless shepherd of Tempe's classic vale, "I, too, have lived in Arcady."

Colon did not merely discover the New World. He spent seven years and one month among the islands and on the coasts of the hemisphere now called after the ship-chandler who helped to outfit his later expeditions. For the greater part of that time he was under the constant burden of knowing that venomous intrigue and misrepresentation were doing their deadly work at home while he did what he believed was his Heaven-imposed duty on this side the Atlantic. He persisted in the one, but he would not remain silent under the other. What he wrote to one of his steadfast friends as he was returning in chains from the new world he had given to Spain, has a peculiar appositeness, now that his name and deeds are on all men's tongues:—

"In Spain I am being judged as though I were a Governor who had gone to Sicily, or to some city or town which is under an established authority, and where the laws can be enforced in their integrity, without fear of losing all; and in this I receive a grievous wrong.

"I ought to be judged as a Captain who has come from Spain to the Indies to make a conquest of a warlike and numerous people, whose habits and faith were wholly different from ours; a people who live among the mountains and forests, and who have no fixed habitations, as our own men can have none. There, by the Divine favor, I have placed another world under the dominion of the King and Queen, our sovereigns, whereby Spain, which was before called poor, has now become the richest of all the nations."

His appeal should not go unheeded. Humanity at large, as well as the Spain he served so faithfully, was infinitely enriched by the labors and sacrifices of this Genoese Admiral of Castile, and by his deeds should Humanity judge him. Not Cæsar only is entitled to his due.

APPENDIX.

NOTE A.

THE BIRTHPLACE OF COLUMBUS.

MUCH controversy has waged concerning the place of Columbus's nativity. It has been variously assigned to the city of Genoa; to several of the lesser towns in the ancient republic of that name; to Florence, Corsica, and even to England. But the declarations made by Columbus himself in the course of his writing should, it seems to us, leave no ground for reasonable dispute, and fix the city of Genoa itself as the spot where he first saw the light.

In the deed of entail, or testament as it is more commonly called, executed by the Admiral in Seville on Thursday, Feb. 22, 1498, and confirmed by his sovereigns in their decree of Sept. 28, 1501, he specifically says that, "*being born in Genoa*, I came to serve their Majesties here in Castile," etc. Later on, in the same document, he directs that some one of his lineage shall always be maintained in becoming state in that city, "as though a native thereof, . . . since from it I started out, *and in it I was born.*"

Moreover, during his lifetime it is evident that no doubt existed that Genoa was the birthplace of the great navigator. Not only do his contemporaries — his friend Las Casas, his son Ferdinand, Sebastian Cabot (whom some would call his rival), the curate of Los Palacios, Peter Martyr, and others — refer to him consistently as "the Genoese," but the Government of Genoa, in the persons of the famous magistracy of St. George, emphatically confirm the truth of the general supposition. In acknowledging to Columbus, under date of Dec. 8, 1502, the receipt of sundry important documents remitted by him to them through

Messer Nicolo Oderigo, the Republic's ambassador to the Spanish Court, the Seignory state that this action of Columbus has given them "exceptional gratification, evidencing as it does that your Excellency is, as your character would imply, devoted to *this your native land* (*questa sua originaria patria*)." Further on, in the same epistle, they refer to the "generosity and benignity which you show toward this, *the country of your birth* (*questa primogenita patria*)." Finally, in alluding to the provisions of the deed of entail above-mentioned, the Seignory declare: "We shall ever be as affectionately inclined toward the before-mentioned Don Diego, your illustrious son, as the very condition of his being your son demands, as well as the pre-eminence of your own deeds and glory, of which *our common country* claims and cherishes its full share." The whole tone of this interesting communication is, indeed, that of the chief-magistracy of a popular government endeavoring to appropriate to the Commonwealth a part of the fame achieved by one of its distinguished sons.

That Columbus, in referring to Genoa, alluded to the city proper, and not to any one of the towns situated in its territory, is obvious from the distinction made by him in the deed of entail. The fifth "Item" from the end reads thus: "I also enjoin my son Diego, or whomever shall enjoy the said entail, to seek and labor always for the honor, well-being, and aggrandizement of the *city* of Genoa, and to exert all his powers and resources in defending and increasing the well-being and glory of *its republic*." Here it is apparent that Columbus discriminates between the city and its dependent territory. That the house wherein he was born has not been discovered and located beyond cavil, does not seem to us to weigh down the repeated asseverations of the man himself.

NOTE B.

THE DATE OF COLUMBUS'S BIRTH.

AT no place in his existing writings has Columbus stated definitely the year of his birth, and none of his contemporaries attempt to fix it with exactness. Historical critics have assigned it variously to 1435, to 1455, and to intermediate years. We shall content ourselves with transcribing such extracts from accredited authorities as may serve to aid the reader in forming an individual opinion.

The remarkable "Book of Prophecies," in which Columbus [1] endeavored to show that the Hebrew Prophets foretold the recovery of the Holy Sepulchre by means of the treasures resulting from his discovery of the New World, contains on folio IV. an address from the Admiral to the Spanish Sovereigns, which opens thus: "From *a very tender age* (*muy pequena edad*) I embarked on the sea, as a sea-farer, and have continued thereon until this day. This career inclines whomsoever follows it to seek to know the hidden things of this world. *More than forty years* are already spent since I engaged in this practice," etc.

Again he says, a little later on in the same address: "I repeat, that I set aside all the navigating I have done *since early youth* (*edad nueva*)," etc.; a repetition which establishes at least the certainty that he first went to sea while very young.

His friend and contemporary, the curate of Los Palacios, writing after the death of Columbus, says that "he died at Valladolid, in the year 1506, in the month of May, in a good old age, — being seventy years old, a little more or less." This would make him about sixty-six in 1502, when the "Prophecies" were written; consequently, upon our assumption that the "more than forty years" during which he followed the sea mean forty-two or forty-four, Columbus would have been twenty-three or twenty-five years old when he entered upon a sailor's life, — an hypothesis irreconcilable with his twice-repeated reference to his "tender years."

The difficulties surrounding the subject are well summed up by the learned Señor Navarrete in his introduction to that "Collection of Voyages" which has proved such a mine to all students of the Discovery. After analyzing the conflicting testimony concerning Columbus's birthplace, the Spanish scholar says (vol. i. p. lxxix) : —

"There is even a greater difference of opinion in fixing the date of Colon's birth and of some of the earlier events of his life. Ramusio says that he was forty years of age when he first proposed to the Seignory of Genoa the project of sailing to the West in order to reach India and carry on directly the traffic in spices, which proposal was deprecated as a dream or idle fable; and that Colon, offended that they should not give weight to his argument, went to negotiate the affair with the King of Portugal. . . . Since we know, through his son

[1] Doubt has been thrown, we think somewhat arrogantly, upon the authorship of this famous manuscript. We have greater confidence in the expert skill of the experienced scholars who unhesitatingly affirmed it to be Columbus's work, than in the guarded scepticism of those who question it. The latter "deny" altogether too much.

Don Fernando, that Colon came to Spain as a fugitive from Portugal toward the close of 1484, we are forced to the conclusion that in 1470 he was already in Lisbon. If he was then forty years old, according to Ramusio, it is clear that he must have been born in 1430. . . . Peter Martyr, also, states that Colon was forty years old when he submitted to the Seignory of Genoa his project of discovery; but as he mentions no date, it is not possible to fix the year in which he was born. Muñoz indicates 1446; and if Colon was of the age stated when, in 1485, he went to Genoa to offer his services and present his schemes, — as the author believes, — his birth would have taken place in 1445. In the letter which Colon wrote to his sovereigns when in Jamaica, the 7th of June, 1503, he says obscurely that he entered their service at twenty-eight years of age, which would show that he was born in 1456; but there is plainly a mistake in the copies of this document, as some writers have already pointed out, and as we ourselves have also remarked.

"About the year 1501 or 1502 Colon addressed to the monarchs his book of 'Prophecies,' and states that for more than forty years he had followed the sea; and his son quotes another letter in which he (Colon) declares that he began to go to sea when fourteen years old. If to these fifty-four years we add the eight which he passed in Spain without making a cruise, — from the end of 1484 to August, 1492, — and the four which elapsed from 1502 to his death, we gather that he lived at least sixty-six years; although Père Charlevoix says sixty-five. The Curate of Los Palacios, who knew and was on intimate terms with him, asserts [1] . . . In this case, he must have been born in 1436; and this appears the more probable if we heed what Oviedo declares, when, in relating the death of Colon, he says that he was 'already an old man;' and when the king, in granting him, in 1505, permission to ride on muleback, states, among other reasons, that it was because of his 'advanced age,' which could not be properly asserted of a man sixty years old."

We differ from Señor Navarrete and those who follow him in supposing that Columbus, when speaking of the long period during which he followed the sea, referred only to the years actually passed in voyaging. If we deduct the years he passed on land in Spain, why not deal in like manner with the years when he was *carteando* — painting maps — in Lisbon? And is it not almost certain that in 1485, at least, he was away from Spain, — as some have it, laying his project before the Genoese and Venetian authorities; or, as others hold, in the sea-fight off St. Vincent? To us the context seems to show that the "more than forty years" embraced the whole term of his sea-faring life. Nor do we read the Jamaica letter as Señor Navarrete does.

[1] Quoted on the preceding page.

"I began to serve ever since twenty-eight years of age," is what Columbus wrote. He does not intimate that he then entered the service of Spain; on the contrary, the sense is that he then began to labor in his scheme of discovery. If he was born in 1445, he was twenty-eight years old in 1473; and this apparently coincides with the year when he began his correspondence with Toscanelli concerning the feasibility of a westward passage to India, since the latter's reply is written in 1474. If the Jamaica letter proves anything, it would seem to be that Columbus was twenty-eight years old in 1473.

Adopting Don Fernando's citation from a lost letter of his father, that the latter was fourteen when he first went to sea, and adding forty-two years as the equivalent of "more than forty," he would be about fifty-six when the "Prophecies" were written, or about sixty-one when he died, in 1506. "Round numbers" are apt to be used where exact dates are not available; and we are inclined to the opinion that the curate of Los Palacios, in stating that his friend was "seventy years old, *a little more or less*," at the time of his death, was only using the common Spanish form of approximation, which may as properly be read sixty-five or sixty-six as seventy exactly. Moreover, the difference between "sixty" and "seventy" in Spanish is but a single consonant, and in crabbed writing an error would be easy. We do not advance these remarks to discredit either the ancient chroniclers or their more recent followers, or to support any theory of our own, but only to evoke a spirit of caution in dealing with a matter far from easy of solution. We know, both from his own and from his contemporaries' declarations, that Columbus was aged for his years, and especially in the bitter lustrum preceding his death was infirm and broken; therefore, if only sixty, he might well have the appearance of and be characterized as an "old man."

NOTE C.

COLUMBUS'S STAY AT THE COURTS OF PORTUGAL AND SPAIN.

THE Admiral himself twice states that he spent *fourteen* years in his applications to the Portuguese Crown for assistance in making a western voyage, and *seven* at the Spanish Court before his petition was granted. We know that he left Lisbon, or rather fled from that city, toward the close of the year 1484; therefore he must have gone there in 1470, or early in '71. In that pathetic letter which, the year before his death, he addressed to King Ferdinand, Columbus says that he first "came to anchor in Portugal because the king of that country was more learned in discoveries than any other." It seems to us doubtful whether at this time his mind was bent upon a westward cruise, or whether he had any more definite plan than to use his knowledge of navigation to the best advantage in the expeditions then frequently sailing under the Portuguese flag in search of a southern passage around Africa. Be this as it may, it was not long before a western voyage became the master idea in Columbus's mind.

How he had passed the earlier years of his life, from the ship-boy age of fourteen to the skilled mariner's of twenty-five or twenty-six, is largely a matter of conjecture. He has recorded, as we have seen, only that he "followed the sea." His contemporaries relate tales of shipwreck, of naval battles, of expeditions against the corsairs of Barbary, even of what would be called to-day deeds of flat piracy, as occurring during the years preceding his arrival at Lisbon. Las Casas quotes from a manuscript of Columbus, which he calls his "Book of Memoirs," allusions to various voyages and adventures, and in our extracts from the Admiral's Diary we have had occasion to notice the extent of his wanderings to distant shores; but most of these cruises are referable to the period of his nominal stay in Portugal. It seems most likely that prior to 1470 his exploits were confined to the Mediterranean waters; and these he seems to have known familiarly, from the Pillars of Hercules to the Bosphorus, both on the European and African coasts. In the first half of the fifteenth century there was occupation enough, both in navigating and fighting, on these sapphire seas.

The first distinct knowledge that we have of the future discoverer is through the medium of his friend Las Casas, who says that Columbus and Fernando Martinez were occupied in compiling and painting charts for King Alonzo of Portugal, and the daring navigators who then made Lisbon their point of departure for the bold ventures along the western coasts of Africa which culminated in 1487 in the discovery of the Cape of Good Hope. At that time Columbus was a diligent student of the learning of the ancients, and in especial seems to have been influenced by the "Imago Mundi" of Petrus Aliacus, — a scholarly dissertation upon and compendium of early cosmography as exhibited in the writings of Pliny, Strabo, Aristotle, Seneca, Ptolemy, and other authors. The original copy of this book, profusely annotated by Columbus's own hand, is yet preserved, and bears evidence on numerous pages of the great enterprise which was fast shaping itself in his mind. Another work which was copiously commentated by Columbus was the "Historia Rerum" of Æneas Sylvius; while his attention was likewise drawn to the travels of Marco Polo and Mandeville; indeed, to the wildly gorgeous accounts given by the former of these two veracious travellers Columbus was indebted for that unshaken belief in the certainty of finding Cipango — the modern Japan — which so constantly influenced him in the first period of his Discovery.

Meantime his collaborator in the compilation of maps, the Canon Martinez, was in correspondence with Paolo Toscanelli, — a deeply learned Florentine philosopher, whose high reputation for geographical skill was based on the practical observations derived from long voyages through the then known seas, as well as upon exhaustive study of all obtainable works dealing with the subject. To this eminent man Columbus wrote, in 1474, and received in reply that fascinating letter in which he applauds the argument of Columbus as to the certainty of reaching India by a westward passage, and urges him to make his contemplated voyage "to the land where the spices are born," where "the temples and royal palaces are covered with planks of gold." The more to confirm his correspondent's confidence, Toscanelli sends him a copy of a recent letter to Martinez, written at the request of the King of Portugal, *and also a copy of the map* which he had prepared for his Majesty, in which the countries referred to by Marco Polo are laid down in their supposed relations to Europe. It is worth while to note that the aged Florentine scientist, in his letter to Martinez, dilates upon the advantages which would accrue to Portugal were she to push her advances across the Atlantic rather than southward along the African coasts; and also that he refers to Columbus, in writing to him, as one of "the Portuguese nation," — misled apparently by the latter's own letter being addressed from Lisbon. The effect of this correspondence on the already ardent imagination of Columbus is traceable throughout his whole subsequent career, and is frequently referred to in our narrative. As we have there seen, he used Toscanelli's map throughout the first voyage; and many of the delusions which he then cherished are directly referable to that ingenious production. Unfortunately no copy of Columbus's letter to Toscanelli has been found. Las Casas says that he himself "saw it and had it in his possession, translated from Latin into Spanish." He adds that the letters from Toscanelli were in Latin. Doubtless Columbus also enjoyed at this period the advantage of Martin de Behaim's acquaintance, and was familiar with the labors which resulted in 1492 in the publication of the globe bearing that cosmographer's name.

The great explorer during these years was diligently accumulating all such maps and charts as professed to give the contour of the world, and pursued indefatigably his questionings of all mariners who had sailed in other quarters than those visited by himself. What to him must have been a priceless collection of charts and accounts of voyages made to the recently discovered Canary Islands and like remote frontiers of the habitable globe came into his possession in 1473, or thereabouts, upon his marriage to Donna Felipa Moniz Perestrello, daughter of a Portuguese nobleman, who had made several voyages of discovery in the service of the sailor prince Dom Henrique. This marriage also resulted in Columbus visiting the island of Porto Santo, one of the Madeira group, where his father-in-law had been governor during his lifetime, and where his widow yet possessed extensive estates. Here Columbus's son Diego was born, in 1474, and from here the father made voyages to Madeira and the Canaries. Other and wider sea-wandering he also did while his nominal home was in Portugal: for we are told that he sailed "many times" to the Guinea coasts, and once to "Ultima Thule," — which some historians think was the Faroe Archipelago, though most believe that Iceland was so called, and rightly, we judge. To this period are to be assigned the other voyages of which Columbus speaks in the course of his writings, — to England, Ireland, France, Flanders. His claim that he had "sailed every sea which until to-day is navigated" was no idle boast.

Notwithstanding his long absences on these distant journeyings, Columbus gained fame and credit as a geographer of supreme ability, and steadfastly pressed his suit for the ships and men he needed to cross the Western Ocean. King Alonzo ended his vacillating reign in 1480, and John II. ascended the Portuguese throne; but neither granted the aid the Genoese asked. To use his own words, "God so closed the eyes and ears and all the senses" of Portugal's king that "in fourteen years I could not make him understand what I was saying." From John II. indeed he experienced that treachery of which he speaks so bitterly in our earlier pages; but these years were far from wasted, for his writings bear constant witness to the vast store of experience and knowledge acquired during this period of alternate voyaging and study; and in his diary it is the familiarity with the Atlantic Ocean in its manifold phases which he then gained that established his faith and led him ever westward when the courage of his stoutest pilots was all but gone.

In 1484, toward the close of the year, he left Lisbon suddenly, and apparently by stealth. His wife was dead, and he was deeply involved in debt. That his flight was connected with money troubles is conjectured from his Testament, already cited; for in the codicil thereto dated the week before his death he directs the payment of sundry sums, reaching the important total of more than one hundred thousand maravedies, to various Jew and Genoese merchants of Lisbon, with the injunction that the payments were to be arranged "in such manner that it should not be known who had caused them to be made." That he was in Lisbon at least a part of 1484 is apparent from the statement in his diary (9th of August, 1492) that, "being in Portugal in 1484, he saw a resident of the island of Madeira come to ask of the king a caravel to go in search of" the phantom land which was so often seen on the western horizon and never found.

In leaving Portugal Columbus's plan seems to have been to go to Paris and lay his projects before the Court of France. From this he was dissuaded by the Duke of Medina Celi, the most powerful of the grandees of Spain, whose protection he sought immediately after his sudden departure from Lisbon, and whose hospitality he enjoyed during the two years which elapsed until, in 1486, he made his first appearance before Ferdinand and Isabella. This, at least, is the positive declaration of the great noble in the letter which his Grace wrote to the Grand Cardinal of Spain, — that famous Pedro Gonzalez de Mendoza, of heretic burning proclivities, — which was dated from "this my town of Cogolludo, the 19th of March [1493]," four days after Columbus's return to Palos from his successful expedition. The letter is worth quoting in its entirety. It will be observed that the Duke had heard of Columbus's arrival at Lisbon; he had not yet learned of his still later entry into the port of Palos. The epistle runs: —

MOST REVEREND SIR, — I am not aware whether your Lordship knows that I had Cristoforo Colon under my roof for a long time when he came from Portugal and wished to go to the King of France, in order that he might go in search of the Indies with his Majesty's aid and countenance. I myself wished to make the venture, and to despatch him from my port [Santa Maria], where I had a good equipment of three or four caravels, *since he asked no more from me;*[1]

[1] This still further disposes of the idea, sometimes advanced, that Columbus, in making his voyage in three small ships, was acting under the stress of necessity. Here we see him, six years before 1492, asking only the same fleet which he afterward received from the Spanish Crown.

but as I recognized that this was an undertaking for the Queen, our Sovereign, I wrote about the matter to her Highness from Rota, and she replied that I should send him to her. Therefore I sent him, and asked her Highness that, since I did not desire to pursue the enterprise but had arranged it for her service, she should direct that compensation be made to me, and that I might have a share in it, by having the loading and unloading of the commerce done in the Port.

Her Highness received him [Colon], and referred him to Alonso de Quintanilla, who, in turn, *wrote me that he did not consider this affair to be very certain;* but that, if it should go through, her Highness would give me a reward and part in it. After having well studied it, she agreed to send him in search of the Indies. Some eight months ago he set out, and now has arrived at Lisbon on his return voyage, and has found all which he sought and very completely; which, as soon as I knew, in order to advise her Highness of such good tidings, I am writing by Suares and sending him to beg that she grant me the privilege of sending out there each year some of my own caravels.

I entreat your Lordship that you may be pleased to assist me in this and also ask it in my behalf; since on my account and through my keeping him [Colon] *two years in my house*, and having placed him at her Majesty's service, so great a thing as this has come to pass. And because Suares will inform your Lordship more in detail, I beg you to hearken to him.

May Our Lord protect your very reverend person as your Lordship desires.

From this charmingly frank specimen of courtly wire-pulling it is evident that Columbus was first presented to Queen Isabella, in 1486, by this powerful noble, and not by the priests, as is so commonly recorded. The letter is too circumstantial to admit of dispute as to the facts alleged, and accounts for the two years between his leaving Portugal and his reception at the Spanish Court in the only manner admissible. If Columbus took part, as Las Casas asserts, in the sea-fight between the French and Venetian galleys off St. Vincent, in 1485, it must have been while nominally under the protection of Medina Celi; and if he went to Genoa and Venice to press his plans upon the consideration of those republics, as some assert, he most probably did so at this time. It is barely possible, indeed, that he was aboard the Venetian galleys, returning to Spain when the fight occurred, and not on the French ships, as is generally alleged. There is no substantial historical basis for any of these conjectures, however, beyond the fact, recorded by Las Casas, that the Seignory of Venice sent to thank the Portuguese king "at the time of the election of Maximilian, son of the Emperor Frederic, as King of the Romans," for aid rendered the shipwrecked survivors of this naval battle. The election mentioned took place in 1486; so the fight may well have occurred in the previous year.

At all events Columbus enjoyed the ostensible patronage of the great duke from some time in '84 to the beginning of '86. He himself says in his diary, under date of Jan. 14, 1493, that he formally entered the service of the Spanish monarchs on the 20th of January, 1486; and this should be conclusive. It was in this same year that those debates, discussions, or conferences took place at Salamanca between Columbus and the learned schoolmen appointed by the Spanish sovereigns to hear the arguments of the Genoese geographer and pass judgment upon their merits. These discussions have passed into history as the "Council of Salamanca," and as such have been celebrated alike by pen and brush; but it is doubtful whether they were more than a series of conferences carried on without especial pomp or circumstance, much as similar conferences are conducted in Spanish countries at the present day. Such, at least, is the character given them by Dr. Rodrigo Maldonado, who, as a member of the Royal Council resident at Salamanca, was deputed by the sovereigns, "together with other learned men, scholars, and seamen," to "argue with the said Admiral concerning his voyage to the said islands," that is, the Indies. Beyond this there is no evidence that the queen or king took any part in the proceedings. The result of the investigation was, according to Dr. Maldonado (and he was a faithful friend and supporter of Columbus later on), that "all agreed that it was impossible that what he said should be true." Doubtless it was about this time also that Quintanilla, afterward so stanch a supporter of Columbus, wrote to his friend the Duke of Medina Celi "that he did not consider the business to be very certain."

The failure of the clergy and pilots to sustain the views of the great discoverer led to the temporary abandonment of the project by Ferdinand and Isabella; but they still retained him in attendance at their Court. In 1487 we find four payments made to Cristoval Colomo (note that the name was not yet Hispanicized into *Colon*), amounting in all to fourteen thousand maravedies, "for certain matters pertaining to the service of their Majesties;" and other like payments in 1488. Beyond this, until he appears at the portal of La Rabida, the details of Columbus's life at the Spanish Court are lost to us. That he persistently urged his project appears both from his own repeated declarations which are incorporated in our narrative and from the testimony of his contemporaries and friends. In the pursuit of his object he gained some powerful and courageous supporters among the highest notabilities of Isabella's Court, but more and equally influential enemies among the envious, the bigoted, and the would-be wise. Thrice during these years was he invited by as many princes to visit them and discuss his proposed enterprise with them, — by the kings of England, France, and Portugal. The latter wrote him on the 20th of March, 1488, seemingly in answer to some communication made to him by Columbus, and urged him to return to Lisbon, adding a warranty of safe-conduct, "since perchance you may have some apprehension of our officers of justice on account of certain matters to which you may be bound." Of the invitation sent by Charles VIII. of France, or rather by the regent Anne, no trace remains. That of the English Henry VII. was no doubt sent in answer to the solicitations of Bartholomé Colon, the navigator's brother, who had gone to London in 1486 to lay Christopher's scheme before that king. All these three flattering commands from royalty were received by Columbus while waiting at the Spanish Court, and by him were laid before Isabella. "I had letters of request from three princes," he says in his letter of May, 1505, to Ferdinand, "which the Queen (whom God have in His holy glory!) saw, and had read to her by Dr. Villalan."

It was in 1491, so far as we can determine, that Columbus, being then in Seville, decided to leave Spain and again start for France, in the hope that the regent Anne would be as good as her written offer, and lend him the aid he had not been able to secure from Spain. It was then, if we read aright the testimony of those who knew best his movements at the time, that he stopped at the Convent of La Rabida, met the warm-hearted friar Juan Perez, and through the entreaties of that kindred spirit and his friend Garcia Fernandez the physician, was persuaded to make the final appeal to Isabella which resulted in the discovery of the western continent.

In this view of the obscure years of Columbus's life we have differed widely from many familiar presentations of the subject; but we have followed faithfully the original documents bearing on the period, and find no other consistent record possible than that here given and adopted in our narrative.

NOTE D.

COLUMBUS AT THE CONVENT OF LA RABIDA.

WE have begun our story with the visit of Columbus to La Rabida, because here, for the first time, we could tread on solid ground with the plain testimony of eyewitnesses to guide us. Most of the critics and historians of Columbus's career attribute to him *two* visits to the convent and its good prior, Juan Antonio Perez; but we fail to find any sufficient authority for such a view. Las Casas, indeed, does give an account of a first visit, made by Columbus on his way from Portugal into Spain, which he says he heard "from one of the old residents of this island," — that is, San Domingo; but he follows it with the story of the single visit as related by Garcia Fernandez, in a manner which indicates that to the latter account he gives the greater credence. According to the former version, Columbus knocked at the convent gate on his journey to the Spanish Court, and was so hospitably received by the worthy guardian of the little monastery that when, in 1491, he abandoned all further hope of aid from the sovereigns of Castile and turned his face toward France, he once more sought La Rabida, and took counsel of Fray Juan Perez. This is, therefore, counted as his second visit. From this point onward accounts agree in most respects concerning the encouragement given him by the liberal-minded priest and the efficient help given by him to Columbus.

We differ radically from this position, and have in our account followed the statements made by Garcia Fernandez the physician, old Juan de Cabezudo, and other villagers of Palos whose evidence was given in unmistakable language twenty-two years later in the *pleito*, or lawsuit, brought by Diego Colon against the Spanish Crown to enforce the fulfilment of all the engagements made with his deceased father the Admiral.

The effort was being made to show that to the Pinzons all the credit for the discovery was due, down to the very money used by Columbus in going from La Rabida to the Court. In reply Dr. Fernandez declares that undoubtedly Martin Alonzo Pinzon had the means to do what was alleged; but that the whole affair happened in a very different manner, which he proceeds to relate: Columbus with his "little boy," the doctor says, arrived in Palos on foot, and "put into La Rabida in distress" (the nautical phrase *á la arribada* is significant). He asked of the porter bread and water for his lad, which were given. Seeing him there,

Fray Juan Perez, guardian, or prior, of the monastery, entered into conversation with him, and discovered at once from his speech that he was a foreigner. In answer to the friar's kindly inquiries, Columbus entered into a frank conversation with him, and described at some length his prolonged efforts to interest the Spanish monarchs in his daring scheme, with the result only that many of the courtiers mocked at him for a dreamer of dreams, and asserted that "it was all thin air, and there was no sense in it." Wearied with such crass bigotry and ignorance, Columbus "had left the Court, and was now on his way directly from Palos to Huelva to see and confer with the husband of his wife's sister, Muliar by name." Struck by his sincerity, and impressed with the soundness of his visitor's arguments, the prior kept him at the convent while he sent to the adjoining village of Palos to summon this same Dr. Fernandez — "with whom he had an affectionate friendship, and because he (the doctor) knew something of the astronomical art " — to come and converse with "the said Cristóval Colon" and examine the correctness of his views "touching this matter of discovery." The doctor went to the convent "at once, and all three conferred about the affair."

The subsequent action of this little band is shown in our narrative; still following the simple and convincing relation of Garcia Fernandez. From all his testimony, which remains uncontroverted to this day, it is evident that this was the first visit of Columbus to La Rabida, and that it was through the aid and encouragement then extended by the two friends, priest and layman, that he was again enabled to visit Granada and secure a favorable hearing from Queen Isabella.

The whole account is detailed and circumstantial, and we have limited ourselves to it, adding only such explanatory and corroborative facts as a careful study of Columbus's own writings and the archives of the period supplied. The substance of the Admiral's conversation is given by the physician himself; but we have preferred to substitute the language of the discoverer's letters for the necessarily brief summary given by Garcia Fernandez in his verbal testimony.

The evidence of Juan Rodriguez Cabezudo is no less emphatic and conclusive than that of the physician. He swore that "he saw the old Admiral [as distinguished from Don Diego, the young Admiral] in this town of Moguer, going about with a Franciscan friar trying to arrange for a discovery of the Indies; and the said Admiral asked him [Cabezudo] to lend him a mule, on which the said friar could go to Court to carry on the negotiation, and he let him have it," etc. Other statements he also made, which have been woven into our narrative.

?Now, the physician Garcia Fernandez explicitly refers to this mLle, and says that Juan Perez set out on it at midnight on his journey to the Court.

In view of the directness of the stories told by both doctor and sailor, we are satisfied that Columbus did not visit La Rabida before the occasion referred to by these witnesses, and that the supposition of any previous visit must be due to a confused mention of the Admiral's return from his finally successful mission to Granada, when he was again an inmate of the friendly cloisters during the preparation of his little fleet in the adjoining port of Palos.

The incidents which we have related concerning the early life of Sebastian Rodriguez, the ex-pirate, and other details up to the time of Columbus's return from Granada, have been obtained by a careful collation of official documents selected from the Archives of the Indies, and printed by Navarrete.

NOTE E.

COLUMBUS'S DEBT TO EARLIER NAVIGATORS.

"YOUR Majesties determined to send me, Cristóval Colon, to the said parts of India to see the said princes and nations and countries . . . and directed that I should not go by land to the Orient by the way it was customary to travel; but by the route to the West, *by which we do not know to this day, of a surety, that any one has passed.*"

In such frank phrase did Columbus begin the journal in which he wrote down from day to day, for the information of his sovereigns, the incidents of the daring adventure he had undertaken. Neither here nor elsewhere in his writings did he claim to have invented the theory of a western passage to Asia. On the contrary, he based his belief in its practicability on the consensus of evidence which for twenty years he had been industriously accumulating, — partly by studying the works of ancient and contemporary philosophers and travellers, partly from his contact with other seafaring men, partly from observation of winds and currents and the spoil they cast on more than one Atlantic beach. To himself we owe our chief knowledge of the sources whence his faith was derived. Pedro de Velasco, pilot to Diego Detiene, told Columbus in the Convent of La Rabida of a lonesome voyage far out into the Ocean Sea, the fruit of which was the discovery of Flores Island. Martin Vincente informed him in Portugal of a voyage four hundred and fifty leagues due west from Cape St. Vincent, which resulted in nothing more than pushing back the horizon that much farther. From Cazaud he learned of the voyage in search of a western land seen by Diaz de Tavera. The blind sailor and his Portuguese shipmate who are mentioned in our narrative told him how they were blown far to the northwest of Ireland, and caught sight of a coast they fancied was Tartary. All these facts, and others, we owe to Columbus's own pen. He did not attempt to ignore his debt to others; he determined to prove "of a surety" that the Dark Ocean was a highway, not a bottomless chaos.

We put aside as futile the argument that he was indebted for his steadfast confidence to the Norse Sagas which describe the voyages of Leif Erikson and his hardy countrymen to Labrador. If, in the "Ultima Thule" visited by Columbus in 1477, we recognize the modern Iceland, it is scarcely credible that at so early a period of his life he should have time or inclination to study Runic lore while on a hasty privateering cruise. Had he done so, or had he learned in later years of Vinland the Good, as some would have it, through the medium of faded parchments "procured from the Vatican for the Pinzons," he would surely have adduced so pertinent a witness when quoting the far less important testimony of Aristotle, Seneca, and Pliny. If he attached weight to the vague tales of the blind sailor of Murcia, why should he have failed to present the positive proof of a voyage which could be so circumstantially established? That Leif Erikson reached Labrador we are prepared to believe; but that Columbus knew of so momentous a corroboration of his theory, we greatly doubt. As to the Pinzon fable, it is refuted by the testimony of Pinzon's own son, who asserts that he was present with his father when the latter obtained in Rome a certain "writing" concerning the western lands, and that it was "of the time of Solomon." Even the Dighton Rock can hardly claim so venerable a pedigree.

The legend of the dying pilot, Sanchez, delivering to Columbus in 1485 a map showing the location of Hispaniola, whither Sanchez had been blown by easterly gales, and whence he had miraculously returned, rests on an equally frail foundation. Las Casas says it was "common" in Hispaniola after Columbus's death, but he gives it no credence. It is so variously and loosely related in other chronicles that we may safely assume, with the doughty Benzoni, "there were many who could not endure that a foreigner and an Italian should have acquired so much honor and so much glory, not only for the Spanish kingdom, but also for the other nations of the world."

Mutatis mutandi the same might be said of those who, under the pretext of "historical criticism," spend their powers in trying to prove that we owe the discovery of our continent to a happy combination of good-luck and fraud.

NOTE F.

THE FUNDS FOR THE VOYAGE.

IN his codicil, dated May 19, 1506, a few days before his death, Columbus mentions that "their Majesties did not spend, or wish to spend, more than one million maravedies, and *it was necessary for me to provide the rest.*" We know that at the time he set out across the Western Ocean Columbus was no capitalist, and the queries naturally arise : How much was "the rest"? Who supplied it?

The Crown furnished 1,040,000 maravedies. This money was advanced by Luiz de Santangel, *Escribano de Racion*, or Comptroller, of the kingdom of Aragon. From existing documents it is apparent that this was no "loan," as is so often and romantically asserted; for on the 5th of May, 1492, — only eighteen days after the capitulation for the voyage was signed between Columbus and the Spanish sovereigns, — we find a part of the sum so advanced being repaid to Santangel, or rather to his order, by the Archbishop of Granada from the coffers of the Church. The language of the entry is plainly that of a mere transfer of accounts, and the money furnished to find "the Indies" is prosaically coupled with another million of maravedies received from Don Isaac Abraham, a wealthy Jew, to carry on the war with the Moors. The Archbishop seems to have been the real lender of the Columbus funds, for as late as August, 1494, we find the prelate still receiving payments on account of *his* payments to Santangel.

The expedition cost more in its preparation than the amount supplied by the Crown, and it has been commonly assumed that the additional sum required was 500,000 maravedies, and that these were contributed by the Pinzons. Las Casas refers to this ; not as a fact, but as his own surmise from certain entries on the notarial records of Palos. It has also been supposed that this sum represented the "eighth" which, under his contract with the sovereigns, Columbus was *obliged* to furnish. A reference to that document, as given in Chapter V. of our narrative, will show that it was wholly optional with Columbus to subscribe this portion of the cost of the expedition. Had he exercised the option (and, as Las Casas suggests, he doubtless did so in order to furnish material evidence of the faith which inspired him), the amount required would have been far less than 500,000 maravedies. On his return in 1493 the sovereigns granted him a special gratuity of 375,000 maravedies; possibly this was designed to afford him the means to repay the debt incurred by him personally to supplement the insufficient contribution of the Crown. Be this as it may, it is not probable that the Pinzons, had they supplied any such sum of money as that alleged and not been repaid, would have failed to lay great stress upon it in the determined and virulent effort which they made in 1519 to rob him of all the credit of the discovery.

NOTE G.

THE PART ACTUALLY TAKEN BY THE PINZON BROTHERS.

GARCIA FERNANDEZ, in his testimony in the *pleito*, or lawsuit, already referred to, twice declares in positive terms that Columbus first met the Pinzons and secured their co-operation *after* his return from his last and successful visit to Granada. "And he came from there," he states in answer to one interrogatory, "armed with authority to take the said ships, which he should indicate as being suitable for the prosecution of the said voyage, *and it is at this time* that the arrangement and association which he made with Martin Alonzo and Vicente Yañez were consummated, because they were both competent men and familiar with nautical affairs. And they, in addition to their own knowledge and that of the said Cristóval Colon, instructed him and assisted him in many things which were of value on the said voyage." In replying to another query, the same witness repeats: "*After the return* of the said Don Cristóval Colon from their Majesties' Court to the town of Palos, the said Martin Alonzo assisted and aided him in everything that was serviceable, and obtained for him the men necessary for making the said voyage." In a third answer he says: "In order to go in company with the said Admiral, the said Martin Alonzo found all the equipment and people, for he was held in much esteem in this town in all that concerned the sea, and was wise in such matters and a man of much courage."

Still more: Arias Perez, the son of Martin Alonzo, although doing his utmost to belittle the achievements of Columbus and transfer to his own father the chief glories of the Discovery, testified in the same suit: "That *when the Admiral returned from the Court* he brought a warrant from their Majesties and a certain order to go with three ships to discover those lands; and that when the said Admiral arrived in this town of Palos there was no man who dared to go with him, or even to let him have ships; all declaring that if he went he would never find land. Seeing that there was no means of getting either ships or men, he exerted himself greatly in persuading the said Martin Alonzo; exhibiting to him the bounties which their Majesties would give him [Columbus] for discovering land, and then saying that he would share with Martin Alonzo the half of these if he went with him, and that he should be the chief captain, and that as a man who, with his relatives, could do it, he ought to undertake it for their Majesties' service."

In the face of this positive evidence we think it idle to argue, as many writers do and as some of Martin Alonzo's own friends (including this very Arias Perez in another place) did, that Columbus met the Pinzons *before* going to Granada, and was indebted to them for the means and encouragement with which he prosecuted his final suit before the queen. The prior and the young physician furnished the moral support, and her Majesty herself the financial help needed, in the manner described in our opening chapters.

That the Pinzons afforded invaluable aid and received therefor a share in the products of the voyage, is beyond dispute; but we look upon their connection as clearly beginning *after* Columbus had adjusted his contract with the Crown and received the peremptory authority conveyed in the decrees of 30th April.

NOTE H.

THE THREE SHIPS OF PALOS.

COLUMBUS signed his contract, or capitulation, with Ferdinand and Isabella on the 17th day of April, 1492. On May 30, the same day on which the decrees were signed which conferred upon him the extensive powers over the ships and mariners of all Andalusia, the sovereigns issued their edict expelling the Jews from Spain. By the harsh terms of this ordinance the unfortunate Israelites had to leave the kingdom by the 31st day of July. According to the most moderate estimates, no less than 200,000 emigrated in the interim; some respectable authorities swell the number to 800,000. Very many of these exiles went by sea to the Barbary ports, to Italy, and to the Levant; and it cannot be doubted that their requirements for ship-room materially reduced the number of vessels available for other foreign service at that season. This may account, in part, for the difficulty in providing a squadron for Columbus, to neutralize which such broad discretion was vested in him.

The careful reader of history will have observed that the royal warrants given Columbus for this end were two in number: the one addressed to the civil authorities of the whole province, calling upon them to provide three ships for his use; the other addressed to the representatives of the Crown in the single port of Palos, referring specifically to the two vessels which that town was obliged to furnish upon demand, in discharge of the penalty imposed upon it by sentence of the Royal Council. From this we may infer that if he failed to find what he wanted in Palos, he was to seek the ships in the other ports of that maritime district; and, in any event, was to call on the superior authorities to assist him.

Palos was an active and enterprising community in those days. Its importance as a seaport may be inferred from a decree of 1478, which bestowed upon it special immunities and privileges for the despatch from its harbor of vessels destined for the jealously guarded foreign trade. Ships were constantly leaving the little port on what were then adventurous voyages, — to the Canaries and Azores, the northern and western coasts of Africa, Flanders, and England; so the presumption must have been that it was a promising place in which to seek the vessels and crews needed for the perilous venture out into the Sea of Darkness. But it has seemed to us, after a painstaking study of all the evidence in hand, and a comparison of the relations existing between the physician Garcia Fernandez, the Pinzons, Columbus, the prior Fray Juan Perez, Diego Prieto, the *alcalde mayor*, and others, and the respective parts taken by them both at this time and in after years, that the possibility of using the penalty under which Palos lay was suggested to Columbus at the time of his visit to La Rabida, and had an important influence upon the action of Fray Juan Perez. The village mayor, Diego Prieto, was certainly summoned to court at the time the worthy guardian was making his appeal to the queen, and was the medium chosen to communicate her Majesty's encouraging response and largess to Columbus while the latter was awaiting the superior's return at La Rabida. When Columbus himself returned from Granada, a few months later, he brought the order to press the two bounden vessels into his service; and since, by the physician's own testimony, it was not until this latter date that Columbus consulted with the Pinzons, we are led again to conclude that the suggestion to utilize this penalty emanated from some one of the townspeople well acquainted with its shipping interests, and from the very outset favorably disposed toward Columbus. This one was, we feel justified in assuming, none other than the sagacious and helpful village doctor.

In relating the embarrassments encountered in fitting out the expedition and the dilatory proceedings of the men of Palos, we have followed the records as they exist in the many documents referring to the period. To bring the events more vividly before our readers, we have transposed literally the evidence given in 1513-1515 concerning the stirring days which fell upon Palos in the summer of 1492.

NOTE I.

THE FIRST SIGHT OF THE NEW WORLD.

WASHINGTON IRVING, following a mistaken conjecture of Navarrete, censures Columbus for having accepted from his sovereigns the bounty promised by them to whomever should first see land, to the manifest injury of that one of the seamen who gave the warning-cry on the night of October 12. "It may at first sight," says Mr. Irving, "appear but little accordant with the acknowledged magnanimity of Columbus to have borne away the prize from this poor sailor; but this was a subject in which his whole ambition was involved, and he was doubtless proud of being personally the discoverer of the land as well as the projector of the enterprise." Passing over the questionable ethics involved in this suggestion, as to the saving grace of ambition as a sufficient justification for an act of rank robbery, we think the charge wholly at variance with the recorded facts. Mr. Irving's "Life and Voyages of Columbus" is, to say truth, but little more than a graceful and elegant English version of the patient labors of Navarrete and the gossiping pages of Las Casas; and the errors of his authors have in many cases been incorporated textually into his own work by the gifted romancer of Sunnyside. Unfortunately the view propounded in Irving's "Life" has found general credence; and very recently we have seen one of the ablest and most conscientious of American critics commenting upon this incident as having "subjected his [Columbus's] memory, not unnaturally, to some discredit, at least with those who reckon magnanimity among the virtues."

In both these cases the American historians base their charge upon the critical note given in Navarrete (vol. iii. p. 611), "On the first sight of land in the New World." With all diffidence we conceive that the learned Spanish scholar, the ingenious novelist, and the acute critic have alike been misled in the premises, and have left erroneously a stain upon the fame of the Admiral which he in no wise merited. Navarrete himself begins his Note by saying: "In order to investigate this point, it is necessary to keep in view *what the Admiral says* in his diary regarding Thursday, Oct. 11, 1492;" and in a footnote he again refers to "what the Admiral says." He then quotes at length from the entry given in the diary under the date named. If we, however, turn to the diary itself, we shall find (the more pity!) that it is not Columbus himself who there is speaking, but Las Casas; summarizing, as was too often his wont, the language of the Admiral from the manuscript journal as it lay open before the pious bishop in his monastic quarters in San Domingo. The record begins: —

"Thursday, 11 of October, *he* sailed to the S. S. W.; *they* had much more sea than *they* had had in all the voyage. *They* saw some sparrows and a green rush close to the ship. Those of the 'Pinta' saw a cane, and picked up another little stick worked, as it appeared, with an iron tool. Those of the 'Niña' also saw other indications of land and a branch covered with blossoms. With these signs all breathed freely and were cheered. *They* sailed this day up to sunset 27 leagues. After sundown *he* pursued *his* original course to the West. *They* made 12 miles [Spanish] per hour, and up to two o'clock after midnight made 90 miles, which are 22½ leagues. And because the caravel 'Pinta' was the swiftest sailer, and was going ahead of *the Admiral*, she found land and made the signals which *the Admiral* had commanded. This land a sailor named Rodrigo de Triana first saw; although the Admiral at 10 o'clock in the night, being on the 'castle' of the poop, saw a light; albeit it was something so dim that he did not wish to affirm it was land, but called to Pedro Gutierrez, chamberlain to the king, and told him that it looked like a light, that he [Gutierrez] should mark it; and thus he [Gutierrez] did and saw it. He [Columbus] also called to Rodrigo Sanchez, of Segovia, whom the king and queen sent with the fleet as Inspector, who saw nothing, because he was not in a place where he could see. After the Admiral mentioned it, it was seen once or twice, and was like a small wax can׳ dle which was being raised and lowered ; which to few would seem to be an indication of land. But the Admiral had been confident that he was near land ; for which reason, when they recited the *Salve Regina* (which all sailors are accustomed to say or sing after their fashion, and gather together for the purpose), the Admiral asked and warned them that they should keep a sharp watch in the 'castle' at the bow, and should look well for land ; and that to whomsoever should first call out that he saw land, he [the Admiral] would give at once a silk doublet in addition to the other bounties which the sovereigns had promised, — which were 10,000 maravedies of pension to whomever should first see land. At two o'clock after midnight the land appeared, from which they were distant two leagues. They shortened all sail, and remained with the squaresail, which is the mainsail without 'bonnets,' and hove to until the morning of Friday, when they arrived at *a small island* [isleta] *of the Lucayos, called in the language of the Indians* Guanahaní."

The careful and always candid Navarrete finds this passage obscure, contradictory, and misleading. After discussing it and comparing it with the testimony of three eyewitnesses (given in the lawsuit in 1519), all of whom speak of Juan Bermejo, or Juan Rodriguez Bermejo, as having been the one who first descried land, he concludes : —

"The final result is, . . . that the reward of the 10,000 maravedies annually which the sovereigns granted the Admiral during his life 'because he first, before any other, has discovered the land of the said islands ' [decree cited], was one of those favors common in Courts; when, after the death of Martin Alonzo Pinzon, the influence of the Admiral grew and spread, as a sequence to the fortunate outcome of an adventure previously regarded with, at least, distrust; and afterward as the most notable and of the greatest consequences which the annals of modern times rehearse."

No one can accuse Señor Navarrete of any bias against the great navigator ; in this criticism of one of the most romantic incidents of a voyage fruitful in all the elements of romantic adventure he is unquestionably sincere. Nevertheless, we think him to be mistaken in laying this charge of petty envy and fraud at the Admiral's door, and for the following reasons: —

First. The whole passage in the diary which records the sighting of land is *not*, as Navarrete twice calls it, "what the Admiral says." It is, beyond all peradventure, the summary condensed by Las Casas from the original text of Columbus. The literal transcription of the Admiral's journal begins on the following day, — October 12, — and both then and thereafter is plainly marked by the use of the first person and the greater prolixity and *naïveté* of the writer's account. This we have utilized in our narrative. But that the language of the entry under Thursday, October 11, is Las Casas's, appears not only from the use of the words "he," "they," "the Admiral," but also from his description of the island discovered. How could Columbus, on the very day of his arrival in the New World, know that the island was called Guanahaní? And, far more, how could he know that it was one of a group to be christened in after years "the Lucayos"?

Secondly. The journal, as it existed for Navarrete and exists for us, does not claim that the light seen by Columbus at ten o'clock at night — or four hours before land was sighted — was on Guanahaní itself. Las Casas, in his own delightful History, gives us his theory of what the light was, based upon many years' life among the Indians of the islands now discovered by Columbus. Unhappily the Bishop's solution of the vexed point will not bear translation. Suffice it to say that he sees no inherent improbability in the claim of Columbus to have seen a light four hours before land showed itself, and even assumes that this light was on land. Whether that land was Guanahaní or another island passed four hours before the latter was sighted, must depend on the identification of the "true Guanahaní." Upon this subject our next note touches. It is enough for our present purpose that we make clear the fact that Columbus did see a light, and that he instantly published the discovery; but that he does not claim that it was on the same island afterward seen by Juan Rodriguez Bermejo from the "Pinta."

Thirdly. The language of the diary impresses us as being straightforward in its relation; if it is somewhat involved in structure, it differs in no wise from the whole literature of the period. There does not seem to be any difficulty in reading a coherent account of the day's incidents, even in the abbreviated version of the Admiral's own words which Las Casas has left. All day long the squadron sailed a south-southwest course; unmistakable signs of nearing land were seen from all the ships; Columbus, in virtue of these, held that land was at hand; and at sunset, when the sailors gathered together to intone the Evening Hymn to the Virgin, he strenuously urged a sharp lookout, and promised a personal reward to whomever should first espy land, in addition to the sovereigns' promised pension; the course was then changed to west (Las Casas was a priest, not a sailor, and his courses may not always be correct); Columbus himself took his station in the tall structure built in the stern of his vessel; at ten o'clock he saw a light, but "did not wish to affirm it was land;" he called one of the royal officers, who confirmed the existence of the light; a second Crown official did not see it, owing to his unfavorable position. That he was called for the purpose is explicitly stated, and has never been disputed. Thus far the record seems clear enough. After showing once or twice again the light disappeared. "To few would it appear to be a sign of land," says the diary. If the words are Columbus's own, his frankness should be the strongest proof of the correctness of his story. If they are Las Casas's, they are a tribute to the Admiral's shrewdness, and not a doubt cast upon his veracity; for Las Casas was a believer in Columbus's account of the incident. The fleet swept swiftly on for four hours; at two o'clock A. M., just as the moon broke through the clouds, a sailor on the "Pinta," Juan Rodriguez Bermejo by name, saw the white sands ahead, and gave the warning signal. The Admiral himself recorded this in his diary; and that diary was written especially for the perusal of the sovereigns of Spain, subject to the confirmation or dissent of Rodrigo Sanchez, their Majesties' Inspector. Where, then, is there any deception,—any attempt to defraud "a poor sailor" of his reward?

Fourthly. The whole question turns on whether Columbus saw a light or not. If he did, we think he was fairly entitled to claim to have been the first to sight land,—as much so as though he had seen a mountain by day. On a fresh, almost stormy night Indians were not likely to be out at sea in their frail craft; and even if by any stress they were, they would not carry lights in their boats as modern yachtsmen would. Therefore we believe that the light was on shore, that it was visible from Columbus's lofty station as the flagship sped on in the darkness, and that whoever descried it "first discovered land" in an entirely legitimate acceptation of the phrase. Such of my readers as have approached a strange coast at night after a long cruise in unfamiliar and shipless waters will at least concur that such a light means land.

Fifthly. The fact that Columbus in his diary calls the "poor sailor" Rodrigo de Triana when the other witnesses call him Juan Rodriguez, Juan Bermejo, or Juan Rodriguez Bermejo, does not seem to be an incoherence. Triana is the name of a castle and its village near Seville,—rather famous, in later days, as a place of incarcaration for "heretics" awaiting the fiery release of the *autos da fé*. One of the witnesses cited says that Bermejo "was a townsman of Molinos, in the Seville district" (*tierra*); another that he was "of Seville." Rodrigo was constantly substituted for Rodriguez; probably the names were often indistinguishable in the crabbed writing of the times; and the substitution of one suburb of Seville for another is scarcely an indication of an intention to mislead.

Under these circumstances, we think that Columbus should stand relieved of the charge of bad faith thus lightly brought against him. We have presented the record as it exists, and submit that there is no sufficient ground for charging the Admiral with so unnecessary and clumsy a fraud.

NOTE J.

WHERE IS THE "TRUE GUANAHANÍ"?

"IT is a matter of controversy which of the Bahama group was Guanahaní, the first land seen by Columbus," writes, in recent days, one of the best informed of Americanists. "The main, or rather the only, source for the decision of this question is the journal of Columbus; and it is to be regretted that Las Casas did not leave unabridged the parts preceding the landfall, as he did those immediately following, down to October 29. Not a word outside of this journal is helpful."

Seven islands dispute the honor of being the "true Guanahaní," and each has its able champions. San Salvador, or Cat; Watling's; Grand Turk; Mariguana; Samaná, or Attwood's; Acklin's, and Crooked islands have in turn been presented as the Gate of the New World. Apart from the testimony of ancient charts, the impartiality of which in applying the name Guanahaní to nearly every one of the islands mentioned robs them wholly of reliability, most of the arguments as to the real scene of Columbus's landing turn upon careful computations of the distances and courses sailed by him after leaving Ferro, as laid down day by day in his diary. That these are confusing and lead to widely varying conclusions, is evident from the several islands fixed upon by the different investigators as being "determined" under this system. For our own part, we have eschewed these ingenious calculations as liable to much inevitable error, — both because, in frequent copying, distances and courses alike must have in many instances suffered more than a sea-change, and because, from the imperfection of his instruments, Columbus himself must often have had to depend wholly upon his skill as an approximator. We have found, however, sufficient data in the diary of Columbus and in the pages of his friend Las Casas to be not only "helpful" in determining this most interesting question, but (under correction be it said) to establish beyond a reasonable doubt which was the "true Guanahaní."

Much importance is attached by some critics to an alleged confusion in the Admiral's own description of San Salvador. In some places he calls it, they say, "a small island" (*una isleta*); and elsewhere "quite large" (*bien grande*). If the Spanish text is carefully examined, however, we think it will be found that no such confusion exists. On the 11th of October, in the diary, it is called "a small island of the Lucayos;" but, as before remarked, this is plainly Las Casas's interpolation. To the good monk, writing thirty years after, on the huge island of San Domingo, any one of the Bahamas would be "small." On the 13th of October the Admiral's own language is given textually; and here he says "this island is pretty large" (*Esta isla es bien grande*). On the 14th, when rowing along shore, he saw a "bit of land which is like an island, but is not one;" and a little later on he refers *to this peninsula* as "the said little island" (*isleta*). This clearly does not refer to the mainland of Guanahaní. On the 16th he calls Fernandina (the present Exuma) "very large," in comparison with Guanahaní. On November 20, Las Casas, in summarizing the Admiral's entry for that date, calls even Isabella (the present Isla Larga) an *isleta*, — a small island, as it surely is in comparison with San Domingo, where he was then writing. Thus it seems to us that, properly studied, no confusion is apparent in the record touching the size of Guanahaní. Columbus himself does, indeed, at a later date refer to it once as an *isleta;* but we must remember that he had then explored the endless coasts of Cuba and Hispaniola, and to him *then* the island first found in the Indies was in truth "small." If it had seemed only "pretty large" when seen for the first time after weeks of tedious voyaging, how could it appear other than small with the images of the vast bulks of the giant Antilles still fresh in his memory?

The only reference to the physical characteristics of Guanahaní, beyond those given by the Admiral in describing his visit to it which we have incorporated in our narrative, is found in his diary under date of Jan. 5, 1493. In speaking of his landing on the island near Monte Christi, on the northern coast of Hispaniola, he says (or Las Casas for him) "he found there many tinted stones, or quarry of such stones hewn by nature, very beautiful for royal or church edifices, like those which he found on the *isleta* of San Salvador." Outside of this the diary makes no further mention which would serve in distinguishing the true Guanahaní from its rivals.

But Las Casas in his own work settles the question for us beyond peradventure. Writing in 1525, or thereabouts, in the adjoining island of San Domingo; possessing Columbus's original journal and many of his other writings, his chart, and a number of relics; a participant in numberless conversations with the Discoverer himself, — the Friend of the Indians was surely competent to know which of the neighboring Bahamas was the island first trodden by Columbus. That he was personally familiar with it is shown by one expression where, in commenting upon the landing, the bishop says, " And I am surprised that he (the Admiral) does not say that he found salt; for there are in that *isleta* (that is, Guanahaní) very good salt-pits " (*salinas*). This is not in itself conclusive, however, since the same might be said of several other islands in the same archipelago. But when, in giving his own account of Columbus's discovery, Las Casas describes the incidents attending the taking possession, he inserts parenthetically this observation of his own: " *This land was and is an island of fifteen leagues in length, a little more or less* " (Esta tierra era y es una isla de 15 leguas de luengo, poco mas ó menos).

This seems to us to be final, when the circumstances are all duly weighed. Las Casas's perfect acquaintance with the facts as related by Columbus in conversation and recorded in his charts and writings; his familiarity with the West India islands (for the good father had visited most of them in the course of his devoted labors in behalf of the natives); and the fact that, as his own writings testify, he had taken pains to interrogate all the accessible survivors of Columbus's first voyage concerning the events of the discovery, — all add credit to the assertion he makes. Moreover, mark the emphatic use of the present tense, — " This island was *and is*." Evidently he intended to establish a point already in some dispute.

The description given by Las Casas, when taken in connection with the many allusions made in the diary to Guanahaní, is applicable *only* to Cat Island, or San Salvador, as it is commonly called abroad. Fifteen Spanish leagues, old style, are forty-five of our English miles. Watling's Island is thirteen miles long; Grand Turk, less than six; Mariguana, twenty-three and a half; Attwood's Cay, nine; Crooked Island, twenty.

San Salvador, or Cat Island, and Acklin's alone have the

requisite length; for accurate surveys make them each about forty-three miles long. The controversy should thus seem to be narrowed down to these two claimants. But Cat Island is the only one which possesses the other requisites for an identification with Guanahaní, — such as its distance from other islands mentioned, its position with reference to them, etc.; while Acklin's Island does not fulfil any of these requirements.

Even considered by itself, we find this explicit declaration of Las Casas to be conclusive. Taken in connection with the admirable arguments of Mackenzie and Humboldt, and the persistency with which from the earliest times Cat Island has held the title of San Salvador, we see no possibility of disputing, in justice, its claim to be the "true Guanahaní," — the first of the Golden Indies visited by the great Genoese and his companions of the immortal Discovery.

Another instance of the interest taken by Las Casas in establishing a correct knowledge of San Salvador is given in the pains which he takes to give the true pronunciation of the Indian name. It should be called Guanahaní, he insists, "with the accent on the last syllable," and not Guanaháni.

www.ingramcontent.com/pod-product-compliance
Lightning Source LLC
Chambersburg PA
CBHW020219240426
43672CB00006B/359